STRANGE

OFFBEAT INSTRUMENTS AND SONIC EXPERIMENTS IN POP

SOUNDS

STRANGE

OFFBEAT INSTRUMENTS AND SONIC EXPERIMENTS IN POP

SOUNDS

MARK BREND

STRANGE SOUNDS
Offbeat Instruments And Sonic Experiments In Pop
Mark Brend

A BACKBEAT BOOK
First edition 2005
Published by Backbeat Books
600 Harrison Street
San Francisco
CA 94107, US
www.backbeatbooks.com

An imprint of The Music Player Network, United
Entertainment Media LLC.

Devised and published for Backbeat Books by
Outline Press Ltd, 2A Union Court, 20-22 Union
Road, London SW4 6JP, England
www.backbeatuk.com

ISBN-10 0-87930-855-9
ISBN-13 9-780879-308551

EDITOR: **John Morrish**
EDITOIRAL DIRECTOR: **Tony Bacon**
BOOK DESIGN: **Balley Design Associates**
JACKET DESIGN: **Paul Cooper Design**
ART DIRECTOR: **Nigel Osborne**

Origination and print by Colorprint (Kong Kong)

05 06 07 08 09 5 4 3 2 1

CONTENTS

Like most musicians and producers, I know all too well the quest for new, old, or simply 'strange' sounds. In my case that might involve hours spent searching for the right sample, trying different analog or digital effects, or perhaps experimenting with various acoustic and electric instruments. But with a little luck, all this trial and error will lead to a moment when a track starts to take on a life of its own and becomes much more than the sum of its parts. Often times, the more unique this 'sonic signature' is, the more likely it is that it will carry the track in a more profound way than the harmony and melody could on their own.

Within these pages, we are invited to follow similar journeys of discovery with many legendary sonic innovators of the 20th century. Collectively, they cut a wide swath across all types of popular music and illuminate many unique applications, utilizing a wide array of instruments and techniques. In reading these stories, a chord is frequently struck with my own experiences. It seems that the most interesting results one can hope for often come from nothing more than willful experimentation. A happy accident may lead to something which takes a piece in an entirely new direction. It is this spirit of openness which is often responsible for making an arrangement new and exciting, by incorporating timbres or ideas that may at first seem oddly out of place.

Although technology and music exist hand in hand, there is a slant to these chapters which I find very appealing: they do not focus entirely on modern instruments or applications. So often it seems that music, and instrument design specifically, is driven by market forces and technological innovation. Yet many of the sounds herein buck that trend, and instead pick up on threads and possibilities that may in some cases be centuries (or even millennia) old. Time and again original contexts, intended uses, and traditions get thrown into a state of disarray, only to arrive in a modern setting completely reconfigured. From children's toys to rarefied electronic creations, it seems that anything is fair game in the quest for sonic innovation.

But having said that, there is an arc of history, and specifically the impact of technology, which can't be denied in the course of this book. To quote the collective improvising group AMM: "The past always seems intentional, but at the time it appears to be accidental." Could one have imagined in Harry Chamberlin's time that the conceptual foundations behind his instruments (drum loops, sampling, etc) would, in 50 years, become utterly ubiquitous – the basis of all commercial popular music? In retrospect it is truly amazing, and even more so with this roadmap in hand.

Though all of their individual experiences are unique, we see many common threads running through the work of the innovative designers, the pioneering producers, and the forward-looking artists contained herein. I believe that this spirit of exploration and curiosity is, in some ways, a metaphor for the essence of musical experience. Though scattered histories on some of these individuals and instruments have been available previously, what a pleasure it is to have this comprehensive collection now together in one place. A book such as this has been long overdue, and Mark Brend has done a wonderful job of covering a vast amount of territory with great depth and care. These pages have given me plenty of inspiration, and sparked all kinds of ideas. I certainly hope they will do the same for you… Enjoy!

John McEntire,
August 2005

John McEntire is a musician and a producer. A leading figure in the Chicago music scene, he is a member of the hugely influential Tortoise, and drummer with The Sea And Cake. He owns Soma Electronic Music Studios, a 24+ track analog and digital recording studio that numbers Stereolab, Teenage Fanclub, and Wilco amongst its customers.

INTRODUCTION

In a 1966 article entitled 'Soundmania,' the British music newspaper *Melody Maker* declared that "almost everybody agrees that as long as far-out sounds retain some sort of slight musical content, the field is wide open."[1] Those words came at a time when the international pop scene had seen, or would soon see, such instruments as ocarinas, Melodicas, sitars, and electro-theremins featured on chart-topping records.

Although its terminology now sounds quaint, the paper put its finger on a thread that has run through 50 years of pop music – the search for new sounds. Every act wants an aural trademark, something that makes its record recognizable, whether it's a serious rock act looking for new sonic options, or a cash-in commercial producer with a manufactured band. It could be a particular blend of voices, or a drum sound, or the way guitars combine. Or it could be an unusual instrument. This book tells the stories of those times when musicians have sat in studios and asked themselves, "If I play this, will it make the record sound different?" – and then decided that the answer to that question was "Yes."

Often, people choose certain instruments because of what is happening in music at the time. Pop music is, and always has been, a hybrid form, a story of ongoing synthesis. The original main constituents were blues, rhythm & blues, country, and gospel. The style and content of many other forms has been absorbed since then, for instance the British and American folk music that pre-dates even the blues. Elements of modern classical experimentation, the orchestral ballads of pre-rock'n'roll singers like Sinatra, jazz, world music – they've all joined the party over the years, bringing with them new turns of phrase, new chord changes, new melodies, and new rhythms. And as each form has been admired, explored, and plundered, so has its instrumentation.

Autoharps and dulcimers, instruments commonly used in folk music, first started to appear in rock and pop during the folk-rock boom of the mid 1960s, when rock performers started to delve into folk traditions, and some folk performers went electric. Early electronic instruments were used alongside explorations into electronic sound by the wider musical community. But if many of the stories of unusual instruments in pop run directly parallel to the absorption of new musical forms into the mainstream, at other times instruments seem to appear randomly. In these pages I've tried to unpick both types of story – those that were obviously of their time, and those that were freakish one-offs, inspired moments of madness.

In music, the dividing lines between definitions tend to become more blurred and less straight the closer you examine them. What that means is that the process of deciding what qualifies for this book and what doesn't has been difficult, and the final list of what's 'in' will no doubt be contentious. I can start to explain why I've chosen my subjects by expanding on the subtitle of the book. This is a study of unusual instrumentation and sound sources in popular music in the rock'n'roll era (roughly from the mid-1950s onwards, with a few exceptions). But what instruments or sound sources qualify as unusual? And what is popular music?

To take the second question first, one way of defining popular music is to say what it isn't. It isn't classical music, New Music, or avant-garde modern music. It isn't jazz, either, although I have included some jazz-influenced music when I have judged that it has permeated the rock'n'roll sensibility, or has been permeated by it. The same can be said of country, folk, and what is now called 'world music.' It could mean film and television music, because many composers and musicians working in those fields draw from pop as much as from jazz and classical vernaculars. Having said that, I have to throw up my hands and say there are no clear lines. I can't map out this territory exactly. No one can.

The other question is what qualifies as a 'Strange Sound?' I have decided on the following four broad categories. (Of course these often overlap, and many instruments fall into more than one category.)

The rare and the obscure

At one end of this spectrum are instruments like the electro-theremin that was used on The Beach Boys' 'Good Vibrations.' It was, literally, one of a kind. The Ondes Martenot would fit somewhere in the middle, as few were made. At the other end there are many instruments that are widely made and used, or have been, but are not well known outside of limited circles. There is a considerable element of subjectivity here, but the question I asked myself when considering an instrument was this: "If I stopped a random person on the street and asked them what a certain instrument was, what are the chances that they would know what I was talking about?" On that basis, I reckon all sorts of dulcimers probably qualify, for example, as do autoharps and Melodicas, to name just a few.

A sub-heading of this section could be obsolete instruments, once common but now fallen into misuse. Early electronic instruments such as the Clavioline fit here. They were made in thousands, but how many people now know what they are, or what they sound like?

The inherently odd

Again, there is much that is subjective about this category, but I contend that it is valid nonetheless. The Theremin is now quite well known, but it is a curious thing because, if nothing else, you don't touch it when you play it. And isn't it odd to use a jug or a washboard as a percussion instrument? And what about those hybrids that proliferated in the middle of the 20th century, like the Marxophone, which were meant to combine the characteristics of several different stringed instruments?

Unusual in the context of pop music

This is a category that changes with the times. These days no one bats an eyelid if a major rock act incorporates world music instruments. But when George Harrison and Brian Jones started using the sitar on pop records, it sounded strange and exotic alongside conventional rock instrumentation. And it caused a sensation.

Early use of instruments or sound-generating techniques that have since become commonplace

In some cases instruments are unusual for a while, particularly in their earliest forms, but then become assimilated. Take the early drum machines of the 1960s. When such devices first appeared on pop records, nobody knew what they were, and the sounds that they made were nothing like the real percussion instruments they were replacing.

So those are the loose criteria that I've used to help me decide what to include. But having said all of that, I admit that I found myself drawn to instruments and stories that I found fascinating in themselves. The Theremin, the Stylophone, the Ondioline, the Marxophone, the Ace Tone Rhythm Ace, the Clavioline, magnetic tape splicing – to me there are compelling mysteries in such a list. And why did The Troggs use an ocarina on 'Wild Thing?' And who was the first rock guitarist to play sitar? Turn the pages and find out.

Mark Brend

London, England, August 2005

chapter 1

WAVES IN THE ETHER AND GOOD VIBRATIONS

the theremin and electro-theremin

The Theremin was not the first electronic musical instrument, but of all the early attempts to make an electronic musical instrument it is the best known. Predecessors include Thaddeus Cahill's 200 ton Telharmonium, which produced music more than a decade before the first Theremin. Cahill's grand scheme was incredibly farsighted. He planned to broadcast the tones of a monstrous electronic organ directly down the telephone lines of paying subscribers into restaurants, theatres, and private homes – a sort of prehistoric muzak Internet. It actually worked for a few years from 1906 onwards, in the New York area, but the technology defeated Cahill. The beast he had created was greedy for power and caused interference on the telephone network. In contrast, the Theremin was compact and simple, and could be run off any domestic electric supply. A mouse to the Telharmonium's elephant, it was invented around 1919, a few years after the plugs were pulled on the Telharmonium. At first glance it didn't look like a good prospect for long-term survival. For a start it is monophonic (it can only play one note at a time); it has no recognizable controlling mechanism (no keyboard or fingerboard); and it is very hard to play. Yet its very strangeness has proved to be its strength. It is the only early-20th century electronic instrument still in production. Indeed, it is currently more than ten years into a surge of renewed popularity that shows no signs of abating.

The Theremin, initially called Thereminvox, gets its name from an anglicization of the name of its inventor, a Russian called Lev Sergeyevich Termen, commonly known in Europe and America as Leon Theremin. An electrical engineer, cellist, and astronomer, he was born in St Petersburg in 1897 (or 1896), and in his extraordinary and long life he lived through the 20th century's great upheavals: the Russian revolution, two world wars, the cold war, and the falling of the iron curtain. He invented the Theremin almost by accident, chancing upon the idea while working in a Soviet sponsored laboratory on a project for measuring gases.

What is unique about the instrument, and perhaps the main reason why it has endured, is not so much the sound the Theremin makes but the manner in which it is played. The player does not touch the instrument, but rather moves his or her hands around its two antennae. The right hand antenna is a straight vertical aerial that controls pitch, while the left is a horizontal loop that controls volume. Thus the thereminist appears to be conjuring sound from, quite literally, thin air. Actually, what is happening is that the player's body's capacitance – its ability to store a small electric charge – alters the electro-magnetic fields around the antennae, which in turn control oscillators that produce sounds. These use the heterodyning (beating together) principle, in which two sound waves at different frequencies combine to create another audible frequency. Theremins are monophonic and have a range of up to five octaves. In skilled hands the cold electronic tone can be made to mimic a bowed stringed instrument like a violin, or a soprano voice. In unskilled hands it sounds like radio interference or a test oscillator.

The absence of visual or tactile cues makes it a challenge to play even a simple melody on the Theremin. Several things compound this. Firstly, the volume loop is operated in a way in which many people find counter-intuitive: volume *decreases* the closer the hand gets to the loop. As for the pitch aerial, moving your hand to and from it only results in a continuous rising or falling glissando. To play a melody line of distinct notes, each with a beginning and end, the volume must be cut with the left hand at the end of one note, while the right hand is moved to the next note, at which point the volume is increased again.

Despite the difficulty of playing the instrument, the Theremin seems to have an innate power to entrance and fascinate. Lenin was impressed when Theremin demonstrated the device at the Kremlin in 1922. Following this, the inventor was charged with the task of popularizing his invention internationally as an example of Soviet ingenuity, a job that occupied him for the next 16 years. He hoped that his wonder instrument would be taken up by the classical music establishment. The first composition to use the instrument was Pashchenko's *Symphonic Mystery, For Theremin And Orchestra* (1924), and others followed, written by such important 20th-century figures as Percy Grainger and Bohuslav Martinu.

Theremin himself toured Europe and America

with his marvel, attracting responses that ranged from interested to bemused to contemptuous. Enthusiasm in America was sufficient for him to extend his stay there from a planned three months to 11 years, during which time he became quite well known. In several newspaper articles in 1930 reporting the arrival of French electronic music pioneer Maurice Martenot (chapter 2), Theremin was mentioned in passing, with the assumption that the reader would know who he was. In 1929, sensing a commercial opportunity, RCA Victor secured a license to produce Theremins commercially, ushering in the first of three distinct periods of popularity that the instrument has so far enjoyed.

About 500 RCA Theremins were built during the early 1930s. They were actually manufactured by General Electric and Westinghouse, but branded as RCA instruments. These were, of course, tube (valve) instruments, with the electronics housed in a large dark-wood cabinet set on legs, which looked, appropriately, something like a radio of the period. A project attempting to track all surviving RCA instruments reckons that about half are still in existence.[1]

The revolution in serious music that Theremin hoped for never happened, and by the 1930s you were as likely to hear a Theremin in a music hall novelty act as at a concert. In England, for example, a performer named Joseph Whitely toured the halls for many years under the name of Musaire, billing himself as "Europe's only thereminist." He played an RCA Theremin that he had bought from Selfridges store in Oxford Street, London, in 1930. This he customized, extending its range, painting it yellow, and installing a door in the case, which opened to reveal a neat drinks cabinet mounted inside.

But the Theremin fell out of vogue by the late 1930s. Economic depression and the threat of war in Europe distracted people's attention from what most still considered to be an expensive gadget. And Theremin himself was no longer around to promote his idea, as he had returned to the Soviet Union abruptly in 1938. It was during this first lull in the Theremin's popularity that Samuel Hoffman, a doctor and part time musician, was given one in payment of a debt. Living in New York at the time, Hoffman used his acquisition to earn extra cash by performing his own nightclub novelty Theremin act.

In 1941, Hoffman relocated to Los Angeles where he set up as a foot specialist. Once there, he got himself listed in the musicians' union directory as a thereminist, seemingly more as a light-hearted afterthought than a serious bid for work. By now in full-time medical practice, Hoffman treated his Theremin playing as a mere hobby. But being the only one of what was presumably a small list of Theremin players in the directory who could read music, Hoffman got the call when composer Miklos Rozsa was looking for someone to play the instrument on the soundtrack for Alfred Hitchcock's movie *Spellbound* (1945).

Rozsa's first choice was reputedly Theremin virtuoso Clara Rockmore, a friend of Theremin's who had developed a degree of skill in playing the instrument that remains unmatched. She was busy with other commitments, and seemed in any case to harbor misgivings about the project, not approving of the use of her beloved instrument for creating 'weird noises.' So Hoffman got the job, and did it well. His playing is used to represent the distress of the character played by Gregory Peck, who, suffering from amnesia, is disturbed whenever he sees parallel lines on a white background. Whenever these episodes occur they are accompanied by a jarring Theremin theme, playing with an orchestra. Rozsa's soundtrack won an Oscar, and Hoffman became Hollywood's thereminist of choice.

For the next decade Dr Hoffman had a lucrative sideline, with performances on sci-fi classics like *The Day The Earth Stood Still*, radio programs, and even a gig with the Hollywood Bowl Orchestra. It was during this busy spell that Hoffman crossed paths with composer and bandleader Les Baxter, whose work in the loosely-defined genre of 'exotica' is mentioned elsewhere in this book. Between them, with the help of composers Harry Revel and Billy May, they made three big-selling records, oddities that blend pre-rock'n'roll light orchestral blandness with the spectral swoops for which the Theremin is famous. These albums, *Music Out Of The Moon*, *Perfume Set To Music* and *Music For Peace Of Mind*, introduced the sound of the Theremin to many hundreds of thousands of new listeners in the late 1940s and early 1950s.

Music Out Of The Moon was first released by Capitol in 1947, as an album of three 78rpm records (it was later reissued as a vinyl 33rpm album). Written by British-born songwriter and composer Revel, and arranged and conducted by Baxter, it was, according to the liner notes, "music that can affect the sensitive mind in a way that is sometimes frightening." That may have been true in 1947 – although it probably wasn't – but to anyone hearing the album now it sounds like the typical light orchestral music of the period: lush, slushy and sentimental. The difference was Hoffman, playing his Theremin along with the small orchestra and choir. More than 20 years later, it would become music out of the moon in a literal sense, when Apollo astronaut Neil Armstrong took a tape of the album into space on the first moon landing. "Armstrong's decision to make it part of his own soundtrack struck me as at once deeply eccentric and absolutely perfect," says Andrew Smith, author of a joint biography of the astronauts. "And ever since, when I've thought of Apollo, I've thought not of the first step, but of him and his little band drifting out there towards the moon, spilling spooky music out at the stars." [2]

Music Out Of The Moon sold well, and the Revel/Baxter/Hoffman team reconvened in 1948 for another themed album, this time on RCA Victor. For this project, Revel composed six impressionistic aural representations of different fragrances marketed by the Corday perfume company. Corday sponsored the project and advertised it heavily, helping it to Number

A recent Moog Etherwave Theremin, made by Bob Moog, who has been building Theremins for 50 years.

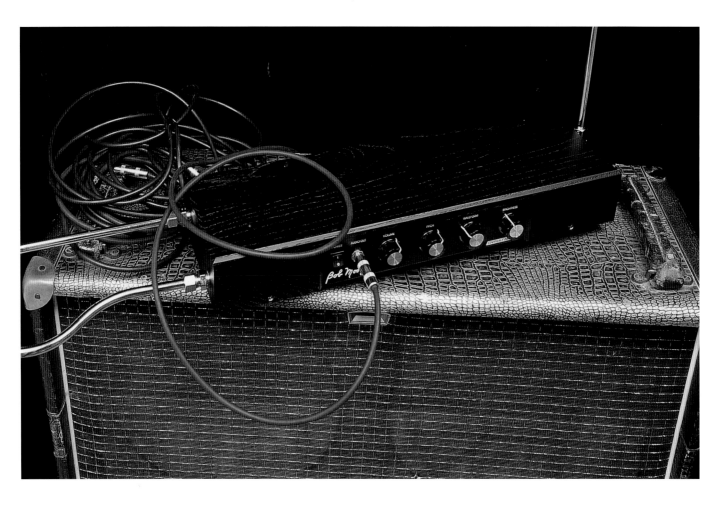

One in *Variety*'s chart in mid-December of that year. Musically, it was a similar blend to the first album, with the addition of a Hammond Novachord, an early polyphonic electronic keyboard (see chapter 3).

It was back to Capitol in 1950, with Revel and Hoffman working with Billy May and his orchestra for the self-explanatory *Music For Peace Of Mind*. "Turn down the lights, relax in an easy chair, and listen," urged the sleeve notes, as Hoffman's Theremin mournfully wailed over the smooth backing once again. It was another huge success.[3] Hoffman carried on with his Theremin for several more years and lived until 1968, but by the end of the 1950s his name had all but disappeared from the scene – the reason for which we will come to shortly.

With Hoffman fading from the picture, the popularity of the Theremin took its second downturn. Bob Moog, who had in the 1950s turned out dozens of make-your-own-Theremin kits, was now giving his attentions to developing his new synthesizers. Although they were played using conventional keyboards, these electronic instruments seemed to offer so much to aspiring electronic experimenters. It seemed as if the Theremin would be confined to the margins permanently, an anachronism and little more.

But in the 1990s a number of events coincided to propel the Theremin back into the spotlight. Moog returned to volume Theremin production, selling kits and complete instruments, first under the Big Briar brand and later under his own name. Several other companies began producing models too, and over the past decade a Theremin squiggle or two has become an almost commonplace way of introducing some ready-made weirdness into your records.

Badly Drawn Boy, Pere Ubu, Portishead, and Jon Spencer Blues Explosion are just a few of many acts who have recorded the sound of conducting the air. In the summer of 2003, British band Goldfrapp appeared on television chart show *Top Of The Pops* performing their hit, 'Strict Machine,' with singer Alison Goldfrapp torturing a handheld Theremin: "Slapping it around a bit,"[4] in her words. Many more Theremin-like sounds have appeared on records, film and TV themes, most of them not from Theremins at all. Modern sampling techniques and flexible MIDI

controller keyboards make it possible to reproduce the key elements of the Theremin sound – the wobbly sine wave, the swooping glissandos – with considerable accuracy. Purists might object, but anyone who has tried to play a tune on a Theremin will appreciate how tempting this option is.

The man who started it all, Leon Theremin, had missed the instrument's second phase of popularity – the Hoffman era of the 1940s and 1950s – but remarkably re-emerged to enjoy the beginnings of the third. He had left America in 1938 and was long assumed dead, maybe falling foul of the Soviet regime for fraternizing with the West for so long. But by the mid 1960s rumors had begun to filter through that Theremin was not only still alive, but that he had continued to work on state-sponsored electronics projects in the USSR. More incredible still, it later emerged that for the whole time that Theremin had toured Europe and lived in America in the 1920s and 1930s, fêted and famous, he had been working as a Soviet spy, passing technological secrets back to the Kremlin. On his return to the Soviet Union he fell in and out of favor with the government several times, spending time in a labor camp before being accepted once again into the dark heart of the Soviet establishment. After the iron curtain fell, in 1989, Theremin, now in his nineties, was found living in penury in Moscow, "with all of his life's work and belongings distilled down into this little heap of furniture and icons sitting around this sad little room."[5] He emerged blinking from 50 years of cultural isolation as the subject of Steven Martin's film *Theremin: An Electronic Odyssey*, which appeared in August 1994, two months before his death.

It seems like everyone knows what a Theremin is now, but despite its apparent popularity examples of melodic use of Theremin on pop records are rare. The simple reason for this is that it is extremely hard to play a tune on the instrument. Clara Rockmore could play the Theremin; so could Hoffman. But most pop musicians who get hold of one soon loose patience with it, and use it not as a musical instrument as such, but more as a generator of strange noises. The most famous example of this trick is Jimmy Page's electronic howling on Led Zeppelin's 'Whole Lotta Love.' Page was wise to the instrument's theatrical as well as sonic possibilities, as can be seen in the concert movie, *The Song Remains The Same*. Here Page uses a single-antenna model (pitch only), played through a Maestro echo unit. With this combination he generates weird swoops, flamboyantly conducting the air around the antennae. Both sonically and visually, it is a performance analogous to Hendrix coaxing feedback from a Fender Stratocaster.

Jimmy Page playing a Theremin on-stage with Led Zeppelin, mid 1970s.

> The Beach Boys, Paul Tanner and the electro-theremin

The record most frequently held up as a prime example of the use of a Theremin in pop features an instrument that isn't a Theremin at all, although it sounds something like one. The sonic strand that runs through The Beach Boys' 'Good Vibrations' is actually an oscillator-based instrument, dubbed, for convenience more than anything, an electro-theremin. To trace the genesis of this hand-made one-of-a-kind gadget, we need to go back to some time in 1958, when Hoffman was at a film soundtrack session with his Theremin. Amongst the other musicians present was Dr Paul Tanner, playing trombone. Tanner was a top-flight session player on the staff of the

American Broadcasting Company, who had worked with Glen Miller, Henry Mancini, and Frank Sinatra, amongst others. He was also on the teaching staff of UCLA. He had, at this point, no interest whatsoever in electronic music. During the course of the session Hoffman appeared to be having trouble pitching his instrument. Tanner says: "He kept coming over saying 'What does a D sound like?' then [he'd] go back to his instrument and try to play it. I thought there must be a much better way than that, so I just decided to dream up a better way of operating."[6]

Tanner's experience at that one session was sufficient to motivate him to set about building an electronic musical instrument. To achieve this he turned for help to his friend, actor and electronics enthusiast Bob Whitsell. Within a week they had made the first version of their instrument. After finishing it at 2am one morning, Tanner debuted it later that same day on a session for an album called *Music For Heavenly Bodies*, a mood music mix of strings and electronics not dissimilar to Samuel Hoffman's previously mentioned recordings. According to the liner notes of the album, Tanner's electro-theremin "provides a sense of the unknown, … of falling off into the whistling world of infinite space."

A second version of the instrument, produced after that initial session had revealed some shortcomings, was the one that Tanner used on all subsequent sessions. And there were to be quite a few. For Tanner, the whole endeavor was nothing to do with exploring the boundaries of electronic music. All he was thinking, he says, "was that it's a nice way to augment the income."[7]

Whitsell and Tanner's invention was beautiful in its simplicity. Essentially, it was a mechanical means of controlling a variable pitch audio oscillator that produced a sine wave tone. The oscillator and the mechanism that controlled it were contained in a simple wooden box, approximately 26 inches wide, 13 ½ inches deep, and 8 ½ inches tall. A slot ran along the length of the box, with a hand-operated slide control protruding through it. This operated a pulley system that in turn controlled the oscillator's rotary pitch control. There was an on/off switch on the slide control that, if pressed, sounded the oscillator's note.

This switch, fashioned by Whitsell, operated without an audible click. Using his right hand, Tanner moved the slide control back and forth along the slot, turning the oscillator's pitch control and thus varying the pitch of the instrument.

The home-spun stroke of genius that made Tanner's instrument so useful was a drawing of a piano keyboard mounted along the length of the slot that the slide control protruded from. This was carefully calibrated. When the slide control was slid to, for example, a C note on the dummy keyboard and the switch pressed down, the oscillator would sound a C note. This meant that Tanner avoided the struggle he'd observed as Hoffman tried to pitch notes correctly. But by moving the slide control back and forth, and keeping the contact switch depressed, he could still create the eerie glissandos at which real Theremins excelled. He had further control over the instrument using a simple volume control, which he operated with his left hand. The instrument was christened the electro-theremin by one of the producers of Tanner's first electronic session, *Music For Heavenly Bodies*, when he was using the early prototype of the instrument. The name stuck, and helped Tanner to exploit the gap in the market he had perceived for an instrument that sounded like a Theremin yet was more controllable.

In the hands of a seasoned studio veteran, who could readily adapt to all sorts of music, such an instrument proved an irresistible combination. Within the space of a few weeks, Tanner was not only a doctor of music and an experienced session player, he was also the most in-demand creator of electronic weirdness on the West Coast commercial music scene. It is no coincidence that from this point on Samuel Hoffman's name appeared very rarely in credits. Now, whenever you wanted an eerie, outer-space sound, Tanner was your man.

"I did anything that anybody wanted to do on TV or movies where there was a ghost or somebody was drunk," he says. "Lucille Ball would do a drunk act, and they wanted some loose music to go along with it, so they hired me in. I was hired to do all kinds of things – anything that was eerie. A thing that featured my playing constantly was [TV series] *My Favorite Martian* – I played whenever the Martian

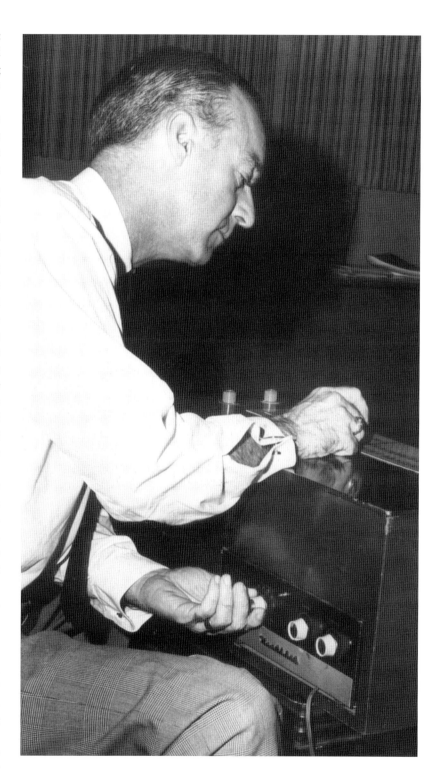

Paul Tanner with the electro-theremin, early 1960s.

fellow levitated. There was a movie [*Strait-Jacket* 1964] where Joan Crawford was a little strange in the head – chopped off people's heads – and they used me to demonstrate that she was losing it mentally. It was so easy; I could just play it like I did any other instrument. I could do it in tune; I could have a lot of vibrato or no vibrato, anything that they wanted."[8] For the next few years, Tanner had a lucrative sideline. The TV and film commissions rolled in, including contributions to the popular mid-1960s children's sci-fi series, *Lost In Space.* It was easy work. So simple was the electro-theremin to play that Tanner never even practiced.

Now the story moves forward to 1966. The Beach Boys' main songwriter, leader, and now producer, Brian Wilson, was planning the *Pet Sounds* album, and a new single of previously undreamed of complexity, 'Good Vibrations.' He wanted to introduce some electronic sounds into both projects. Wilson knew of Tanner and his electro-theremin and decided to call him in for a session. It is unclear whether Wilson, when first booking Tanner, thought he was getting a real Theremin or not. Speaking later he has tended to refer to Tanner's instrument as a Theremin, thereby feeding the confusion that the instrument on 'Good Vibrations' and *Pet Sounds* is a conventional aerial-controlled instrument. This confusion was compounded still further when books about the Beach Boys, and CD liner notes on reissues of their recordings, quote 'observers' who appear to be describing Tanner's instrument as a Theremin.

But whatever confusion has been sown about the nature of the instrument that made the sounds, and whether or not Wilson knew exactly what he was getting when he booked Tanner, he (Wilson) was clear about what *sounds* he actually wanted. Speaking later, he said: "When 'Good Vibrations' was forming itself in my mind I could hear the Theremin on the track. It sounds like a woman's voice or like a violin bow on a carpenter's saw. You make it waver, just like a human voice. It's groovy!"[9]

So it was that Tanner found himself, on Valentines Day 1966, alongside rock session luminaries like Hal Blaine and Glen Campbell, recording what would become 'I Just Wasn't Made For These Times,' a song on *Pet Sounds.* Not that

Tanner knew that at the time. He recalls the sessions as "little bits and pieces – I never had a clear picture of what I was working on. He [Wilson] did everything in piecework. I never saw the singers. Three or four instrumentalists would sit around and we'd play and they'd tape it and Brian would put it all together later."[10] Another thing that Tanner found unusual, having been used to playing scored orchestral and big band sessions, was that he wasn't given any music to read. "Brian came over to me and sang such and such a thing, and I said 'Well, write it down and I'll play it,' and he said 'Write it down? We don't write anything down – if you want it written down you have to write it down yourself.'"[11]

Tanner, ever the professional, wrote down the part and got on with the job. Wilson must have been happy, because a few days later Tanner was back for the first sessions for 'Good Vibrations.'

During the course of the many takes of 'Good Vibrations,' Wilson and Tanner discussed the workings of Tanner's instrument, and the parts Tanner should play. Bootlegs and later legitimate issues of early takes of the sessions show Tanner's playing prominent from the start, but becoming more so as time went on. Wilson was clearly impressed with the sound Tanner coaxed from his home-made gadget, and by the final take, the distinctive wobbling electronic whirr was mixed high.

The first Beach Boys fans heard of the electro-theremin was when *Pet Sounds* was released in May 1966, including the elegiac 'I Just Wasn't Made For These Times.' Tanner's brief solo, just before the long fade, demonstrates perfectly the electro-theremin's appeal. The pitching is accurate to a degree that only the very best 'real' thereminists could ever achieve, yet the tone retains the Theremin's haunting, ethereal quality – somehow both human-sounding and alien at the same time.

Five months after *Pet Sounds* came 'Good Vibrations,' routinely acclaimed, and rightly so, as one of the greatest pop productions of all time. It astonished fans and critics when it was released in October 1966. Other artists and producers, notably The Beatles and Phil Spector, had used varied instrumentation and multi-tracking to create complex studio productions before. And others, like Roy

Orbison, had written complicated pop songs before. But 'Good Vibrations' eclipsed all that came before it, in both its complexity as a production and the liberties it took with conventional notions of how to structure a pop song.

Crammed into its three and a half minutes are previously untried mixes of instruments, unexpected jumps from one section to another, and of course, unparalleled harmony pop vocals. Yet in all of this, the real triumph of the recording is that it fits together as a catchy, hummable, radio-friendly pop song. Tanner's electro-theremin can be heard most noticeably when pitted against the juddering rhythm cellos, in themselves a first in a pop hit, that underpin the "I'm picking up good vibrations" section, the closest the song gets to a conventional chorus. The final fade of the song reprises this section without the vocals, so one of the last things you hear as the song quickly fades is Tanner's electronic wail. A suitably unconventional way to end this least conventional of singles.

'Good Vibrations' went on to be one of The Beach Boys' biggest hit singles, rising to high chart placings all over the world. Yet its success posed a problem for the band. Then, more so than now, bands were expected to play their recent hits during live appearances. For most artists, most of the time, this wasn't a problem, as songs were routinely knocked into shape during endless months of touring before they were recorded. 'Good Vibrations,' though, was a studio creation, not a song that had been refined on the road, and there was a pressing need to find a way to perform it live. And this included finding a way to recreate Tanner's parts on stage. With this in mind, at some point shortly after the recording of 'Good Vibrations' Wilson asked Tanner to perform on stage with The Beach Boys. Although The Beach Boys were offering good money, Tanner had too many commitments to consider taking the job. He was conscious, too, that he would have looked out of place with the band, being a generation older. He recalls saying to Wilson: "I've got the wrong sort of hair to be on the stage with you fellas," to which Wilson replied, "We'll give you a Prince Valiant wig."[12] It wasn't enough to persuade Tanner.

With Tanner unavailable and The Beach Boys touring to promote their new masterpiece, an alternative was urgently sought. Electronics genius Bob Moog was commissioned to design and build a special ribbon-controlled sound source to mimic Tanner's electro-theremin. With a delicious irony that you feel must have been deliberate on someone's part, Mike Love, who objected to Wilson dragging The Beach Boys out of the frothy surf, was handed the job of playing Moog's Tanner substitute live. To Love's credit, he entered into it gamely. Film and photographic evidence show him sometimes standing awkwardly at a microphone, managing the considerable feat of coordinating both singing and playing the ribbon controller. At other times he is seen striking splayed-leg guitar hero poses with Moog's little electronic box.

Tanner's association with The Beach Boys didn't end there, though. In September 1967 he was called up again to contribute a two-note hook to the title track of The Beach Boys' *Wild Honey* album. Not much was heard of the electro-theremin after that performance. Some time shortly after his last Beach Boys recording, Tanner found himself at another session with someone playing a synthesizer. He recognized at once that the new instrument's capabilities far exceeded his humble, homemade device. The electro-theremin was retired to a hospital, where it was used to conduct hearing tests. A few years later, the hospital was destroyed in an earthquake, and the electro-theremin was buried in the rubble.

With the electro-theremin gone, Tanner once again devoted all of his energies to his session and teaching work, before embarking on a long and active retirement. He has written many books, including volumes of memoirs, and a jazz tutor that is currently in its tenth print edition. Although gone for ever, Tanner's electro-theremin enjoys a sort of afterlife. When Brian Wilson re-emerged in the late 1990s with The Wondermints, to tour *Pet Sounds*, he took on stage with him an instrument designed by Theremin enthusiasts David Miller and Tom Polk. Miller had previously done much work investigating the electro-theremin's history. The instrument he and Polk built is a modern recreation of the electro-theremin. It is called, affectionately, The Tannerin.

FrENCH
CONNECTIONS

the ondes martenot and the ondioline

F or a few decades in the middle of the 20th century, the French seemed to have a particular knack for making advances in electronic musical technology. Constant Martin designed the Clavioline in the 1940s (chapter 3) and Pierre Schaeffer pioneered the tape editing and sound manipulation techniques of musique concrète in the 1950s (chapter 4). Before them came two men who designed and made the instruments discussed in this chapter: Maurice Martenot and Georges Jenny.

Maurice Martenot was born in 1898. He trained as a cellist, but during World War I served as a radio operator in the French army. During this time he noticed that electrical equipment could sometimes create audible pitches. When the war was over he set about finding a way to harness this phenomenon for musical purposes, a quest which culminated in the launch in 1928 of what was originally called the Ondes Musicales (musical waves) and later became known as the Ondes Martenot (Martenot's waves).

The instrument Martenot launched in Paris, playing the solo part to a work he had commissioned from Dimitri Levindis – *Symphonic Poem For Solo Ondes Musicales And Orchestra* – was not the model that later went into limited production. Nor was the version Martenot took on a demonstration tour of America in late 1930 and early 1931. Both of these early instruments had mechanisms that allowed the player to produce Theremin-like glissandos, but with more control. But the familiar model, which dates from 1932, was more sophisticated. Martenot extended the scope of the instrument to include *two* ways of pitching notes: a ribbon controller for glissandos, and a conventional piano-style keyboard.

Although the sound production technology Martenot used for his instrument was the same heterodyne principle used by Theremin, and both instruments excel at sweeping glissandos, they have little in common beyond that. The Ondes Martenot has a host of expression controls and up to four different speakers, which combine to give a much broader sonic palette and greater interaction between the player and instrument than the Theremin. It is these features that set the Martenot apart from the primitive devices it was competing against in the early 1930s, and which continue to attract composers and performers today. Ondist and film composer François Evans puts it this way: "There is a sensual relationship between yourself and the sound the Martenot gives out. It is not like an electronic instrument you get nowadays that gives you exactly what you might put in. The instrument is alive."[1]

There are two ways of selecting notes on the Ondes Martenot. Firstly, you can use the conventional piano-style keyboard, which is usually seven octaves, although as instruments were built to order this can vary. Screws can be loosened to allow the keyboard itself some lateral movement, which if activated by moving a finger from side to side while depressing a key produces vibrato.

The Martenot is a monophonic instrument, so players use their right hand only to select notes, leaving the left free to control dynamics and timbre using a number of controls to the left of the keyboard, which are housed in a tray that can slide in and out of the body of the instrument. The oddest of these controls is a carbon-filled bag with the consistency of a sponge – sometimes referred to as a 'lozenge' – which controls timbre and can be thought of as the equivalent of the bowing action of a violinist. There is also a knee lever that controls volume.

The other way to pitch notes is by using the ribbon in front of the keyboard. The player operates this by inserting his or her index finger into a metal ring in the middle of the ribbon, and sliding up and down the octaves. A row of indentations (for white notes) and small brass 'nail heads' (for black notes) between the ribbon and keyboard mark out semitones, giving a tactile reference point for the player. Like the slider on Paul Tanner's electro-theremin (chapter 1), the ribbon controller can produce the wide range of inflexions, glissandos, quarter tones and the like, so characteristic of the Theremin, but, on account of the tactile cues, with much greater accuracy. While using the ribbon controller the left hand is free to operate the expression controls, as it is when the keyboard is being played. Two foot-controlled pedals (mute and intensity) give further dynamic control.

The Martenot keyboard unit, which houses the sound producing electronics, is connected to as many as four speakers, or diffusers, which are selected using

The Ondes Martenot keyboard (main picture), 'palme' and 'metallique' acoustic
chambers (below, left and right), and slide-out control panel (below, center).

buttons on the left-hand control panel. One of these is a conventional loudspeaker. The other three are unique to the Martenot, their distinct sound characteristics the result of an integration of the instrument's electronic tones with acoustic treatments. The most visually striking is the *palme*, which looks like some kind of ancient psaltery. Its body is an acoustic chamber fitted with guitar-type strings on both sides – 12 on the front and 12 on the back. These resonate in sympathy when an electronic signal is sent to the speaker. The *metallique* is in effect a standard speaker with the cone replaced with something like a cymbal, which produces a crash like a gong. The last, the *resonance*, a reverb chamber, is not always fitted.

From its inception, Martenot thought of his instrument as a new voice for the orchestra. As the music critic in the *New York Times* put it when reporting on Martenot's first promotional visit to America, "The inventor asserts … that his primary aim is not to imitate the sounds of other instruments, but to provide new resources of expression for composers and novel color effects to enrich the orchestral palette."[2]

Initially, Martenot went some way to achieving this aim. Many symphonic works, operas, ballets, and other works were composed for the Ondes Martenot in the mid 20th century, most famously by Olivier Messiaen, whose *Turangalîla Symphony* remains the instrument's definitive orchestral work. Martenot himself was a professor at the Paris Conservatoire from the 1940s until 1970, where he taught a method of playing his instrument to budding ondists, including, in the late 1950s, the British TV composer Barry Gray (see chapter 5). But his high aspirations for his invention would ultimately limit the appeal of what is still, in the age of apparently limitless sonic options, a remarkable instrument.

Production of the Ondes Martenot remained a small-scale affair, overseen by the inventor in Paris until his death in a road traffic accident in 1980, four days before his 82nd birthday. As each instrument was made to order by hand, there were many minor differences throughout the whole range. The biggest change came in the late 1960s, when what had up to that point been a tube instrument became a solid-state one. These later models had the advantage of being considerably louder than the rather polite older versions. In his long and productive life, Martenot also devised a system of musical education that is still is use in France, Canada, Spain, and Portugal, and wrote a book on how to relax. Production continued for a short while after his death to meet outstanding orders. Most of these last models went to Japan.

The instruments, particularly the earlier ones finished in light-colored wood casings cut in art deco shapes, are as much works of art as working musical gear, and are highly prized today. Expensive, fragile and beautiful, they look at home on a stage in a concert hall surrounded by an orchestra, but only a very rich or very foolhardy person would take one on a tour of clubs, or around a few recording studios. They were intended as specialist instruments for the musical elite, and by and large that is what they still are. It wasn't until the late 1950s, by which time the Ondes Martenot was 30 years old, that it first appeared in popular music, courtesy of British TV composer Barry Gray (see chapter 6).

Shortly afterwards it started to get some exposure as a tool for film soundtrack composers, first in the hands of Maurice Jarre, father of Jean Michèle Jarre. He used it in many films, including, contrastingly, *Lawrence Of Arabia* and *Mad Max*. But with the exception of a very obscure Canadian band called Et Cetera, operating in the 1970s, it wasn't until the 1990s that a rock band used the Ondes Martenot.

Radiohead's Jonny Greenwood nurtured a fascination for the Ondes Martenot before even seeing one. "I first heard the Ondes Martenot when a teacher at school played us Messiaen's *Turangalîla Symphony* and I heard it swooping along with the strings," he says. "But I had no idea what it looked like, and then finally, when we were doing *Kid A*, I found one in Paris."[3] The model Greenwood found was one of the very last Ondes Martenots built, one of a production run of just 50 overseen by the grandson of Maurice Martenot after the inventor's death. Greenwood used the instrument on several songs on that album, and all of the others that have followed, including his solo debut *Bodysong*. It has become a pivotal component of the Radiohead sound, its eerie sweeps an ideal foil for singer Thom

Yorke's quavering sustained notes. Indeed, at times the two sounds seem to become one. On 'Pyramid Song' from *Amnesiac*, a disjointed piano ballad, Yorke starts the song with a wordless melody line. When he returns to it later in the song, it is overlaid with a Martenot harmony to haunting effect.

Greenwood loves the instrument for its sound and the possibilities it offers for expression: "It puts you in total control of the pitch and expression, and it's as close to singing as I can get. It's a living thing."[4] Martenot would have approved of these sentiments. He would have approved, too, of Greenwood's work composing new pieces of classical music for the Ondes Martenot. But Greenwood's assertion that, because the instrument is monophonic, "anyone can play it and it should have had the populist appeal of the Stylophone,"[5] would have the French inventor turning in his grave. The last thing Martenot wanted was that the instrument that bore his name would become a simple gadget with populist appeal. On the contrary, so intent was he on promoting it as a serious addition to the classical range of instruments that the playing method he taught at the Paris Conservatoire was rigorous and thorough, extending to correct posture and hand positions.

Radiohead are a commercially and critically successful band, and Greenwood's enthusiastic endorsement of the Ondes Martenot may yet result in some enterprising company taking up production of the instrument again. If that were to happen the inevitable result would be that more rock bands would get hold of the instrument, thus pulling it further away from Martenot's original vision. Greenwood, though, would welcome this, taking up the Stylophone comparison again and saying: "It just needed a Rolf Harris. Although I'm not quite sure if that's me."[6] But until that happens, if it does, the Ondes Martenot will remain infrequently used in pop on account of its scarcity. Like some nearly extinct exotic bird, it will glide tantalisingly into view fleetingly, before returning to its rarefied natural habitat.

But although the Ondes Martenot itself will most likely remain obscure, Greenwood's enthusiasm for it has led directly to a modern interpretation of its unique set of controls. In 2000, Greenwood approached British company Analogue Systems,

asking if they could develop a Martenot-style controller keyboard that he could use on stage to control his modular synth set up, as he had reservations about taking his Ondes Martenot on tour. The company took on the commission, and the French Connection was made. Analogue Systems owner Bob Williams says: "Jonny's tech Peter Clemence (Plank) brought the Martenot down to us for an hour or two to take detailed notes, photos, and measurements. A few weeks later French Connection Number One was personally delivered to Jonny for initial evaluation. A few tweaks and adjustments were made, as per his instructions, then the first two production French Connections were delivered to him and then consequently used."[7]

The French Connection is a 'dumb controller.' That is, it does not have any sound-creating circuitry or the Martenot's speaker system. What it does have, though, are replications of the Martenot's unique expression features: a ribbon controller in front of the four-octave keyboard, and a wooden button to mimic the Martenot's expression sponge.

Greenwood first used the French Connection in performance on the BBC's *Top Of The Pops* program in May 2001, performing 'Pyramid Song' from *Amnesiac*, which in its recorded form makes extensive use of Martenot. Since then many other pop acts have purchased the controllers, including Athlete, Red Hot Chili Peppers, Aerosmith, Sigur Ros, and Nine Inch Nails.

In contrast to Maurice Martenot, Georges Jenny had the big idea of making an instrument that could do many of the things the Ondes Martenot could do, but in a simpler, cheaper package that could be used in the popular arena. He went some way to achieving this. Jenny (born circa 1900) first conceived of his Ondioline in 1938, while recovering from tuberculosis in a sanatorium. He completed his first instrument during the war, and put it into production in 1947. For nearly 30 years, until his death in 1976, he continued to refine the instrument. Jenny never licensed the Ondioline for mass production, preferring instead to assemble completed instruments himself, or sell them as kits. Yet despite this, more than 1,000 were sold in the US alone, where it became briefly popular in the early 1960s.

French electronic pop pioneer Jean-Jacques Perrey with his Ondioline in the mid 1960s.

In its original form, the Ondioline is a monophonic vacuum-tube keyboard instrument housed in a wooden cabinet with a hint of art deco styling. As with the Ondes Martenot, the technology switched to solid state in the 1960s and the cabinets were updated to look more like contemporary speakers and amplifiers. With both basic models there are two components, the keyboard unit and the amplifier/speaker combination. The amp/speaker cabinet stands about three feet high, and houses a single nine-inch speaker, a small amp, and the Ondioline's sound controls. The small three-octave keyboard is designed to stand on top of the amp/speaker or on a stand of its own.

The Ondioline keyboard is the instrument's feature that most obviously betrays a debt to the Ondes Martenot. It is mounted on leaf springs, which allows for playing a note and simultaneously moving the key from side to side, which gives vibrato. In front of the keyboard is a flat metal braid mounted on a brass plate, which runs the entire width of the keyboard. Unlike the Martenot's ribbon controller, this device does not control pitch. Rather, it adds attack to a note if pressed at the same time as selecting a note with the keyboard. The keyboard also has a volume knee-lever for expression.

The Ondioline's sounds are created by a number of filter controls on top of the amp/speaker. These can be used in many combinations, and produce a range of tones unique to the Ondioline, as well as others that mimic orchestral instruments. As Jenny developed the instrument over the years, he added more sound control features, including, on later solid-state models, an air pipe that allowed the performer to control expression by blowing.

Ondiolines produce a range of sounds far broader than the other popular early electronic keyboards that they competed with, but their success was hindered by unreliability. Wanting to keep costs down, Jenny often used poor quality components, which meant that unless carefully maintained the instruments often failed after a few years. Despite this, Jenny's Ondioline almost became the popular instrument he wanted it to be. Along with the roughly contemporaneous Hammond Solovox and the Clavioline, made under license by Gibson and Selmer (see chapter 3), it was among the very first reasonably cheap, purely electronic keyboards. But unlike the Solovox and the Clavioline it was not pushed by the promotional muscle of big, established musical instrument companies. Yet despite its comparative obscurity, it marks a sea change in the development of musical electronics. Before the Ondioline, electronic instruments were either obscure failures built in tiny numbers, or, like the Theremin and Ondes Martenot, originally designed with higher purposes in mind. Ondiolines, on the other hand, were meant for the popular musician. Given this, it is fitting that the star of the Ondioline story was a musician who unashamedly made pop music.

By the time Ondioline production stopped, with Jenny's death in 1976, the instruments were obsolete curiosities, superseded by the first generation of small analogue synthesizers. But in the late 1940s, when they first started to appear in significant numbers, they were marvels, much admired for their ability not only to mimic existing instruments but also to create their own unique sounds. In America in particular they attracted significant media attention. This was due to another Frenchman, whom Jenny had employed as an Ondioline salesman, electronic pop pioneer Jean Jacques Perrey.

Perrey is an artist who has been rediscovered by later generations after years of bargain bin obscurity; there are many of them in this retro-obsessed age. This has led to sweeping claims being made on his behalf about his musical importance that most listeners, when they actually hear his music now, struggle to accept. In fairness to Perrey, he doesn't make such claims himself, and always says that what he was trying to do as a musician was to make fun music. His live act was from the age of variety – a sort of electronic music hall turn that combined demonstrations of the Ondioline with comedy. His records, excepting a few exceptional songs including the much-sampled 'E.V.A.,' are kitsch period pieces. Making a version of 'Flight Of The Bumble Bee' out of recordings of bees buzzing, using tape-editing techniques, as Perrey did, was an impressive technical feat. But it still sounds like a novelty. He is an important figure, though, less for the actual music he made, and more for being one of a few pioneers who dragged electronic musical instruments out of the stiflingly austere world of modern classical music into the bright, cheerful pop landscape that has turned out to be their natural home. History has proved him to be a true visionary. When Perrey started on his eccentric career as an Ondioline salesman and musician, in 1953, pop's use of electronics was in its infancy, whereas in modern classical music electronics were the coming thing. Now, virtually all pop music uses electronic instruments, whereas they are marginal items in classical music.

Born in 1929, Perrey was studying medicine in Paris when he met Georges Jenny in 1952. He was fascinated by Jenny's Ondioline and within a year had given up his studies to work with Jenny promoting the instrument. Later, Perrey became interested in tape manipulation, following a meeting with another French musical innovator, musique concrète creator Pierre Schaeffer. He would go on to combine tape manipulation and the Ondioline in a number of the instrumental pop albums on which his current reputation rests. After a few years of traveling around Europe giving Ondioline demonstrations at music fairs, Perrey met Edith Piaf, who was much impressed with the instrument. He played the Ondioline on stage with her at the Paris Olympia in 1959, and she in turn gave him money to pay for studio time to make some recordings with the instrument. Piaf then sent these recordings to a friend in New York called Carroll Bratman. His company, Carroll Music Service, hired out musical instruments to orchestras and studios throughout New York. Bratman liked what he heard and ordered an Ondioline. He also invited Perrey to visit New York in 1962, sending him tickets and providing accommodation and studio space for him once he arrived.[8]

Once established in New York, Perrey set about composing and recording, while promoting the Ondioline wherever he could. He toured the country giving demonstrations, and appeared many times on television as 'Mr Ondioline,' a cheerful Gallic eccentric. The American public had already got a taste for the instrument on account of its use by composer Alex North in the Stanley Kubrick film *Spartacus* (1960). North had bought his Ondioline in Paris, but with Perrey's arrival in 1962, the instrument became more widely available in America, and for a short while it was in vogue.

The following year the Ondioline appeared in the American singles charts for the first time, thanks to popular jazz trombonist Kai Winding, a one-time musical director at the Playboy club. His 1963 instrumental hit, 'More,' from the movie *Mondo Cane*, was drawn from the album *Soul Surfin'*. On this and a subsequent follow up, *Mondo Cane 2*, released to cash in on the single's success, Winding himself is credited with playing the Ondioline. Perrey has claimed since that he was the performer, which seems plausible given that Winding's records were made in New York when Perrey was the resident Ondioline gun for hire.

The first rock musician to get interested in the Ondioline was sometime Dylan sideman Al Kooper. He first came across the instrument at a private demonstration at Carroll Music, set up by a friend's aunt who worked there. From there on, whenever Kooper wanted to use an Ondioline on a session, he hired one from Carroll.

Kooper first recorded Ondioline on the Gene Pitney album, *I Must Be Seeing Things* (1965), returning to the instrument several times after that, most notably on The Blues Project's 'No Time Like The Right Time,' a minor hit that later found a wider audience after being included on the *Nuggets* compilation. You can hear the instrument clearly when the band drops out at 1 minute 7 seconds for Kooper's raga-style solo.

"[I liked] the fact that I could play it with the heel of my hand and play Coltrane-ish scales that way,"[9] Kooper says, and this style that turns up on later Kooper solos with Blood Sweat & Tears, and on the *Super Sessions* and *Live Adventures* albums with Mike Bloomfield. These later solos are sometimes said to be played on the Ondioline, but Kooper says: "I later purchased (in 1967) an early Japanese synth called an Ace Tone Canary and a tube-shaped one from Sweden called a Tubon, which was referred to as the Kooper-fone because nobody else knew what to do with it. I played the Canary on the BS&T album *Child Is Father To The Man* and on the albums *Super Sessions* and *Live Adventures*. I had outgrown the Ondioline by that time."[10] The Ace Tone Canary is a rare bird indeed. It was displayed by Ace Tone at the

NAMM instruments show in 1964 alongside an early version of the famous Rhythm Ace drum machine (chapter 5), but was only ever produced in very limited numbers.

Meanwhile, Perrey was continuing his varied activities in commercial music making. He made adverts and jingles, performed live, and embarked on a series of four instrumental electronic pop albums for Vanguard, two with collaborator Gershon Kingsley. The first of these, *The In Sound From Way Out* (1966), was made entirely with tape manipulation and the Ondioline. The other three albums in the series also used the then new Moog synthesizer. Perrey returned to France in the late 1960s. Now in his eighties, he lives in Switzerland and is still active in music.

Just as Kooper and Perrey introduced the Ondioline into pop, it was already on the point of being trumped by a new keyboard, the Moog, which could apparently do anything. By the late 1960s, the French oddity was drifting inexorably into obscurity. It was already an anachronism when, in 1978, New York new wave band Television used one for a song called 'The Fire' on the *Adventure* album. Television's debut *Marquee Moon* had been instantly acclaimed as a classic, and *Adventure* suffered in comparison. With hindsight it is a good album, although it does lack the tightly-drilled energy of its predecessor. Nearly six minutes long, 'The Fire' starts side two of *Adventure*, a slow, spacious guitar arrangement, with the hovering Ondioline a distinctive aural signature.

By the 1990s, the Ondioline was known only to collectors and students of kitsch, but in 1993 the name at least came back into pop consciousness with the release of Anglo French band Stereolab's 'Jenny Ondioline' single. Stereolab's reference points include 1960s experimental electronic music and French pop, and it is a part of their aesthetic to make reference to their odd cultural anchors in song titles ('John Cage Bubblegum,' 'Melochord Seventy-Five'). The 'Jenny Ondioline' single is an example of this, although the lyric is an apocalyptic polemic that makes no mention of the instrument, and the music – 17 minutes of hypnotic synth pulses sweetened with a pop sensibility – doesn't feature it.

There is a third electronic instrument in the lineage that started with the Ondes Martenot and continued with the Ondioline. But although it was a French design, it also bore the marks of the Hammond Solovox. The coming together of these two lines, the French and the American, in the form of Constant Martin's Clavioline, marked another giant step forward for electronic musical instruments. The Clavioline became the first truly popular electronic keyboard instrument, produced in thousands in several countries for many years, and itself spawning several close imitations. It is also featured on two of the biggest hits of the 1960s. It is the subject of the next chapter.

A FULL ORCHESTRA AT YOUR FINGERTIPS

solovox, clavioline, univox, maestrovox, and musitron

T he Hammond Novachord was not a commercially successful product. But as Hammond's first electronic tube-based instrument, marketed between 1939 and 1942, it is historically significant. Also, it shares some technology with a smaller, simpler Hammond electronic instrument, the Solovox, which has a more important place in the evolving story of electronic instrumentation in pop music. But more of that shortly.

The 1,000 or so customers who were brave enough to buy a Novachord found themselves with a large, heavy, and complex machine. In a walnut body, and with a full size piano-type keyboard, three sustain foot pedals, an expression pedal, and 14 control knobs, the Novachord was over four feet wide, three feet deep and more than three feet high, and weighed in at 500 pounds. Designed by John Hanert, it was a marvel of pre-transistor ingenuity, polyphonic, with 12 oscillators, which gave a six-octave range through the use of frequency-dividing tubes.

The Novachord could muster up what were in the 1940s considered to be passable simulations of conventional instruments such as the piano, harpsichord, and various stringed and woodwind instruments. It also generated a few of its own unique sounds. The Novachord was featured on at least one pre-rock'n'roll best seller, *Perfume Set To Music* (1948), composed by Harry Revel and arranged and conducted by Les Baxter. This oddity was also a showcase for the Theremin playing of Dr Samuel Hoffman (see chapter 1). Baxter used the Novachord again, on a 1961 album called *Jewels*, which returns to many of the themes Baxter explored on the earlier record, but without the Theremin.

Yet despite its versatility compared to other contemporary electronic instruments, the Novachord never quite caught on. It was big and cumbersome, the electronics were unreliable, and both pianists and organists found it hard to adapt their playing styles to the instrument's unique demands. The Novachord was something of a folly, a grandiose but doomed instrument, a footnote in the history of electronic music. Novachords were not imported into England in great numbers, but an odd postscript to the Novachord story took place in London in 1957, when two brothers, Ken and Eddie Palmer, built a new Novachord. Their choice of a launch event, a

furniture exhibition at Earls Court, contributed to the venture's complete failure.

While the Novachord had no direct descendants, another electronic instrument designed by John Hanert for Hammond, the Solovox, was to have a longer life and a lasting legacy. The Solovox was the first of several instruments that are sometimes collectively referred to as piano attachments. These were very popular in light entertainment music throughout the 1940s and 1950s, and have dramatically made their presence felt in rock'n'roll on several occasions since, which is why the Solovox earns a place in this story.

The first Solovox, the Model J, appeared in 1940, a year after the launch of the Novachord. Production was suspended in 1941 when US industrial resources were diverted to the war effort. Production started again after the war, with a revised Solovox, the Model K, produced from 1946 to1948, and the final version, the Model L, from 1948 to 1950.[1]

Although the Solovox used some similar technology to the far bigger Novachord, it was not simply the poor relative of the earlier instrument. Hanert always intended it as an entirely new concept: a solo voice for playing melodies, which would be attached to a piano or organ. To realize this idea Hanert designed a small monophonic electronic keyboard with its own separate 'tone cabinet,' an amplifier and speaker combo. The keyboard was designed to be physically fitted beneath a piano or organ keyboard, using metal brackets that were supplied with the Solovox. The tone cabinet, a slimline rectangular shaped wooden box with a curved front, was designed to be fitted, using small chains and hooks also supplied on purchase, either to the side of an upright piano or underneath a grand piano. Thus equipped, players would key melodies using their right hand, while still having their left hand free to play chords on the piano or organ. Or, as the Solovox owners' manual put it: "The beautiful sustained tones of the Solovox blend in thrilling fashion with the percussion tones of your piano, greatly enriching even the simplest music."

Hanert housed the sound-generating electronics of the Solovox in the three-octave keyboard unit, not the tone cabinet. Beneath the keyboard itself are a number of large rocker switches that select the Solovox's various sounds. In the Model L, for example, there are 12 of these, divided into three groups. The first group are called register controls (bass, tenor, contralto, soprano); the second are tone controls (deep tone, full tone, first voice, second voice, brilliant); the third group is untitled, and consists of mute, fast attack, and vibrato off. To get a sound from the Solovox one or more of both the register controls and tone controls must be switched on. A total of 77 different combinations of controls were suggested in the owner's manual, many of which correspond to orchestral instruments or organ sounds. For example, selecting the bass, vibrato off, and deep tone controls gives you a tuba sound (or an approximation of one, at least). Some 20 of the suggested combinations were not intended to correspond to any other existing instrument, but are simply "interesting combinations."

Further possibilities for expression are provided by a knee-operated volume lever. The maximum and minimum volumes between which the knee lever operated are set by two volume controls. Rough and fine tuning controls are also provided.

The Solovox was quite widely used in American popular and light orchestral music in the 1940s and early 1950s, although it was not exported in great numbers. Its sonic capabilities were highly regarded, and still are by those aware of them. But it was to be a short-lived instrument, quickly eclipsed by the other piano attachment instruments that followed it, which were both more portable and more versatile. This meant that there would be very few uses of Solovox recorded in the rock'n'roll era. Its importance lies more in the later instruments it influenced. You can hear one, though, on 'Sugar Shack,' a 1963 US hit for Jimmy Gilmer and The Fireballs.

Of all the piano attachments, the Clavioline was the most successful and is the best remembered. It took some design cues from both the Solovox and the Ondioline, with other piano attachments that followed, including the Univox and the Maestrovox, taking those same cues from the Clavioline rather than their original sources. Each had a monophonic sound-producing keyboard with a separate amplifier/speaker combination. The sounds of each were chosen by selecting combinations of tones and

voices. And each had a knee-operated volume control for expression. While the Ondioline is musically a more versatile instrument, with its manual keyboard vibrato and percussive strip, the Clavioline was more practical for the gigging musician. Its great advantage over both the earlier French instrument and the Solovox is that the Clavioline keyboard unit packs into the back of the ten-inch speaker/amp combo, making a single portable unit.

Max Crook, Del Shannon's keyboard player, was one rock'n'roller who found this feature persuasive. He had considered a Solovox in the late 1950s, but discarded the idea, as the instrument was "very heavy, not to mention awkward to carry."[2] The two Solovox units, the keyboard and speaker, had a combined weight of about 60 pounds. Crook, like many others, eventually chose a Clavioline. The combined keyboard and speaker/amp weight of Claviolines is about 45 pounds, with some variation between different models.

The Clavioline's keyboard unit is similar to that of the Solovox. It too is three octaves, monophonic, and houses the sound generating technology. The keyboard includes another feature that gave it an advantage over the Solovox – a sliding switch that can transpose the whole instrument an octave either up or down, making a total of five octaves available. The first Claviolines have 18 rocker switches beneath the keyboard for controlling timbre, vibrato, and so on. The later Concert model, introduced by Selmer in 1954, has four more switches, which add sub-octaves. According to the adverts of the time, by selecting different combinations of the various switches the Clavioline reproduces "with amazing fidelity the tonal quality of more than 30 different musical instruments." These include the obvious – various orchestral stringed, brass, and woodwind instruments – and the unusual, including musical saw, zither, banjo, bagpipes, and 'Arabian Flute.' Today, most listeners would beg to differ with those claims. The sounds are all constant tones, with sharp attack and no decay. They do vary from each other, sometimes bright and buzzy, sometimes warmer, but all are inescapably electronic tones. And using the onboard vibrato only makes them all sound more like an organ, and less like the instrument they are supposed to be mimicking.

An American Clavioline keyboard and amp made by Gibson's parent company, Chicago Musical Instrument.

Only the bass saxophone sound is plausible in itself, although passable violin and woodwind sounds can be obtained with subtle use of the knee lever for expression. Yet despite this, the Clavioline was much admired in its day for its ability to mimic reed instruments like clarinets and oboes.

The Clavioline was designed by Constant Martin, of Versailles, France, in 1947.

As well as being a clever electronics engineer, and the author of a book on electronic music, Martin was a canny businessman. He licensed the rights to manufacture Claviolines to Gibson in the USA, Selmer in the UK, and to several other smaller manufacturers around the world. The combination of this commercial muscle with improved portability meant that as soon as the Clavioline was introduced it rendered the Solovox obsolete. The Ondioline was able to survive alongside the Clavioline on account of

its greater musical range, but its sales never came anywhere near those of the later keyboard.

Selmer was the first company to start manufacturing the Clavioline, in about 1950, with Gibson launching its model at 1952's NAMM (National Association of Music Merchants) instruments show. It caused quite a stir, with a *New York Times* feature on the event reporting, "Hot news here is not the world premiere of a new piano concerto, but the [Gibson parent] Chicago Musical Instrument Company's new Clavioline."[3] Footage of the Clavioline was broadcast several times a day to the show's 300,000 visitors, over a closed television circuit.

Claviolines were originally marketed by both Selmer and Gibson as instruments mainly for home use. In those days, the early 1950s, the way many people enjoyed the hits of the day was by buying the sheet music of popular tunes, so that they could play them on their pianos at home. It was to these people that Claviolines were pitched. Clavioline adverts and brochures of the period were full of enticing come-ons like "have a full orchestra at your fingertips," and showed refined ladies in their comfortable drawing rooms delighting in the possibilities of the new purchase fixed to their upright pianos. But both companies quickly caught on to the fact that the Clavioline, being portable and capable of generating many interesting sounds, offered a great deal to the working popular musician, whether organist or pianist. In Britain, Claviolines also became popular as additions to church organs. A trade publication of the time reported that, according to the magazine of St. Augustine's Church, Gillingham, in Kent, the installation of a Clavioline meant that "brides with their bridegrooms can now march down the aisle with a flourish of trumpets."[4]

In Britain, the Clavioline was embraced by mainstream light orchestral and dance band musicians. All but forgotten now, these artists flourished not only in the years immediately before rock'n'roll, but also alongside the new music through to the late 1950s. Once popular names like Bill McGuffie, Cyril Grantham, Harold Smart, and Sandy MacPherson used the instrument, a fact that Selmer was quick to exploit in its adverts. Those same adverts also told you that if you tuned into the BBC radio Light

Programme at 10pm on Mondays in the latter part of 1958 you could hear a Clavioline played by one Peter Yorke. Selmer went on to boast that Claviolines had been installed in all sorts of important places in London, including the RAC club, an exclusive gentlemen's establishment, the BBC organ at Bush House, Streatham Ice Rink in the south London suburbs, as well as on the Queen Mary ocean liner. Claviolines had a lower profile in the United States, perhaps because Gibson's attention always tended to wander towards its guitars.

Given the Clavioline's popularity in the British music business mainstream in the 1950s, it was only a matter of time before rock'n'rollers picked it up. The first British rock'n'roll band to use the Clavioline was led by a man who also had a background in many branches of the era's classical, jazz, and popular orchestral music, and would no doubt have come across the instrument in the course of his other work.

The John Barry Seven are best remembered now as an early vehicle for film composer John Barry. They used the Clavioline on their only album, *Stringbeat* (1961). In the late 1950s and early 1960s, The Seven were a popular live band on the British dance hall circuit, although they failed to achieve much chart action. It would be another band that would have the first big British rock'n'roll hit to prominently feature a Clavioline, in 1962, towards the end of the instrument's production run. That record, 'Telstar,' was credited to The Tornados, but it was really the work of its composer and producer, Joe Meek.

By any standards, Meek was an unusual man to succeed in the music business. Born and raised in the rural west of England, he was poorly educated, barely literate, and could neither sing, read music, nor play an instrument. But he was fascinated by electronics, recording technology in particular. His mother had wanted a girl, and it is said that Meek wore dresses until he went to school. From a very early age he didn't fit in. He was sensitive and often bad tempered. While his brothers and school-friends were absorbed in typical country pursuits like fishing, shooting, and stealing apples, Meek preferred the solitude of a garden shed that his parents had allowed him to colonize. Here he dismantled old radios and gramophones.

Meek left school at 14 with few career options open to him. After several jobs in radio shops and a spell doing national service in the Royal Air Force, Meek found his way to London. He soon joined the country's leading independent recording studio, IBC, where he worked as an engineer. There he recorded several big hits of the time, including Lonnie Donegan's 'Cumberland Gap' and Frankie Vaughan's 'Green Door.' In those days, recording was a formal process with its own unwritten rules and established hierarchy. The roles of engineer, producer, songwriter,

Early Clavioline promotional literature included in a British Selmer catalogue.

and manager rarely overlapped. Meek, having scant regard for convention, found that frustrating. He wanted to do everything. He also had his own ideas about how to record and mix records, which didn't always coincide with those of the traditionalists he found himself working with. He craved independence.

Meek, the gauche, unsubtle iconoclast, lasted three years at IBC before setting up Lansdowne studios with independent jazz producer Denis Preston. The pair lured many IBC clients into Lansdowne, and the relationship thrived for a while before Meek once again started to bridle against what he perceived as the endless obstacles other narrow-minded people were intent on putting in his path. In time this tendency to be suspicious of, and fall out with, colleagues and competitors was to descend into the paranoia that contributed so much to Meek's tragic end. He walked out of Lansdowne in late 1959.

By that time he had already set up the first of his home studios, in a flat in Holland Park in west London. But it was in his second home studio, in a rented flat above a leather goods shop in Holloway Road in north London, that he was to achieve his greatest triumph. Here he wrote and recorded dozens of songs for his roster of artists, making finished masters that he then hawked around to major labels under the aegis of RGM Productions (named after his own initials).

Home studios and independent production companies are commonplace in the recording industry these days, but back then they were unheard of. So Meek's run of hits in the early 1960s, admittedly interspersed with many more flops, was a staggering achievement. And 'Telstar' is the greatest hit of them all.

There are several slightly different accounts of the writing and recording of 'Telstar,' from which a broadly consistent story emerges.[5] It starts in July 1962, when the Telstar 1 satellite was rocketed into orbit. Although just one of many satellites to go spinning around the earth since the launch of Sputnik 1 in 1957, Telstar 1 was intended for special things: it was to be the means by which the first transatlantic television broadcast would take place. This broadcast turned out to be little more than a hazy, ghostly,

indistinct image of a man sitting at a desk, but it was sufficient to captivate Meek when it appeared on British television screens in the early hours of a July morning.

Meek was fascinated with the idea of space travel and the possibility of life on other planets. Indeed, he had made a bizarre concept album in 1960, *I Hear A New World*, which explored these themes (see chapter 4). That fascination and Meek's love of all things electronic meant the Telstar broadcast fired his imagination. At this point some accounts diverge, but what is certain is that Meek, dwelling on the night's events, was struck with a tune. He then began his idiosyncratic and laborious compositional method, which involved singing a very vague approximation of the tune in his head over a pre-existing backing track. One of Meek's associates, Dave Adams, was then charged with deciphering the music encrypted in Meek's out of tune wailing. This was a process of trial and error, with Adams playing a fragment of melody, based, as best he could, on what Meek had sung. Meek would then either say "Yes, that's it," and the two would proceed to the next line of the song, or he would say "No," in which case Adams would have to try something else.

Eventually Adams' work was finished, and a few days later The Tornados were called in to record the new song. The band was a part of Meek's stable of artists, pursuing a career as an instrumental rock group and also backing British rock'n'roll star Billy Fury, whom Meek was keen to sign. At the time Fury was playing a summer season in Great Yarmouth. During a Sunday break in performances, The Tornados drove back to London and further developed the song, under Meek's strict guidance. On that day, and for a few hours the following morning, the band recorded the backing track to 'Telstar,' and what would become the single's b-side. But by the time they had to load up their van for the drive back to Great Yarmouth on Monday lunchtime, the memorable melody line had yet to be recorded.

At this point Meek called on another collaborator, Geoff Goddard. Meek and Goddard shared an interest in spiritualism and a belief that the late Buddy Holly communicated with them. They also had a successful working partnership. Meek's great production of the previous year, 'Johnny Remember Me' by John Leyton, had been written by Goddard. As Goddard sat down to begin several hours of recording Clavioline and piano parts, with Meek calling instructions from the control room, the magic visited them again.

The finished result was, by a very long way, the most radical British rock'n'roll record yet recorded. Coming in at 3 minutes and 14 seconds, then quite long for a pop single, 'Telstar' is an essentially simple, rousing tune. It is the sound of the record that grabs attention, right from the bubbly, fizzing electronic trickery that the listener first hears.

'Telstar' comprises two sections, one led by the Clavioline and one by a twangy electric guitar typical of the era and broadly similar in style to the works of contemporary instrumentalists like The Shadows and The Ventures. After the electronic intro, an ascending Clavioline line introduces the galloping rhythm track that is a constant throughout the song. 'Telstar' then breaks into two runs through the main Clavioline theme. It is followed by one guitar section, underpinned by harp-like arpeggios performed by Goddard on a piano with tacks stuck in the hammers. Both sections then repeat at half the length before a key change leads into a final run through the Clavioline tune, backed by "ah ah" vocals, also provided by Goddard. An outro disappears into yet more electronic noise.

It is the Clavioline tune in 'Telstar' that stays with you after the record ends. But if you were to play that theme on a Clavioline you would not recreate the eerie sound that Meek achieved. This is because Meek multi-tracked Goddard's performances at different octaves, making at least two, maybe three layers of Clavioline. The result is a much thicker, fuller sound than a solo Clavioline creates. Some reports suggest an electric organ is also mixed into the final sound. The inevitable slight irregularities in each of Goddard's recorded performances mean that the Clavioline's vibrato cycles are slightly out of phase with each other. This creates the distinctive wobbly sound you hear on the finished record. Add to that the fact that the multi-tracking process involved much bouncing together of tracks, during which Meek would layer on the reverb and pump up the compression, and subtle

layers of hiss and distortion are integrated into the final sound on the record, too.

Various Tornados expressed doubts during the recording of 'Telstar,' but they recognized that Meek had created something special when he played them the final, mixed version. The layered Clavioline tune embodies perfectly the sense of innocent optimism and hope in technological progress that characterized the early days of the space race. Listening to 'Telstar' now, more than 40 years later, that innocence and optimism seem all the more poignant, given the knowledge of what happened to its creator a few years later.

First released on Decca records in the UK, then London records in the USA, 'Telstar' went on to become one of 1962's biggest hits, topping the charts in both countries. That Meek should score a big British hit wasn't such a surprise. He had done it before and would do it again. What was astonishing, though, was that the single climbed to the top spot in the USA, the first British rock'n'roll record to do so. It went on to sell more than five million copies worldwide on first release, and remained in Decca's catalogue continually until the mid 1980s. It is said to be the favorite record of former British Prime Minister Margaret Thatcher.

'Telstar' was Meek's greatest triumph, but it also contributed to his downfall. A French composer, Jean Ledrut, claimed that the tune was stolen from a piece he had written for a 1960 film called *The Battle Of Austerlitz*. He sued, and Meek's royalties for 'Telstar' were frozen while the case meandered through the French courts for several years. Eventually Meek got his money, but the anxiety and financial hardship that the episode caused him must have further damaged what was already a fragile state of mind.

There were more Meek hits after 'Telstar,' but eventually his career faltered as his life disintegrated. Always unstable, and prone to fits of temper, he became increasingly paranoid, believing his competitors, among them Phil Spector, were bugging his studio to learn his tricks. He took pills to stay awake as he worked too hard, which increased his jumpiness. A gay man at a time when homosexuality was illegal, he was arrested for importuning, and was terrified that his family would see the brief newspaper report about the resultant court case. His interest in the occult became an obsession. Then, on February 3rd, 1967, Meek argued with his landlady and shot her dead, before reloading and turning the gun on himself. He was 38 years old. It was eight years to the day since his hero, Buddy Holly, had died.

After Meek's death a cult gradually grew up around him, which has so far produced several fan clubs, two books, a stage play, and a number of television and radio documentaries. From time to time, people announce that they have in their possession 'Joe Meek's Clavioline,' a sort of holy relic of the fallen god of British pop.

As for The Tornados, they suffered diminishing returns after 'Telstar.' A sizeable follow-up hit, 'Globetrotter,' once again used a Clavioline, as did many of the band's other recordings. But they were swept away by the tide of 1960s British beat bands, led by The Beatles and The Rolling Stones. At the beginning of 1963, The Tornados were the great hopes of British rock; by the end of the year they were has-beens. The hits dried up and the band drifted apart. Drummer Clem Cattini, who had provided 'Telstar' with its galloping beat, went on to become an in-demand session drummer, performing on dozens of hits.

Given the number made, it is not surprising that Claviolines turned up in all sorts of music for many years before and after 'Telstar.' John Barry and Sergio Leone both used them in film scores. The Beatles are often credited with using a Clavioline, on 'Baby You're A Rich Man.' Indeed, a monophonic electronic keyboard instrument – or at least, a keyboard sounding one note at a time – can clearly be heard through most of the song. 'Baby You're A Rich Man' was recorded for the animated feature film *Yellow Submarine*, at Olympic Studios in London, not the group's usual recording venue. The story goes that the Clavioline was left lying around in the studio after the preceding session, and that John Lennon decided on the spot to play it. This is quite plausible, as Claviolines were still commonplace at the time (1967), although they had been out of production for three years. But intriguingly, an engineer on the session, Eddie Kramer, has this to say: "It had a little strip which you put your thumb on and moved it up and down the

length of the keyboard as you played, to get vibrato …"[6] No Clavioline has such a strip, although Ondiolines have something resembling this feature, which controls attack, not vibrato. So assuming Kramer's recollections are accurate, this particular Clavioline sighting must remain unconfirmed.

Even if your tastes extend to the furthest extremes of avant-garde jazz, there is a Clavioline performer for you. Sun Ra had one attached to his piano during the recording of many of his 1960s and 1970s space jazz freak-outs, using the instrument's reed-like tones to play spiraling improvisations.

Whereas many early electronic instruments were designed by creative individuals motivated at least in part by the exciting musical possibilities suggested by electronics, the story of another of the piano attachments, the Jennings Univox, is one of straightforward commercial opportunism. The Clavioline was already being manufactured and distributed in the UK by Selmer when Tom Jennings, whose company produced accordions, spotted its potential. He produced a design with enough circuit changes to ensure that it wouldn't infringe the existing patent for the French instrument, while at the same time doing more or less the same job. From this, the Jennings Univox was born, in 1952.

Given the origins of the Univox, it is no surprise to find that it is very similar indeed to the Clavioline, both technically and in appearance. Like the Clavioline, the Univox has a three-octave monophonic keyboard, which could be extended an octave up or down, making five octaves in total. Fifteen stops and buttons gave different voice options and several types of vibrato, and there's the obligatory volume knee lever. The two instruments look very similar when packed up, too, although the Univox is slightly more compact, and weighs a few pounds less. One unique feature of the Univox is that it has a device that simulates the effect of a mandolin tremolo, with runs of rapid staccato notes.

Initially the Univox was supplied with clips to fasten it under a piano keyboard, like the Clavioline. Later an adjustable z-shaped stand was produced so that the instrument could stand on its own. In time, Claviolines too had their own stands.

The respective manufacturers of the Univox and

the Clavioline .waged what was, in the clipped terms of 1950s Britain, a fierce advertising war in the pages of *Melody Maker* from 1953 to 1956. Both claimed the virtues of their instruments over other 'similar products,' and both lined up endorsement from celebrity musicians of the day. Jennings scored a particularly impressive hit in November 1954 when they got huge-selling light-orchestral conductor and arranger Mantovani to recommend the Univox. But although the Univox was considerably cheaper than the Clavioline, coming in at about 75 guineas (£81.15 or $230) compared to 125 guineas (£135.25 or $380) for the top of the range Selmer (Gibson launched theirs at $395, or £140), it was the Clavioline that prevailed in the end. Jennings all but gave up pushing the Univox by the late 1950s, although there was a late flurry of adverts in the early 1960s, more of which later.

But although the Univox lost the war with the Clavioline, it was a successful commercial product. Initially, it was electronically and mechanically unreliable, but problems were ironed out as the instrument was developed through successive models. In time it became a big-seller, being particularly popular with pub entertainers. The Univox earns its place in pop history, though, not only for being one of the first cheap electronic instruments, but also for the later developments its strong sales funded. Encouraged by the instrument's success, Tom Jennings formed Jennings Musical Instruments, the company that went on to produce Vox organs, guitars, and guitar amplifiers, including the beloved and revered AC30 combo. Indeed, the distinctive diamond patterned speaker cloth to be seen on AC30s was probably first used on the Univox amp/speaker combo. Similarly, the Univox z-stand design later turned up supporting Vox Continental organs.

The rivalry between the Univox and the Clavioline extended to the biggest piano attachment hit, 'Telstar.' Although all authorities, including Meek's biographer John Repsch, insist that Meek used multi-tracked Claviolines to produce the distinctive keyboard melody line on The Tornados hit, claims are still sometimes made that he in fact used a Univox. There are several possible sources to this rumor, one being simply that the instruments

looked and sounded similar. Also, The Tornados used other Vox equipment, which might have led some poeple to the assumption that they used *only* Vox equipment, and therefore the Univox. This doesn't stand up, though, as the keyboard melody on the 'Telstar' recording was not actually played by Roger Lavern, The Tornados' organist.

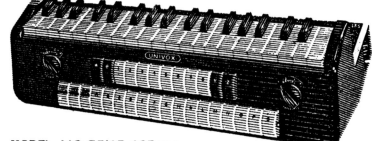

Whatever the original source of the rumor, Jennings Musical Instruments ran a *Melody Maker* advert for the Univox in 1962, the first for a while, claiming that it was the instrument used on 'Telstar.' By this time the Univox was probably already out of production. The advert only seems to have appeared once, so maybe a polite call from Selmer was made. Whatever happened, there remains a very faint possibility that Meek used a Univox on 'Telstar,' maybe mixed with a Clavioline. After Meek's death his musical equipment was auctioned off. Records of that auction show that he owned both a Clavioline and a Univox.

Several other unsuccessful piano attachments surfaced briefly in the 1950s. One of these, a British design called The Maestrovox, was available for a while in 1953. Its only known use in rock music came 25 years later, when British experimental art-rock band This Heat used one on many of their recordings, played by drummer Charles Hayward.

> Runaway and the Musitron

There remains one more chapter, and a significant one, in the piano attachment's legacy in pop music. It is the story of an instrument that started life as a Clavioline before mutating into something else, literally one of a kind. It was used on a record, Del Shannon's 'Runaway,' which was an international hit single that pre-dated the other great piano attachment hit, 'Telstar,' by a year.

'Runaway' and 'Telstar,' revolutionary records both, came at a time of musical conservatism. Rock music was in one of its periodic declines. Elvis had gone into the army, Little Richard had found religion, Eddie Cochran and Buddy Holly had died in accidents, and Gene Vincent had begun his long, alcoholic tail-spin. Meanwhile, the lifestyle choices of Jerry Lee Lewis and Chuck Berry attracted the unwelcome attention of the authorities, to the detriment of their career. By 1960, this first generation of rockers was being nudged out by clean-cut show-biz facsimiles, pale reflections – now largely forgotten figures like Frankie Avalon and Fabian. The charts were clogged up with syrupy ballad singers who too often sounded suspiciously like the syrupy ballad singers rock'n'roll had supposedly consigned to

the cabaret circuit for good. It was almost as if rock'n'roll had been nothing more than some kind of freakish hormonal reaction – an unsightly crop of zits on the face of music. It would be a few years yet before The Beatles and The Rolling Stones proved that this temporary lull was merely a part of the evolutionary process, the ebb before the flow. But until then, there was little new ground being broken in the pop world. That is the received wisdom on the period, and it is largely true.

Yet even during this fallow period, after Elvis and before the beat era, there were a few artists carrying the torch for authentic rock'n'roll. American artists Dion, The Everly Brothers, and Roy Orbison were making great, innovative, exciting, influential records between 1959 and 1963. Another was Del Shannon, whose sharp good looks, voice that could both soar and rasp, and songwriting ability put him into the charts in 1961. These attributes meant that Shannon was one of just a few artists from his generation to sustain an international chart career beyond the nearly all-conquering British invasion of 1964-65. And apart from the looks, the voice, and the songs, Shannon had another card up his sleeve, a sonic trademark that made his biggest hit records immediately identifiable.

Shannon's first hit was his biggest. That hit, 'Runaway,' is a great record – engagingly catchy without being trite, unusual yet accessible, a true pop classic. Unluckily for Shannon, that debut hit set a standard so high that he never quite matched it again, despite making many other very good records.

A few things set 'Runaway' apart when DJs started spinning it in 1961. The first is the way Shannon uses his falsetto so effectively and prominently in the song's chorus. And there's the song's unusual structure, which eschewed conventional verse/chorus repeats. Max Crook, Shannon's keyboard player and his co-writer of 'Runaway,' says: "When we first took it in to be recorded the complaint was that it was too complex and non-commercial, but they didn't realize that every part of the song is a hook."[7]

A little over two minutes long, the song has no repeated sections until it reaches its last quarter. The minor key first section ("As I walk the streets I wonder …") moves into a major key section ("I go walking in the rain …"), which then moves into the stabbing chords and falsetto vocals of the chorus ("I wonder, I why-why-why-why-wonder …"), by the end of which the record is half over. The second two of those three sections are repeated again later in the song; the first, the section most listeners perceive as being the verse, doesn't appear again. At the end of the first chorus, at 1:10, a flighty, fluid instrumental break of approximately 25 seconds duration comes in out of nowhere, played by Crook on an instrument he dubbed the Musitron (a contraction of *music* and elec*tron*), the already-mentioned modified Clavioline.

This other-worldly sound continues as a counter-melody underneath the vocals to the end of the song, as Shannon sings again the "walking in the rain" and falsetto sections. But what exactly was the Musitron? The roots of the answer to that question reach back several years, to Michigan, USA.

In 1959, as Joe Meek was first tinkering with his Selmer Clavioline in London, Max Crook in Michigan had found a Gibson model. Although separated by thousands of miles, the two men had much in common; both were intrigued by the musical possibilities suggested by electronics, and both were given to modifying, building, and playing around with gadgets. Both, too, were given to sticking thumbtacks into the hammers of their pianos in the search for new sounds. The difference between them was that Crook's curiosity found its ultimate outlet in one customized instrument, whereas the outcomes of Meek's inventive zeal were scattered liberally throughout his recording work over several years.

Crook says, "My inspiration came from an intense desire to create something new and different in the sound of music. Electronic principles applied to the field of music seemed to me to be the primary way to accomplish this goal."[8] That could be Meek speaking. Or Kraftwerk or Bob Moog, for that matter.

At the time, both Crook and Meek had no idea that they were thinking along similar lines, although they became aware of each other's records soon enough. They were two very different men propelled in similar directions by their own inventiveness, ingenuity, and the possibilities of a new, emerging technology. Both men first used their Claviolines in 1959, and just a few years later both of them would

introduce sides of proto-electronica into the international pop charts.

The guitars that Gibson has made over the years have secured a place for the company in the history of pop music. The history books tend to overlook, though, the Claviolines the company made on license in the 1950s. It was one of these Gibson Claviolines that caught Crook's eye. He says: "I came across the Clavioline at the Gibson factory in Kalamazoo, Michigan. Then I found one in a pawnshop for a good price and decided to try out my vision on it. I don't recall ever seeing or hearing anyone play one of these, but I could see great potential with the basic instrument. I had considered some early electronic instruments, including the Solovox, but decided that the Clavioline was most suitable for modification, portability, and adaptation to the external effects that I built and incorporated into the Musitron package.

"Way before that I'd been looking for unique sounds and ways of making instruments sound differently – tweaking pianos, putting tacks in hammers, de-tuning notes, anything I could do to make something sound different. I thought that I might be able to put together some kind of a keyboard that had voices that were actually generated within the instrument. I started getting bits and pieces of various things and seeing if I couldn't get a combination together that would be useful."[9]

The Musitron package that Crook refers to is, in one sense, simply a modified Clavioline, although the extent of the modifications are such that it deserves attention as a unique device. The basic keyboard Crook used was a standard Gibson Clavioline model, although he didn't use the amplifier that Gibson supplied with it, only the pre-amp. That original keyboard was modified in several ways, and then matched with a collection of other custom-built components. It is that modified Clavioline keyboard and the other custom-built components that make up the Musitron.

In the early 1960s Crook was secretive about the workings of the Musitron, not wanting to lose the advantage he had over other mere organists or Clavioline players. And no doubt he realized that a dash of mystique does a pop career no harm at all. He says he was approached more than once by companies

Max Crook's keyboards, 1960s (top to bottom): Moog
synthesizer, Wurlitzer piano, Lowrey organ, Musitron.

wanting to produce Musitrons commercially, but declined the offers. All he cared about was having something that could create the sounds he heard in his head. Now, Crook is a little more forthcoming about the Musitron's inner workings, although he can still be vague about how he made the Musitron do what it does. But several themes emerge.

The Clavioline keyboard itself, which, as Crook says, has "a wide range of sounds and pitch to start with," was modified by "putting in pots and resistors and switches into the circuit to make changes." Amongst other things, this enhanced the instrument's range, from "two-to-three cycles per second right up to where the dogs and cats are screaming." He also achieved "differences in timbre, vibrato, and bending of notes," using "spring-loaded levers and knobs, most of which were added to the basic instrument."[10] His pitch bend function, for example, is an alteration of the tuning circuit operated by a spring-loaded, mechanical device attached to the keyboard.

The effects Crook developed to complete the package included vibrato and reverb units. "At that time there were no commercial vibrato units, vibrato meaning the wavering of the note in pitch, so I took a potentiometer, which would change resistance and therefore pitch, and I mounted it on a box which had a concentric cam arrangement on it and a small DC motor, and the motor would turn this pot back and forth, and you could control the speed of the motor because it was a DC motor. My first reverb used springs from a garden gate and transducers. Eventually they started making some reverb units commercially, so I employed those, then finally I was using solid state stuff."[11] At one time there was also a multiple-head tape recorder in the mix too, that Crook used to create slap-back echo. The Musitron wasn't a static invention – rather, it evolved over time. But Crook started using it live and on recordings as soon as he had an operational instrument.

Del Shannon first heard the Musitron at an early stage of its development. "When I first brought the Musitron into the Hi-Lo Club in Battle Creek, Michigan [in 1959], where I was serving as the piano [player] in Del's band, Del was fascinated by the sounds it produced. He was anxious to integrate it into his overall sound."[12] Two years later, Crook and

Shannon were in the studio doing just that, and the result was 'Runaway.'

'Runaway' is a single with a preternatural ease about it. The vague adjectival phrases musicians are so found of seem perceptive and accurate when talking about the record – it flows, it's bright, it feels right, everything works. Despite this, Crook says that the 'Runaway' session was rather fraught. First there was concern from the producer about the perceived non-commercial aspects of the song. Then Crook further ruffled the feathers of the studio staff by wanting to put microphones inside and underneath the Steinway piano he plays throughout the record (the Musitron being overdubbed afterwards). Then, after the song was recorded, the tapes were sped up to make them sound more commercial, and, some say, to disguise Shannon's wayward pitching. The released record, originally recorded in A minor, is pitched somewhere just below B flat minor. Yet for all this, 'Runaway' became one of those records that transcends its time and origins. Shannon's voice, while lacking either the operatic grandeur of Roy Orbison or the effortless swagger of Dion, and suffering whatever pitching problems there may or may not have been, has a lived-in rawness that was a testament to the years of treading the boards in Michigan in the 1950s. The band's playing was tight and crisp, and the song so immediate that its oddness seems natural. It was a Number One hit in the USA and the UK.

Although Shannon never scored as big a hit again after 'Runaway,' he was a major worldwide star for several years afterwards, and scored many US and UK chart entries.

'Hats Off To Larry,' the follow up to 'Runaway,' was another good record and another big international hit. It shares many features of its predecessor, a minor-key guitar intro, a falsetto chorus, and the Musitron, this time double-tracked. The hits kept on coming for Shannon after that, some with the Musitron. When Crook wasn't on hand to help out, Shannon or his producers clearly felt his absence, as several attempts were made to imitate the Musitron's sounds on later singles. Usually, these imitations were performed on organs, but amusingly on kazoo for the solo of 'So Long Baby' (chapter 8). Crook and the Musitron were brought back for a

couple of late minor Shannon hits, 'Handyman' and 'Do You Wanna Dance' (both 1964). The latter demonstrates the Musitron's pitch-bending capacity. But by then Shannon's chart career was almost over. There was one last big UK hit with the excellent 'Keep Searchin' (We'll Follow the Sun),' before a drift into management, production, cabaret work, and occasional comebacks.

Despite the pioneering nature of his work, Crook did not sustain a musical career. He played in an electronic pop duo called Sounds Of Tomorrow played in the mid-1960s without releasing any recordings. Perhaps things would have been different if he had pursued the option of commercially manufacturing the Musitron.

There is a sense, though, that Crook was neither particularly motivated by commercial gain nor the need to establish himself in a career. Rather, he was someone interested in sonic exploration for its own rewards. Yet despite this he is forthright about his achievements: "At the time of my experimentation with and the development of my Musitron, there was no electronic music out there. Thus, the employment of the Musitron on Del Shannon's 'Runaway' recording was the first pop music recording featuring electronically synthesized sound."[13]

If you define pop music as either music aspiring to popularity in sales terms, or as widely heard music, then Crook's claim isn't strictly true. As we've already seen, Meek had used Claviolines on pop records, or rather, bizarre records that aspired to popularity, as early as 1960, a year before 'Runaway.' John Barry used them on a 1961 album. Earlier still, many light-orchestral musicians had used Claviolines on popular recordings.

As for other early electronic instruments, in 1947 Harry Revel and Les Baxter's *Music Out Of The Moon*, featuring the Theremin playing of Dr Samuel Hoffman, had sold very well. And by 1961 there had been many widely heard movie soundtracks that featured Theremins, Ondiolines, Ondes Martenots, and other early electronic devices. But to give Crook his due, the extensive use of the Musitron on 'Runaway' was the first time an electronic keyboard appeared so prominently as the lead instrument on a big-selling rock'n'roll record, an international chart

hit. In that respect, it is a crucial landmark in the evolution of electronic popular music.

Electronic music pioneers come in many curious guises – a Russian spy, reclusive German cycling enthusiasts, and a paranoid poorly-educated boy from rural England who blew his own head off. By contrast, Crook seems like a regular guy, the ordinariness of his life outside music and his down-

Ex-Del Shannon keyboard player Max Crook pictured recently with his Musitron.

to-earth, polite straightforwardness somehow at odds with his singular musical journey. His pop career after 'Runaway' was eccentric. There were the occasional collaborations with Shannon, an appearance, with the Musitron, on a Liberace album (*Autumn Leaves*), and experiments with one of the earliest Moog synthesizers. By the 1970s, Crook had given up playing music professionally to work, amongst other things, as a firefighter. Now in his sixties, he has returned to his first love, and performs as a MIDI-aided one-man-band at retirement centers and holiday parks. The Musitron, still extant but in semi-retirement, still sometimes accompanies him to events commemorating the life and works of the late Del Shannon. Shannon, reputedly depressed at his inability to relaunch his pop career, took his own life in February 1990.

The importance of the piano attachments is often overlooked. In some ways they were the victims of their success. Some claims have Selmer manufacturing more than 15,000 Claviolines, which seems quite plausible. In October 1956, when the Selmer Clavioline still had another eight years of its production life to run, the company was placing adverts claiming sales of more than 7,000 units. Jennings made thousands of Univoxes too. Being quite cheap, mass-produced, and widely used in popular music and as home instruments, piano attachments can seem rather prosaic compared to other early electronic instruments. They lack the built-in oddness of the Theremin, the highbrow cachet of the Ondes Martenot, and the Gallic eccentricity of the Ondioline. Yet for many thousands of musicians, and many millions of listeners, the piano attachments were an introduction to the possibilities of electronic musical instruments.

The last Clavioline variant was introduced by Selmer in 1964, consisting of the keyboard unit only, which could be plugged into any amplifier. This was a sensible move, as by then the Clavioline's little combo would have been sounding rather tame compared to the various more powerful Vox and Selmer amps then in production. Selmer Clavioline production seems to have stopped later that year, with Gibson having given up a few years earlier. A German company, Jorgensen, reintroduced the Clavioline in 1965, but it didn't last long. By then, it looked dated compared to the dozens of polyphonic organs, electric pianos, and other keyboard instruments on sale. Within a few years Moog synthesizers became commercially available, and the humble Clavioline, along with its rival piano attachments, was consigned to a dusty corner of history. It's a comment on how quickly, then as now, electronic music technology progresses that in 1974, just ten years after the Clavioline went out of production, Greek keyboard player Vangelis described it as if it came from another age. By then he was one of very few professional musicians still using Claviolines — incorporating two into his multi-keyboard set-up because he favored the instrument's clarinet sounds. Speaking to *Sounds* magazine, he said: "It's a very old thing … they don't make it any more because nobody buys it. But it's beautiful … it can give you many, many things."[14]

MAGNETIC TAPE AND THE LOST ANALOG SAMPLING

"Who knows, it may even be the 'music of the future.'"[1]

If you traveled back in time to the early 1950s and engaged someone in a conversation about electronic music, they would understand the term to mean two things, if they had heard of it at all. Firstly, it was music that combined conventional orchestral instruments with one or more of the few electronic instruments then around, like the Theremin or Ondes Martenot. Secondly, it was tape music. That is, music using a new invention, the magnetic tape recorder, not simply to record conventional music but to create sounds never heard before.

During World War II, Jack Mullin, an American serviceman and electronics engineer stationed in England, was intrigued by the radio programs broadcast from Germany that he sometimes listened to in the middle of the night. These broadcasts featured symphony orchestras, but the sound had none of the scratches and crackles that came when the source was a 78 rpm record. It seemed possible that Hitler had ordered his orchestras to play live in the early hours, but Mullin was not convinced. Towards the end of the war, with the German army in rapid retreat, he went to Germany and was able to solve the conundrum.

The magnetic tape recorder or 'Magnetophon' had been invented in Germany, before the war, by electronics giant AEG and the IG Farben chemical company. It was publicly displayed at the 1935 Berlin radio show and an example sent by AEG to General Electric in America in 1938. The American company, which was part owner of AEG, scorned the machine. Nonetheless, the Germans used them throughout the war as low-quality battlefield dictating machines.

Mullin knew that the sound he had heard could not have come from something so primitive. But while investigating German electronics, towards the end of the war, he heard rumors of a very different tape recorder being used by radio stations. At a satellite studio of Radio Frankfurt, in Bad Nauheim, he discovered the machines. They used an advanced technique called AC biasing to record with a very wide frequency range and low distortion. Unknown to the Allies, these hi-fidelity tape recorders had been in use in German broadcasting since 1941. The broadcasts Mullin had listened to were not live: they were playbacks of tape recordings.

The canny Mullin immediately recognized the potential of the new technology. He got permission to send two of the machines, in pieces, back to the US for his own postwar use. He later reassembled them, building new electronics, and in the immediate post-war years demonstrated the machines to many people in the music and radio worlds, including Bing Crosby. All were impressed by the sound quality. In 1947 Mullin recorded a Bing Crosby radio show on one of his German machines, and soon after broadcast a taped Crosby radio show – the first tape recorded show to be broadcast in the US.

In 1948, tape recording technology became commercially available when the Ampex Corporation introduced the Model 200 reel-to-reel tape recorder, based on German Magnetophon technology. It was the beginning of a new age.

Very quickly large commercial studios were fitting tape recorders, and at a stroke greatly improving the quality of their recordings. The new technology had an immediate impact on how musicians worked in studios, too. In contrast to the wax disc recorders they replaced, reel-to-reel tape machines could be stopped and restarted quickly and easily. This meant that pieces of music no longer had to be recorded in their entirety, from beginning to end. If anyone made a mistake, the machines could be stopped and started again, with musicians starting to play in the middle of a piece if a suitable 'drop-in' point could be found, or starting again from the beginning and recording over the previous take.

The practice of tape editing was a natural development of this. Because tape played so fast during recording and playback (playing speeds on tape machines could run at up to 32 inches per second), engineers soon realized that it was possible to edit different pieces of magnetic tape together by literally attaching one piece to another with sticky tape, a process called splicing. If the splicing was correctly executed, the physical join between the two pieces of tape would pass over the playback head in a fraction of a second, with no audible consequences. So, assuming that the music on separate pieces of tape matched up, the illusion of a live performance could be created by splicing together several sections of music from different performances to make a complete piece or song. Musicians had mixed feelings about these advances. They appreciated the continuity that tape machines allowed. Now, if someone made a mistake in a performance there was no longer a need to wait while a wax disc was changed.

But concerns were raised, as they always are when new musical technology is introduced, that tape recorders would somehow do 'real' musicians out of a job. Surely, the doubters said, it was now no longer necessary to have a command of your instrument or voice, and a firm grasp of the music you were performing? Now any half-trained amateur could go into a studio and record bits and pieces that engineers could make into something coherent. And surely this wasn't the proper way to make music?

In time these sorts of concerns died down, when the overwhelming superiority of magnetic tape as a recording medium became accepted. But there would be further controversy, when the editing of magnetic recording tape opened up a route not only to recording conventional music in a new way, but to making a previously unheard type of music. The unwinding spools of tape were a path into a new music that seemed so strange that many people refused to accept it as music at all.

When commercially available magnetic tape recorders first started to appear in the late 1940s, they were expensive. This meant that they tended to be bought only by successful commercial studios, or by institutions in receipt of some kind of state or private funding. It was in one of these institutions that the tape music revolution had its beginnings.

Pierre Schaeffer was a radio engineer, lecturer, theorist, broadcaster, and writer. He was not, in the conventional sense, a musician or composer. Yet his experiments with assembling musical collages from snippets of pre-recorded sound, conducted in the 1940s and 1950s, had massive musical implications. The repercussions of these experiments echo still, in hip-hop and other sample-based contemporary music. Schaeffer was born in France in 1910. His parents were both engineers, and Schaeffer initially followed in their footsteps, working as a telecommunications engineer in Strasbourg, before moving, in 1936, to Radiodiffusion-Télévision Française (RTF) in Paris. This gave him access to

recording and broadcast equipment, and a vast collection of sound effects recordings.

During World War II, RTF fell under the control of the occupying German forces. It was during this period that Schaeffer persuaded the authorities, answerable to the Nazi occupiers, to allow him to begin his sonic explorations using the corporation's resources, while at the same time taking part in clandestine operations with the French resistance movement against those same occupiers.

When the war was over, Schaeffer continued with his sound work. In 1948 he broadcast on the radio his *Concert de Bruits* (Concert of Noises), a number of compositions that included sounds made by, amongst other things, trains and saucepan lids, along with many other manipulated conventional instruments and voices. Schaeffer called this *musique concrète* (concrete music), the 'concrete' sounds being sounds from 'real life,' rather than specially produced musical sounds. (Actually, many of the concrete sounds used in early compositions were carefully recorded in studios.) Schaeffer's first broadcast got a hostile response from many listeners; others found his work simply risible. But a few were fascinated by what he was trying to do.

At this stage, Schaeffer was working with the severe technological imitations of the wax-disc recording equipment he had at his disposal, manually synchronizing several turntables during performances. But that was all about to change.

In 1949, Schaeffer and composer Pierre Henry founded the Group de Recherche de Musique Concrète (GRMC) which was recognized by the RTF in 1951. The GRMC was given a new studio, which included a tape recorder. At last Schaeffer had a more flexible tool to achieve his ideas. From this point until the end of the decade he pioneered the use of the tape recorder as a musical instrument, not just a means of recording musical performances, while continuing to develop the idea of using concrete sounds in a musical context.

In the following years Schaeffer's studio became the focal point for many important music experiments as the tape music revolution fermented. He had contact with many forces in new music, including Luc Ferrari, Iannis Xenakis, Olivier

Messiaen, Karlheinz Stockhausen, and Pierre Boulez. Yet by the end of the 1950s the *musique concrète* and tape music revolutions appeared to have lost momentum. Composers became frustrated and disenchanted with the meticulous, painstaking work of 'playing' tape recorders – constructing new compositions from pieces of magnetic tape.

Even Schaeffer had had enough, and he all but retired from composition in the late 1950s. He went on to work in research and radio production, all the while lecturing and writing, including producing a 1975 essay titled 'Musique Concrète: What Do I Know,' which poured cold water on the revolutionary flames he had fanned into life. Schaeffer died in 1995 after a long illness.

Schaeffer might have come to doubt the value of his work, and indeed his compositions are not highly regarded in themselves. Yet he left an incalculable legacy. Much of the work of Schaeffer and the GRMC did not feature musicians who played instruments or sang. For the first time, non-musicians (and Schaeffer was one of those) could make music. Today, many electronic and dance records are made by people who can neither play an instrument nor sing; they simply manipulate and order sound using computer technology. Schaeffer was their father, whether they know it or not.

Also, Schaeffer and his contemporaries introduced the idea that noise – whether it came from 'real' life or was created it the studio – could be a part of music. It could be used for texture, rhythmically, and even melodically. This too has now become an established notion in many forms of popular and serious art music.

Schaeffer and other early tape music pioneers developed a number of techniques for creating and arranging music using tape machines. If the tape machine was indeed a musical instrument, then mastering these techniques was learning to play it. The first technique was a development of the tape editing used in more conventional forms of music to assemble complete performances. In tape music, though, the basic technique was extended to encompass composition, sound creation and arranging. Schaeffer and others quickly recognized that the way a piece of tape was cut and spliced to

another piece of tape – the actual angle of the join – affected the sound. For example, a diagonal cut created a soft attack or decay that may not have been a feature of the original sound recorded. So by using different types of diagonal splices, sounds could be altered and musical expression created.

A vertical cut, on the other hand, gave an abrupt attack or finish to a note or sound, again, creating a dynamic in the music and also a new sound. Tape composers often created their work by sticking together literally hundreds of short pieces of tape. Each piece, maybe only an inch long, would be carefully measured and the cuts angled to create a particular length of note and the desired degree of attack or decay.

In recognition of the importance of tape editing, manufacturers soon began equipping their machines with splicing blocks. These were small channels in which tape could be placed, with different angled guide slots to aid the cutting of the tape.

But how did they tune these isolated notes or fragments of sound that existed on bits of tape? This depended partly on the original sound source. If the source recording was of a conventional musical instrument, pitch variation could be achieved by simply playing different notes. Tape editing would then be used to alter and modify those notes. But if the original sound source was a non-musical sound – a concrete sound – different notes could be created by using a tape recorder's variable tape speed control. For example, hitting a glass with a fork sounds a single note. The tape composer would record this note – for argument's sake, a C – on to a piece of tape. Played back at different speeds, that note changed: the faster the tape speed, the higher the note; the slower the tape speed, the lower the note.

The tape composer then decided how many different notes the composition required – for example 20 C notes and ten D notes. He or she then worked out at what speed the tape recording of the original C note had to be played to sound the D notes. At this point the tape composer needed at least one more tape machine. The original C note was copied from one machine to another, 20 times, at the speed it was recorded at. This created 20 C notes. The original C note was then played ten times at the different speed, to sound the D notes, which were also recorded onto the second tape machine. The second tape now contained the raw musical material with which the composer worked. He or she cut up that tape into 30 pieces, one for each note, and then carefully stuck the notes back together in the order the piece of music required, taking care to angle each edit for the desired degree of attack or decay, as previously described. The end result would be a recording of one 'instrument,' the struck glass, playing the piece of music.

In the days before multi-track tape recorders, to build up the composition from a simple melody at least one more tape recorder was needed. Imagine that the composer wanted to add a counter melody to the first part. To do that, he or she had to create the new part using exactly the same technique as before, taking particular care that the note changes (in other words, the tape edits) corresponded appropriately with the original part as the composition demanded. These would then be recorded from two synchronized tape machines onto a third, creating a single-track recording of two parts. Incidentally, the synchronization might well have been manual, which simply meant hitting two play buttons at the same time.

Another thing the tape composers noticed was that changing the speed of a note or sound not only altered its pitch, but if taken to enough of an extreme, also changed its timbre and tonal properties. If bass piano notes were sufficiently sped up they didn't sound like higher piano notes, they sounded like something else. Additionally, changing the speed of a tape during playback was a way of creating glissandos. Vari-speeding offered many sound creating options, but there were yet more techniques available to the tape composer.

The creation of tape loops allowed composers to make repetitive, hypnotic melodic and rhythmic patterns, or constant drones, as the basis for a composition. A tape loop was a piece of tape that had both ends spliced together. It was threaded between the playback heads and back around both spools, so that whatever was recorded on it played constantly from beginning to end and back to the beginning again, over and over the playback heads ad infinitum,

until the tape machine was stopped. Playing tapes backwards, a trick later beloved of so many psychedelic bands, was another way of making new sounds. A recording of a single piano note, when played backwards, sounded nothing like a piano. Rather than the note starting with a percussive hit and gradually decaying, it faded in before coming to an abrupt stop.

Composers often combined backwards tapes with splicing techniques, maybe editing together a reversed piano note with a forward playing piano note, but using a diagonal splice to remove both the abrupt stop of the reversed note and the attack of the forward note. This would then create a sound that swelled gently to a peak before fading away.

Tape echo was another device much beloved of the early tape composers. This was achieved by setting up the machine so that sounds recorded on to the tape by the recording head would be played back immediately from the near-adjacent playback head, rather than being played back after recording as a separate operation. When the sound played back was mixed with the original input sound, the result was an echo. The length of the echo depended on the distance between the heads. This technology would later become available to guitarists in the form of tape echo units like the Watkins Copicat, which featured a number of playback heads, different distances apart.

Today, in a world of easy to use digital samplers, these techniques seem extraordinarily archaic, complex, and time-consuming. But what the tape composers were doing was, in effect, analogue sampling. They took snippets of sound, either concrete sounds or musical sounds, and edited and manipulated them to make new sounds. When affordable digital samplers began to appear during the 1980s, it suddenly became a considerably easier task to do this.

It is often the case – in art and elsewhere – that revolutionary ideas originate with a small intellectual elite, before gradually filtering down into common use and acceptance. So it was with the techniques of tape editing and some of the ideas of *musique concrète*. And it was just as Schaeffer and the first wave of pioneers – the intellectual elite – were beginning to tire of their explorations that more populist manifestations of their ideas began to emerge. As tape machines became cheaper, more efficient, smaller, and lighter as the 1950s progressed, so more and more musicians, engineers and producers operating beyond the confines of academia and the big commercial studios began to get hold of them. And as the technology became more available, so the musical ideas associated with it became more widely used. Many began to see that tape machines offered possibilities beyond the simple recording of a musical performance. The guitarist Les Paul, for example, experimented from the late 1940s with primitive overdubbing techniques, and vari-speeding to create devilishly fast guitar lines.

By the late 1950s, there were tape-manipulators working in the popular arena who were aware of what was happening in the rarefied world of *musique concrète*. In London there were the staff at the BBC Radiophonic Workshop, for instance (see chapter 6). A few years earlier, in New York, the husband and wife team of Louis and Bebe Barron produced the first entirely electronic movie score, for the science fiction film *Forbidden Planet*, using tape manipulation alongside other electronic sound-generating methods.

The Barrons had set up what was probably America's first electronic music studio in 1950, using tape recorders and self-built tone generating circuits. Much of their work before and after *Forbidden Planet* was soundtracking experimental art films, although they also produced music for commercial adverts. But the *Forbidden Planet* project was their one big public artistic statement in the commercial arena.

Released in 1956, *Forbidden Planet* is the sort of science fiction film that seems quaint now, but at the time was deemed impressively futuristic. So controversial was the idea of having a soundtrack created without any conventional musical performance that the Barrons' contribution was credited as "Electronic tonalities by Louis and Bebe Barron," to avoid unwelcome attention from the reliably conservative musicians' organizations. Judging from what Louis Barron said about his and his wife's work, it is just as well musicians weren't involved: "We can torture these circuits without a guilty conscience – whereas if we did it musically we might have to torture a musician. ... We look on these circuits as

genuinely suffering, but we don't feel compassion."[2]

Intriguingly, one of the earliest popular tape experimentalists, Joe Meek, had no idea what had happened on the tape editing blocks of the RTF or any other avant-garde operation. Rather, he arrived through his own circuitous route at startlingly similar conclusions to Schaeffer and others about how tape technology could be used to create new sounds. It was as if the technology itself was suggesting possibilities to all sorts of musicians, producers, and engineers: as if the machines themselves had ideas about their potential and displayed no prejudice when sharing them. They didn't care if you were a sound theorist from the academy or, like Meek, a self-taught garden-shed tinkerer from the sticks, they wanted you to know what you could do with them.

Meek's experiments with tape technology began in earnest when he started his first home studio, in Holland Park in west London in 1959. He had already tinkered with tape manipulation and other recording techniques like extreme compression and massive reverb in his jobs at IBC and Lansdowne studios. Having some recording gear at home gave him the freedom and time to experiment further, though, and before long he was hatching plans for a project that would give free reign to his ideas.

Although now 30 years old, Meek was still full of boyish enthusiasm. Along with music and electronics, one of Meek's other passions was outer space. He was absorbed by the nascent space race between the USA and USSR, and believed passionately in extra-terrestrial life. It was this passion that would give Meek a theme for his first truly independent album, one of his most feted works.

I Hear A New World is credited as being composed and produced by Joe Meek, and performed by The Blue Men, directed by Rod Freeman. Who were Rod Freeman and The Blue Men? They were a seven-piece rock'n'roll band with skiffle leanings, just a few of the hundreds of musicians Meek co-opted in his singular recording career. Although *I Hear A New World* is a Joe Meek record, and in truth it may not have made much difference who played on it, Freeman deserves credit for translating Meek's ideas for songs into communicable music for his band to play. This involved first deciphering melodies from Meek's

Joe Meek in his studio in Holloway Road, north London, where he recorded 'Telstar.'

tuneless singing, accompanied by a rhythm track of a piece of cutlery hit on a table, and then fitting chords to those melodies. Meek needed trained musicians to perform this role for him, and most of his best records were made with the help of one or more often anonymous collaborators helping out in this way.

Conceived and recorded over about six weeks in late 1959, this homemade curio was produced at Meek's Holland Park home studio. There is a possibility, too, that some work may have been done in Meek's last days at Lansdowne. *I Hear A New World* was literally a kitchen sink production – treated recordings of running tap water being one way Meek conjured up the spooky space effects that permeate the album.

In more ways than one it was a groundbreaking venture. The use of manipulated sound effects mirrored the techniques used in the experiments of the *musique concrète* composers – one of the first times the full range of such techniques had been employed in pop music. Or at least, music aspiring to popularity. The effects Meek conjured up pre-date the experiments of psychedelia in the 1960s, 'Krautrock' in the 1970s, and much dance, indie, post-rock, and electronic music of the present day. *I Hear A New World* was also one of the first concept albums. Meek was enthralled by the pre-Apollo sci-fi world of silver spaceships, little green men on the moon, and the enticing possibility of space travel. The 12 tracks that make up the album are an aural approximation of that naïve imaginary world. Apart from the treated sound effects, the album's instrumentation mixed conventional pop colors – electric bass, electric guitar, and drums – with a swooping lap steel guitar, a newly-acquired Clavioline, and a deliberately out of tune piano with thumb tacks in the hammers (what John Cage might have called a 'prepared piano'). The whole lot was siphoned through Meek's collection of homemade reverb and echo units, compressors, and the like, and recorded onto several semi-professional tape recorders he then owned. The songs are notionally about three different species of alien – the Globbots, the Dribcots, and the Saroos. It's here that

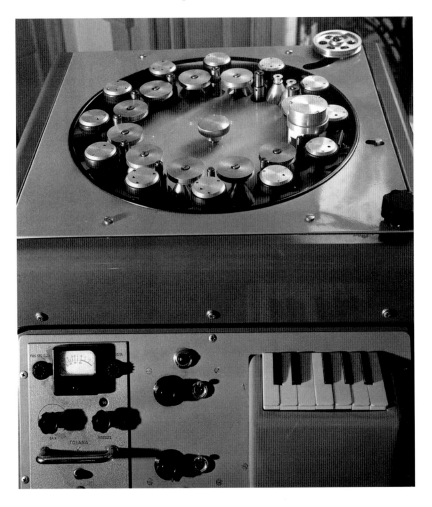

The Phonogène, a primitive tape-replay device designed by Pierre Shaeffer.

the major weakness of the album surfaces, with Meek using absurd sped-up Chipmunk-like voices to represent the speech of the imagined aliens, thus stamping the project with unfortunate novelty credentials. Consequently the instrumental tracks work best, and thankfully there are quite a few of them. Two in particular stand out, 'Glob Waterfall' and 'Magnetic Field.'

Meek described the impression he was trying to create with 'Glob Waterfall' in the notes on the sleeve of an EP drawn from *I Hear A New World*. These are quoted in full to illustrate the fevered pitch to which Meek had worked up his imagination:

"This may contradict the belief that there is no water on the moon; I still hope there is, if it's not external then it's inside the crust. Gravity has done a strange thing, and has formed a type of overflowing well. The water rises to form a huge globule on top of a plateau, and when it's reached its maximum size it falls with a terrific crash to the ground below, and flows away into the cracks of the moon; then the whole cycle repeats itself again and again."

For all their artlessness, these words do a good job of describing the music Meek was writing about. 'Glob Waterfall' is a suspenseful instrumental built around a heavily treated ascending run on the bass notes of a piano, which represent the gradual build-up of water. This plays repeatedly against a backdrop of bubbling water-like noises that, whatever their original source (and it may have been someone blowing bubbles with a straw in a glass of liquid), were definitely *concrète* rather than traditionally musical. There is a regular pattern to these noises indicating that a tape loop might well have been used.

They are drowned in a sea of reverb that helps create a connection with the distant, echoed piano. Periodically, the music reaches a climactic gong-like crash, most likely an over-recorded cymbal hit with a beater rather than a stick, representing the bursting of the water globule Meek had imagined on the moon. It is an extraordinary piece of music for a non-musical pop producer to have made in a home studio in 1959. Apart from the layers of hiss generated by Meek's rudimentary equipment, it would sit quite happily alongside a Gavin Bryars or Brian Eno record made during the 1970s.

Half of 'Magnetic Field' is a much more straightforward piece of instrumental pop, in which The Blue Men betray their skiffle roots with a brisk two-step backing. It is distinguished only by the unusual multi-layering of Clavioline, electric guitar, and lap steel guitar. But that is only half the story. The total track length is just over three minutes, of which the first one minute and twenty seconds is a sound collage that once again showcases several *musique concrète* production techniques. An overlapping of treated noises that may include taped radio interference and the sound of electrical short circuits points to the use of layering of different sounds. And the characteristic swell to an abrupt climax clearly demonstrates the use of backwards tapes.

I Hear A New World was never released in Meek's lifetime. The previously mentioned sampler EP trickled out in very limited numbers in February 1960, with a second EP and the full album planned for March. Distribution problems with Meek's own new Triumph independent label, on which the EP was released and for which the album was slated, scuppered the project. *I Hear a New World* lived on only in a bootleg netherworld until 1991, when British reissue label RPM first released the album in its entirety.

Claims that Joe Meek's *I Hear A New World* is a lost masterpiece should be resisted. The material is often poor, and the performance of it variable. It would not have been a success if properly released. Too many instruments and voices are too out of tune for it to have been palatable to public tastes, and the sped-up vocals would have sounded as ridiculous in 1960 as they do now. What it is, though, is an extraordinarily prescient test-bed for recording techniques that until that point had been largely confined to the rarefied world of academic electronic music studios. As Meek worked often on his own in a home studio, and he was anxious to the point of paranoia about people finding out how he did what he did, many of his sonic secrets went with him to the grave. But enough evidence survives in the form of statements from people who worked with him, and the records themselves, including *I Hear A New World*, to conclude that Meek was using all of the standard *musique concrète* tape-manipulating techniques to blend

'real' sounds into pop music, and to treat conventional musical instruments, in the early 1960s. In later years these techniques would become more widely used in pop – first in the psychedelic era of the mid-to-late 1960s, and then in the early days of electronic pop music in the 1970s. Backwards tapes, vari-speeding, tape loops, electronic oscillations, non-musical sound-effects twisted out of all recognition by echo, reverb and compression, distorted electric guitars, even distorted pedal steel guitars, monophonic electronic keyboards – they all find a place in Meek's wild musical imagining of extra-terrestrial life.

And not only did *I Hear A New World* pre-date by many years much better-known experimental pop music, it also held up a mirror, apparently completely accidentally, to then-current developments in art music – an unknowing reflection of avant-garde high seriousness for the uneducated pop masses. For Meek, the source of a sound quickly became all but irrelevant; it was simply sonic raw material to be pulled this way and that, chopped up and reassembled, stretched, shrunk, changed, and spewed out in all but unrecognizable form. In that respect, he had much in common with the father of *musique concrète*, Pierre Schaeffer, another non-musician fascinated by the musical possibilities of raw sound, a fact that Meek, the poorly educated working class boy from the rural west of England, was completely ignorant of.

Yet despite the undoubtedly pioneering nature of Meek's work, his direct influence on what came later is hard to quantify. He did not spawn a wave of imitators keen to recreate the 'Meek sound'. Even during his commercial peak he was viewed as an oddball outsider – a refreshing alternative or a minor freakish side-show, depending on your point of view – rather than someone driving change in the mainstream of the popular music world. As soon as The Beatles and The Rolling Stones, and The Byrds and The Beach Boys, came along, he very rapidly seemed old-fashioned. This was due to the weakness of his material rather than his recording techniques. Meek wrote or co-wrote many of the songs his numerous artists recorded, and most of those songs simply were not very good, even in the context of their time. With a very few exceptions, they certainly haven't stood the test of time. Had Meek's creative production skills and willingness to experiment been married to stronger material it would have been a different story. But we had to wait a few years before a younger generation of musicians did that.

If Meek pioneered the use of the recording studio and everything in it as a musical instrument, it was The Beatles who formalized this approach into what is now an accepted option for pop music making. Early in their career, The Beatles' recording sessions were much like virtually all other pop sessions of the time – short and efficient exercises in committing to tape live renditions of songs, with maybe a few overdubs for decoration. This changed with *Revolver* (1966). Sessions for the album took months rather than days, during which time the recording studio ceased to be just a room in which the band were recorded playing, and became an environment for wide-ranging sonic research. It was perhaps inevitable that four talented and inquisitive musicians left in a studio for weeks on end with an equally talented producer and engineers would arrive at tape composition as a means of making music. Indeed, those months of work bought many of the experimental techniques discussed in this chapter to a huge international audience.

First evidence of this appears on track three of *Revolver*, 'I'm Only Sleeping.' Here, controlled backwards guitar by George Harrison was fed into a conventional guitar pop arrangement. Unlike many backwards guitar parts, which have a random element, Harrison's part was a carefully worked out melody that was then recorded backwards, so that when the tapes were reversed it would play the melody as it was written. But it is the closing song on *Revolver*, 'Tomorrow Never Knows,' which displays the most radical use of tape manipulation. Actually the first song of the album to be recorded, it features Lennon singing over a planned cacophony created by layering tape loops, sped up tapes, and backwards tapes over a metronomic drum and bass pattern.[3] The techniques the band, producer George Martin, and engineer Geoff Emerick used to build this sound were not new; using them to create what came out still as a recognizable pop song was, though. It is the most fruitful marriage of pop and the avant-garde in The Beatles' career.

The Beatles would return to tape manipulation techniques in later recordings, to more extreme effect. Lennon's 'Revolution No 9' (from the *White Album*) was recorded in June 1968. A sound collage assembled from dozens of tape loops and sound effects, it was a realization on record of what McCartney had attempted 18 months earlier with the unreleased 'Carnival Of Light' (see chapter 6). But by this time tape manipulation was a commonly recognized sound-creating option in rock, and remained so for as long as magnetic tape remained the dominant recording medium. One of the best-selling albums ever, Pink Floyd's *Dark Side Of The Moon*, has a tape loop, the beginning of 'Money' being probably the only time cash registers have rung out a 7/8 time signature.

Although magnetic tape recorders have been all but superseded in the recording of pop music, and hardly anybody now actually creates sound using tape editing and manipulation techniques, the influence and nomenclature of those arcane arts live on. The digital sampler is one of the most widely used instruments in the creation of music today. What it does, more quickly and conveniently, is chop up, isolate, change, and rearrange sounds – either musical or non-musical – so that they can be used in recorded works. In other words, samplers have made available to all what a few tape pioneers did in the 1950s.

Sampling technology is commonly used to record sounds that are then assigned to a piano style keyboard for ease of playing. This in itself is a digital realization of a concept that was first explored in the age of magnetic tape. The potential musical uses of magnetic tape beyond the simple recording of performances found expression in a series of keyboard-based tape replay musical instruments produced from the late 1940s through to the mid 1970s. The most famous of these is the Mellotron, which was preceded by the Chamberlin.

Because Mellotrons play tapes of real instruments, rather than create unique sounds, they are on the fringes of qualifying for these pages. After all, the point of them was not to make new sounds, so much as to make existing sounds more accessible. But as a monument to mad ambition coming up against the very limits of the technology of its time, the Mellotron is worth a brief mention.

The Mellotron was made in England, but its story starts in California with an American named Harry Chamberlin, who we will come across again in the next chapter. At some point, probably in the late 1940s, while playing around with a new tape recorder, he was struck by the idea that magnetic tape technology offered musical possibilities. He conceived of a machine that would play tape loops of real instruments playing notes or patterns, which could be triggered by buttons or a keyboard. Samples, in today's parlance. The date of this eureka moment is sometimes given as early as 1946. This can't be the case, as commercial tape recorders didn't exist then. Most likely it was right at the end of the decade.

Chamberlin's first effort was a rhythm machine with 14 loops of drum patterns. It was followed by a succession of keyboard instruments, with ever more sophisticated internal workings that played a wider range of orchestral and rhythm samples. These instruments, which bore the name of their maker, were ingenious but flawed.

Like many inventive pioneers, Chamberlin seems to have been a very clever man with little idea of how to make a successful business out of his big idea. His instruments were prone to breaking down and his rate of production painfully slow, things which frustrated a salesman Chamberlin hired around 1960 by the name of Bill Fransen.

In early 1962 Fransen took two of Chamberlin's instruments to England in search of commercial opportunity. This he found in Birmingham, where three brothers, Leslie, Frank, and Norman Bradley, ran a company called Bradmatic Ltd, which manufactured tape recorders and magnetic heads. The Bradley brothers saw the potential of Chamberlin's instrument, but believed they could improve it. By the end of 1962 they had set about making the first Mellotron – a virtual copy of the Chamberlins Franzen had bought over from California.

There followed an uncertain period of wrangling between the Bradleys, Fransen and Chamberlin, which culminated in Chamberlin selling his idea to the Bradleys. From there on, Mellotrons were produced in England, while Chamberlin continued to develop and make his own instruments in California. Chamberlin production continued until 1981, with a total of under 1,000 instruments made.[4] Mellotrons were made in England until the early 1980s, too. About 2,700 of all models were made, some of the later ones being branded Novatrons.[5]

Most big British bands of the late 1960s and early 1970s used Mellotrons, including The Beatles, The Rolling Stones, and Led Zeppelin. The most famous use of the instrument is on 'Strawberry Fields Forever,' by The Beatles, recorded in late 1966. Here Paul McCartney plays a MkII Mellotron that John Lennon had acquired in the summer of 1965. A flute sound was used on the familiar single version,[6] although a brass sound had been tried on an earlier version.

The Moody Blues were another British band of the time who used Mellotrons, their sweeping orchestrations all generated by the many frantically whirling tapes of a modified instrument played by Mike Pinder. He had worked for Streetly, as the Bradley's company was renamed, before joining The Moody Blues, his job being to play each Mellotron as it came off the production line to check that it worked properly. Pinder became something of an evangelist for the instrument, although his devotion provoked the usual furrowed-brow harrumphing from the musical establishment. Band member Ray Thomas said: "We've had trouble with the unions, who've said we plug it in and press a note and it puts half an orchestra out of work."[7]

Although tape replay instruments were killed by digital sampling, which could do the same job in a package about a tenth of the size, they began to enjoy a revival in the mid 1990s. The Chamberlin instruments in particular have featured on many recent recordings by major-label artists, including Mercury Rev, The Flaming Lips, and Crowded House. As is often the case when musicians turn to antique equipment, the characteristics of the machines that are now so appealing – the grainy taped sounds, the abrupt cut-off of notes from instruments that would, in reality, have a natural decay, the sometimes wayward tuning – were the very things criticized as limitations when the instruments were made.

ACES AND KINGS

Early drum machines

nce the notion of electronic musical instruments became established, it was only a matter of time before people started to think about the possibilities of electronic rhythm. Early rhythm machines began to appear as far back as the late 1940s, although it wasn't until the early 1980s that the drum machine, as it was by then known, became widely used. In the years between those first instruments and the final acceptance of the drum machine, electronic rhythm was an oddity in pop music.

It was rarely used in recordings, and when it was it invariably made those records sound completely different to the way they would have sounded if real drums had been used – not least because the sounds generated by early rhythm machines aren't really comparable to real drum sounds at all. The individual voices are percussive, and the machines play the voices rhythmically, but the end result doesn't sound like a drum kit.

Rather, what you hear is a vague electronic approximation of a snare, or a bass drum, or a hi-hat (with the odd exception of claves and woodblocks, which always sound quite plausible). Early rhythm machines also played with a rigid exactitude way beyond the most tightly drilled human drummer. As drum machine technology developed, both the performance of the machines rhythmically, and the sounds they generated, came to mimic ever more closely the playing of real drummers. But before that there was a stage when rhythm machines made sounds that were new, that had never been heard before. It is these that are the subject of this chapter.

Since the 1990s, the drum machine has become all but ubiquitous in electronic dance music, hip-hop, and rap. It is also common in reggae, soul, R&B, commercial pop, and rock. Now, most records in most pop charts use drum machines. Most records use samplers and synthesizers too. But whereas the key stages in the development of these other electronic instruments can be traced back to inventors or academics in the world of experimental classical music, or well heeled commercial operators in the mainstream of the music business, the first steps in making the dream of electronic rhythm come true were made by people with more modest concerns. The early story of the rhythm machine is inextricably bound up with the aspirations and needs of home musicians and small-scale light entertainers in general, and electric organists in particular. And it is a story driven by the uniquely Japanese aptitude for electronic innovation.

Rhythm has always been a problem for any musicians playing in a reasonably confined space. Drummers are loud, they annoy the neighbors, and their drum kits take up a lot of room. They also often play out of time. Yet most music, particularly pop music, needs rhythm. What a joy it would be to have drummers and drum kits that were completely reliable, space efficient, and with volume controls. This was the dream that consumed the rhythm machine pioneers.

The ancestor of the modern drum machine was introduced by visionary Californian Harry Chamberlin in 1949. Chamberlin's drum machine, the Chamberlin Rhythmate, used a number of continuous tape loops, not electronically generated sounds. Each contained a recording of a different drum pattern played live on an acoustic drum kit. Selecting a particular loop would result in the recorded pattern playing indefinitely, until the Rhythmate was turned off or another pattern was selected. The Rhythmate came in a combo-type package, with its own amplifier and speaker. As it was designed to sit next to an organist or pianist, the controls were located on the top of the cabinet.

The Rhythmate was hand-made in very limited numbers, and only for a few years. No other drum machines evolved directly from the first Rhythmate, but the tape loop technology it pioneered was developed in a succession of Chamberlin keyboards that made use of orchestral instruments. Some of these later Chamberlins had split keyboards, which used both rhythm loops and orchestral instrument loops. Although Chamberlin was to remain an obscure figure, his ideas lived on through several generations of musical instrument. The Chamberlin technology would eventually re-emerge, much refined, in the British-produced Mellotron tape keyboard of the 1960s and 1970s. The Mellotron was itself rendered obsolete by digital samplers, which offered a much more convenient (and ultimately smaller and cheaper) way of realizing Chamberlin's original concept of using recording technology to play looped recordings of real instruments, included among which were drums.

It was ten years after Chamberlin's first efforts that the next giant step in the evolution of the drum machine was made, when organ manufacturers Wurlitzer introduced their Sideman rhythm machine. The Sideman bore a superficial external resemblance to the Rhythmate. It too had its own speaker and amplifier housed in a wooden cabinet, with the controls mounted on top, and was designed to stand next to the organ it would accompany. But the technology inside the box was completely different.

The Sideman's sounds are electronically generated, rather than taped samples, but its operation is electro-mechanical. An electronic motor drives a wheel, to the rim of which are attached rows of contact points. Each row of contacts triggers a particular drum sound. The points are spread around the wheel and the spacing of the contacts in each row generates a particular rhythm. This technology offered the performer a number of presets familiar to all users of the first generation of drum machines – waltz, foxtrot, and so on. These were selected using a rotary control dial. Individual percussion sounds could also be triggered manually using a set of buttons. Volume and tempo controls gave further control.

Although individual musicians often lead unconventional lives, collectively they can tend towards conservatism. In what has become a familiar refrain in the story of technical advances in music, musicians' unions were concerned when the Sideman appeared, fearing that automated rhythm would put drummers out of work. There were even rumors that attempts were made to stop Wurlitzer making the new device. Similar rumblings of discontent plagued the drum machine's evolution for decades.

The Sideman – "the uncanny new rhythm instrument" as adverts described it – was expensive when introduced around 1960: $375 (£135) for a walnut or cherry model, $10 less for a mahogany version. Yet in spite of the cost, and the grumbling from organized musicians, the Sideman sold well, finding favor with home organists and small-scale professional light entertainers. Now, any organist deft enough with the bass foot-pedals and twin manual keyboards could become a whole band with just a

flick of the Sideman's switch. However, its real importance lies not in its modest commercial success, but in the inspiration it provided to a few musicians and technicians to design and produce the first solid-state, fully automatic rhythm machines.

This is the point where the prehistory of electronic rhythm blends into the history of the drum machine as it is known today. It is also the point in the story when the action moves to Japan.[1]

Ikutaro Kakehashi and Tsutomu Katoh, as the founders of Roland and Korg respectively, are two of the most important figures in the popularization of electronic musical instruments. Of the same generation, their early lives had much in common, and not least because both produced pioneering machines that helped introduce the idea of electronic rhythm to musicians other than organists.

Tsutomu Katoh was born in the mid 1920s. There has been speculation about his first 35 years or so, and much remains unknown. It is thought that he served in the Japanese navy during WWII, and after the war moved to Tokyo. By the late 1950s, he owned several shops and a nightclub. It was at this nightclub that accordionist Tadashi Osanai performed, one day in the very early 1960s, accompanied by his new Wurlitzer Sideman. Osanai could see the potential of an automatic rhythm-generating device, but found the Sideman limiting and unreliable. As well as being a musician, Osanai had an engineering background. This gave him the confidence to believe he could build a better rhythm machine than the Sideman.

No doubt recognizing that Katoh was an entrepreneurial spirit, Osanai approached him for backing, and in 1962 the pair opened a small factory, a venture they named Keio Gijutsu Kenkyujo Limited. The company's first product came a year later, the DA-20 Disk Rotary Electric Auto Rhythm Machine, also known as the Donca Matic. As its name suggest, this was an electro-mechanical device that used similar technology to the Sideman, and was housed in a box with its own amp and speaker. Once again aimed very much at the electric organist, it sold well in Japan, and Osanai and Katoh were inspired to develop their concept further.

Just as Katoh's company was getting established, a fellow countryman, Ikutaro Kakehashi, was setting up

The first product from Japanese maker Korg came in 1963, the DA-20 Disk Rotary Electric Auto Rhythm Machine – also known as the Donca Matic.

another electronic musical instrument venture. Born in 1930, Kakehashi faced considerable hardship in his early life. He was orphaned at the age of two, and towards the end of WWII worked as a child laborer, building submarines for the Japanese navy. After the war, while still a teenager, he started a watch and radio repair business. Then, at the age of 20, he contracted tuberculosis and almost died. By the mid 1950s,

having recovered fully, Kakehashi started an electrical goods and repair business, soon after branching out into designing electronic musical products. Over the next few years he tried making a Theremin, an organ, and an amplifier, none of which was successful. But he finally got a break when, in 1960, he designed an organ that was taken on by Technics (the SX601). It was a modest success, and opened the way for Ace Electronics, as Kakehashi's company was now called, to develop more electronic musical instruments.

Like Katoh and Osanai, Kakehashi had come across a Wurlitzer Sideman. He too thought he could do better. His first attempt, though a commercial failure, is notable as the first fully electronic rhythm machine, unlike the electro-mechanical Donca Matic and Sideman.

The Ace Electronics R1 Rhythm Ace appeared in 1964, and was presented at that year's NAMM instruments show in Chicago. It aroused some interest and a few sample orders, but nobody came forward with any offers substantial enough to ensure that the device would be made in large numbers. The reason for this was simple: the R1 had no preset automatic rhythms, but instead sounded individual percussion hits when its buttons were pressed. This made it useless for an organist, then the most likely customer for a rhythm machine, who needed a constant background rhythm, not a selection of one-off hits.

It was Katoh, maybe inspired by Kakehashi's electronic rhythm machine, who pushed the drum machine's evolution to its next stage. In 1966 a new generation of Donca Matics appeared that combined the virtues of both the original DA-20 Donca Matic and the R1 Rhythm Ace, while eliminating their respective weaknesses. These new devices were purely solid-state drum machines, like the Rhythm Ace, without the original Donca Matic's electro-mechanical workings. But they could play constant, automatic preset rhythms, unlike the Rhythm Ace.

The new generation of Donca Matics was important, and not only because they were the first fully automated solid-state drum machines to go into production. They also showed an understanding among manufacturers that rhythm devices could be used as practice and compositional aids for all sorts of musicians, and not just as accompaniment for organists and light entertainers. Several new models of Donca Matic were offered in 1966 and 1967, the most successful of which was the DE-20, which like all previous drum machines had an integrated amplifier and speaker. Others were simply rhythm-generating devices that needed an external amplifier. These were small, and aimed at guitarists – something to keep time while you practiced your licks.

Later in the 1960s Korg issued several new rhythm machines. This brochure shows the DE-20 Donca Matic, the first solid-state automatic drum machine.

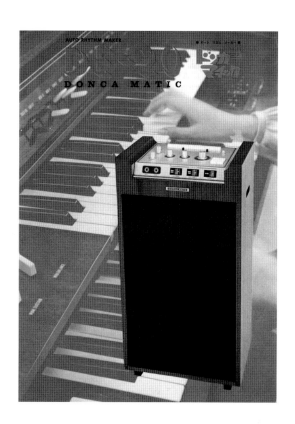

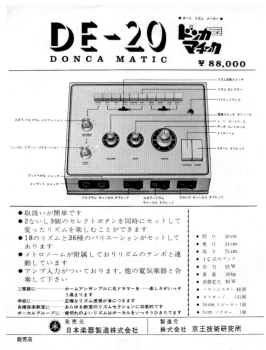

One guitarist who got hold of a Donca Matic and made good use of it as a songwriting tool for many years was Lowell George, best remembered as the slide guitarist, singer, and songwriter of 1970s critics' favorites Little Feat. When a Little Feat career retrospective boxed set, *Hotcakes And Outtakes*, was released in 2000, it included a number of home-recorded Lowell George demos. Many of these feature George singing and playing along to the insistent tapping of a Donca Matic preset.

George's friend and sometime collaborator Van Dyke Parks believes that the Donca Matic did much to set the groove for many early Little Feat classics. "The Donca Matic was very important to the soul of Lowell's work. He would take a drum figure, which would have been predesigned by some farseeing Japanese sound technician, and he would offset it two beats. This would provide the most amazing kind of zero gravity of rhythm, which was highly deceptive. … It informed his music; you could hear it in so much of his work."[2] This capacity of early drum machines to produce a metronomic, insistent groove was exploited by many early drum machine pioneers, more of whom later.

George's Donca Matic is briefly audible on one 'proper' Little Feat release. At the beginning of 'Cold Cold Cold,' from the band's second album *Sailin' Shoes*, it is audible for a mere 12 seconds before being obliterated by drummer Richie Hayward's pulverizing tom-tom fill. It becomes very faintly audible again during the fade-out. The band had been playing along to it throughout the song.

A year after the second generation of Donca Matics was introduced, Ace Electronics replied with a new rhythm machine, the Ace Tone FR1 Rhythm Ace. This marked a great leap forward technically, and in terms of usability. The FR1 has 16 preset rhythm patterns, which are selected by pressing a button, the tempo being set by a separate control. By comparison, the DE-20 Donca Matic offered ten presets. But there is much more to the FR1 than those 16 beats. Each of the presets can be combined with one or more of the others by simply pressing two or more buttons at once. This gives the user hundred of different options, and can result in some very interesting polyrhythms. Even more control is offered by four 'defeat' buttons,

which mute the sound of cymbal, claves, cowbell, or bass drum, so each preset or combination of presets can be further modified. The defeat operation and switching between rhythms can be performed while a rhythm pattern is playing, so that somebody can 'play' the FR1 live, bringing individual percussion sounds in and out of the mix and changing beats. And not only did the Rhythm Ace offer a huge range of sounds for its time, it was also well made and reliable. Not surprisingly, it was a favorite amongst all sorts of musicians for many years. Crucially, it sounded good enough for some musicians actually to record with it. The Hammond Organ Company was impressed, too, and incorporated the FR1 presets into many of its organs from the late 1960s into the 1970s.

A technically similar machine, the FR2, was introduced in 1969, aimed at the home organ market and housed in a slim-line cabinet designed to sit on top of an organ console.

By the late 1960s, after the success of the FR1 Rhythm Ace, many other companies introduced rhythm units. Some of these were clearly aimed at the home organ market, while others were intended as rehearsal aids for guitarists or for more general use. Kent, Seeburg, and Maestro are just a few of the names that clambered on to the bandwagon of electronic rhythm.

With such a choice of electronic rhythm machines, it was only a matter of time before questing rock and pop musicians began to explore the musical possibilities the new devices offered. Sly Stone and JJ Cale are both heralded, rightly, as drum machine pioneers. But their recordings are predated by the often forgotten solo work of Robin Gibb, better known as a member of The Bee Gees.

Gibb's brief late-1960s solo career is an object lesson in the fickleness of pop fame. The Bee Gees rapidly established themselves as one of pop's biggest acts after scoring their first international hit in 1967, with 'New York Mining Disaster 1941.' A string of successful albums and singles, accompanied by massive press interest, saw them hailed in some quarters as rivals to The Beatles. Although they were originally a five-piece band, The Bee Gees' trademark harmonies and songs were the work of twins Maurice and Robin Gibb, and older brother Barry. So when, in February

The Ace Tone FR2 Rhythm Ace drum machine of 1969. Ikutaro Kakehashi's Ace company later became Roland.

1969, at the peak of the band's first flush of success, Robin left over a dispute about what song should be the A-side of the next Bee Gees single, it was big news indeed. Imagine George Harrison leaving The Beatles in 1964. The British music press in particular was full of features, interviews, letters, and editorial comment about the story.

Robin Gibb, although remaining tactful about his brothers, seemed to be enjoying his new-found independence. He was full of grandiose plans for films, books, and solo albums. Speaking to *Melody Maker*, he said: "I shall do concerts, 'An Evening With Robin Gibb,' doing my own songs backed with a 30-piece orchestra. I am also writing musicals and plays."[3] When his first solo single was released in June 1969, just four months after the split, Gibb claimed to have written 100 songs in ten weeks.

That first single was 'Saved By The Bell,' a soaring ballad delivered by Gibb in a mannered, near-operatic style somewhere between Gene Pitney and Roy

Orbison. Instrumentally, it is a swirling mass of lush orchestrations, underpinned, oddly, by a simple tapping rhythm machine pattern. This almost certainly comes from a FR1 Rhythm Ace, then by far the most common rhythm machine around, as the pattern sounds identical to the 'slow rock' preset on the Ace Electronics machine. It is the first use of rhythm machine on a major hit record.

'Saved By The Bell' was a massive international hit (although it didn't chart in the USA). Gibb's solo career was off to a flying start, and it is hard not to speculate that he must have enjoyed the fact that his first single outperformed the contemporaneous efforts of the remaining Bee Gees. But the success was shortlived. A second single, 'One Million Years,' also used a drum machine. It failed to chart, but Gibb was undeterred. In January 1970, a third single and a debut solo album, *Robin's Reign*, were released. Yet with the press and fans caught up in speculation about the future of The Beatles and the murder at Altamont, Gibb's new releases were all but ignored. He had gone from being one of *the* faces of the pop scene to a near has-been in six months.

Despite its commercial failure, *Robin's Reign* is deserving of attention. It is a lost eccentric pop masterpiece. Lyrics about house repossession and Admiral Nelson, epic strings, and a choir of multi-tracked Robin Gibbs are just some of the ingredients strangely juxtaposed. And then there's the rhythm machine, to which Gibb was obviously attached. Of the 11 songs on the album, five feature it, including 'Saved By The Bell' and Gibb's third single, 'August, October.' (The second single, 'One Million Years,' was excluded.) Another five songs use a conventional drum kit. One, the hymnal 'Lord Bless All,' does not have any percussion at all.

'August, October' opens the album with a faded-in rhythm machine waltz preset, overlaid with plaintive mandolins. It creates an impression reminiscent of a Bavarian folk song, which may go some way to account for the album's popularity in Germany. Of the remaining three rhythm machine songs, the ballad 'Down Came The Sun' uses the same slow rock preset as 'Saved By The Bell,' at a faster tempo. From a rhythm point of view, the remaining two, 'The Worst Girl In This Town' and 'Mother And

Jack,' are more ambitious. If indeed Gibb was using a Rhythm Ace machine, he made careful use of the preset-combining and sound-canceling features already described.

Partly because of Gibb's apparent evasiveness on the subject, little is known about the recording of *Robin's Reign*. Bee Gees researcher Joseph Brennan has established that it was put together in several sessions between March and October 1969, in London. Gibb sang and played guitar and organ. Twin brother Maurice probably helped out on a few tracks, and arrangers Kenny Clayton and Zack Lawrence did the charts.[4] The producer's credit went to Gibb himself and Vic Lewis. Speaking in a rare interview about the album, Gibb referred to recording it on two-track.[5] Given that the five songs that use the rhythm machine tend to be built on a foundation of electronic percussion and basic strummed guitar, it is reasonable to speculate that Gibb recorded these on the two-track he mentioned, maybe as a demo. These tapes would then have been dubbed onto a multi-track facility to accommodate the cavernous strings and multi-tracked backing vocals that complete the arrangements.

In later years Gibb has seemed reluctant to talk about this phase of his intermittent solo career. Perhaps it is all a bad memory. There are rumors that Gibb, barely 20 years old when all of this was happening, became unwell. Or perhaps he simply wants to emphasize The Bee Gees' filial strength at the expense of his own efforts. Whatever he thinks now, this part of his life was over by the end of 1970 (although he continued to make the occasional solo album alongside his later Bee Gees work). A second solo album, the dark and bizarre *Swing Slowly Sister*, was completed after *Robin's Reign* but remains unreleased, a much-bootlegged artifact circulated amongst collectors of period pop weirdness. Gibb rejoined his brothers Maurice and Barry, and after a few lean years came to prominence once more with the falsetto harmonies and disco beat of the *Saturday Night Fever* soundtrack.

Reviewers paid little heed to the unconventional timekeeper on Gibb's landmark recordings. Although rhythm machines were widely available by this time, they had not been much heard in recorded music, so it is quite possible that most people simply didn't know what they were listening to. Perhaps they thought Gibb had found himself a particularly strict and economical drummer.

Although Gibb's recordings were pioneering, they did not start a trend. It would be the best part of two and a half years after 'Saved By The Bell' and two years after *Robin's Reign* before drum machines appeared again on major pop records, this time by two very different American artists.

It is often overlooked now just how big Sly & The Family Stone were in the late 1960s. A male/female multi-racial collective combining taut funk, psychedelic rock, and leader Sly Stone's knack with an infectious chorus, the band scored many international hit singles and albums with an exuberant and optimistic sound that was in keeping with the spirit of the age. But by 1971 Sly Stone (real name Sylvester Stewart) was disillusioned with the previous decade's utopian dreams that he had so eagerly championed. Beset with drug problems, he retreated further and further into a paranoid, closeted world. A feature in *Rolling Stone* in November 1971 paints a depressing picture of an indulged, drug-addled rock star surrounded by flunkies.

The US-made Maestro MRK-2 Rhythm King drum machine, as used by Sly & The Family Stone.

But he was still a powerful chart force. With a Sly & The Family Stone greatest hits package riding high in the album chart, *Billboard* was reporting advance orders of 800,000 for the band's eagerly anticipated forthcoming studio album. By Christmas that album, *There's A Riot Going On*, was topping the charts. 'Family Affair,' lifted from the album, held the top spot on the singles chart.

There's A Riot Going On is a dark, murky, and ominous album, with slurred vocals, elastic bass, scratchy guitars, ambiguous lyrics, and a casual-sounding mix. It has all the hallmarks of an obscure cult album, except that it was a huge seller. In 50 years, pop music has turned up many classic cult albums that should have been huge. *There's A Riot Going On* is that much rarer thing, a classic album that probably wouldn't have been a hit at all if it hadn't been for the goodwill and reputation that preceded it, which translated into advance orders.

The circumstances surrounding the making of the album remain vague, but there were rumors that other members of the band apart from Stone had drug problems and absented themselves from sessions. And although many of the songs are full ensemble workouts, others are dominated by the sound of Stone himself overdubbing many of the parts. His use of drum machine – a Maestro Rhythm King – was born out of this chaos. Probably originally intended as a

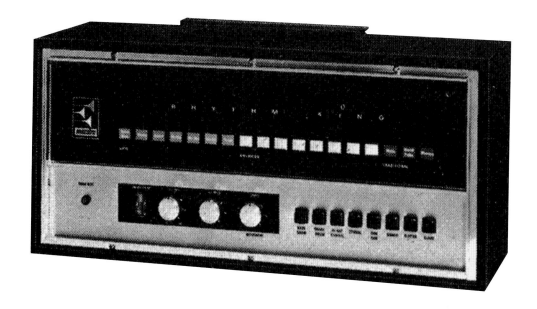

simple time keeper, around which Stone could build up arrangements, it would remain the only percussion part on many of the songs, while on others it was combined with real drums.

The Rhythm King was produced by Maestro, a brand owned by Gibson's parent company, CMI. Several models were offered, the most popular of which was the MRK-2, launched in October 1970. Although it is not a programmable unit – like its main competitor, the Acetone Rhythm Ace, its core sounds are presets that can be played at varying speeds – it does offer a number of useful features that were considered advanced when the unit was launched. The 18 rhythm presets on the MRK-2 can be modified with a balance control, which alters the levels of bass or cymbal sounds within each preset. Additionally, eight different percussion voices can be manually added into a preset to vary it. The MRK-2 proved popular with musicians when launched and is frequently sampled now.

There's A Riot Going On wasn't the first Sly Stone recording to use the Rhythm King, nor was it the first drum machine record to enter the American charts. An earlier recording marked with Stone's distinctive stamp gets both honors. Little Sister was a shortlived R&B vocal group produced by Stone and featuring his sister Vet Stewart. Their single 'Somebody's Watching You,' a minor US hit in early 1971, was driven by a chugging drum pattern from Stone's Maestro Rhythm King, a dry run for the Family Stone recordings later that year.

Of the 11 songs on *There's A Riot Going On*, only four have no trace of the rhythm machine. Of the remaining seven, three songs, 'Family Affair,' 'Africa Talks To You, "The Asphalt Jungle" There's A Riot Goin' On,' and 'Time,' use rhythm machine only, with no live percussion. Of these, it is 'Family Affair' that is the best known, and the most influential. A slow paced funk song with a hook sung by Rose Stone, around which Sly growled a rather obscure lyric, it is a hypnotic record. There is something distant, out of focus, and washed-out about the sound, as if someone has accidentally pressed a wrong button on the noise reduction. Some have attributed this to Stone's repeated overdubbing actually wearing the magnetic coating off the tape. However it came about, the

muffled vagueness only enhances the record's mysterious appeal.

The arrangement of 'Family Affair' is sparse: a syncopated electric piano, bass, spidery wah-wah guitar and little else. It is held together by the persistent repetitions of the Maestro Rhythm King, which a reviewer described as "the most incredible bubbling going on in the background."[6] It serves both as a ballast – keeping the other elements of the arrangement from drifting too far away from each other – and it sets up a groove. Not for nothing did Stone call it the 'funk box.' Critics of drum machines say that they can't replicate the feel of live drums. The early ones like the Maestro Rhythm King definitely couldn't, it's true, but they could do something that a drummer couldn't do. The loping, inevitable forward momentum of 'Family Affair' was down to the Rhythm King. It was a new sound.

In choosing to go with the Maestro's automated rhythm patterns as the anchor to his lazy, loose funk on 'Family Affair,' Stone was unintentionally setting the rhythmic template for much black music that followed. Funk, hip-hop, and rap have long relied on the drum machine to generate the groove, but it started here. Not that anyone seemed to notice at the time. As with Robin Gibb's recordings two years earlier, reviewers singularly failed to pick up on the musical history they were listening to on the Sly album, although *Melody Maker's* reviewer, writing in January 1972, did praise the drummer for his exemplary work throughout.

Stone's star waned after *There's A Riot Going On*. He managed one more strong album, 1973's *Fresh*, which also featured the Rhythm King. After that he gradually slid into critical and commercial obscurity. In the late 1980s he was imprisoned for drugs offences. He hasn't released a new recording for two decades, and his current whereabouts are unknown.

Released at almost exactly the same time as *There's A Riot Goin' On* was another pioneering drum machine record, *Naturally* by JJ Cale. The album established Cale's trademark style – economical, understated, husky, laid-back country blues – which Mark Knopfler later polished up for Dire Straits. Although musically a long way from Sly Stone's languid funk, *Naturally* is another example of the same phenomenon that defined Stone's record: it is swinging groove music created on a foundation of strict, basic drum machine presets.

Many of the tracks on *Naturally* started out with Cale playing a few instruments along with a Rhythm Ace drum machine, which was played through a Fender Twin Reverb amp and then miked up. On some other songs, musicians were then called in to add further parts, although a few of the tracks make do just with the basic arrangements. 'Crazy Mama,' the hit single from the album, chugs along to the simplest of Rhythm Ace rock presets.

British eccentric Arthur Brown had one moment of chart glory, in 1968, when, fronting The Crazy World Of Arthur Brown, he scored a massive international hit with 'Fire.' The song is a classic, but Brown is remembered as much for his flamboyant stage persona as he is for his music, at times wearing robes, painting his face, staging mock crucifixions on stage, and most famously wearing a tin helmet that would burst into flames at an appropriate climax in his show. Actually, there is more to him than risky pyrotechnic stunts. He had been active as a singer and all-purpose counter-culture eccentric for many years before 'Fire,' and has continued on an individual career path ever since.

After The Crazy World Of Arthur Brown spilt in the late 1960s, Brown formed a new band, Kingdom Come, a progressive art rock ensemble with theatrical leanings. That band went through several incarnations, the most interesting of which, for this story, was the one in which Brown replaced his drummer with a Bentley Rhythm Ace drum machine. In doing so, Kingdom Come becoming the first rock act to rely entirely on electronic percussion.

The Bentley Rhythm Ace was in fact an Ace Tone Rhythm Ace, badged and distributed by Bentley, a now-defunct British piano manufacturer, for the UK market in the 1970s.

Like much progressive rock of the early 1970s, the music Kingdom Come made with the Rhythm Ace hasn't aged too well, overburdened as it is with lofty lyrical conceits and unnecessary complexity. But in using electronic percussion, Brown saw a new direction in which music could be taken. Speaking in 1972, he talked not in terms of the Rhythm Ace replacing live drums, but as offering new possibilities instead. "It's just like having a different percussion instrument. … You can go in a tenth of a second from a rock beat through a tango to something else. … There's so much more you can get into than with a drummer. You can't really compare them. We're not trying to make it sound like a drummer."[7]

What Arthur Brown said expressed what all of the rhythm machine pioneers sensed, that automatic electronic percussion opened up new roads for pop music to travel down. The insistent, hypnotic quality of an early rhythm machine preset could provide a secure, unobtrusive, gently arresting backbeat on which chords and melodies could sit comfortably, without having to fight for dynamic space with the more powerful sound of live drums.

After Kingdom Come, rhythm machines continued to be used from time to time throughout the 1970s. The first generation of rhythm machine was obsolete by the early 1980s, when much more sophisticated and usable new drum machines, as they were now called, became available. Many of these were produced by Roland, Kakehashi's new company that built on his experiences at Ace Electronics many years earlier. And as drum machines became more versatile, and the sounds they produced more realistic, so they became more widely used.

For a while, the trend was to program drum machines to sound as much as possible like a live drummer. Now much contemporary music that uses electronic percussion has reverted to Brown's principle, using electronic rhythm as an alternative to a live drum kit, not an imitation of it. In most contemporary dance music, for example, there is no pretence that the rhythm tracks sound like live drums. The parts may not even be playable by a drummer, and the sounds bear little resemblance to any real drum sounds. In fact, what the currently favored electronic drum sounds *do* resemble are the dead, thin, toneless sounds of the early rhythm machines. Indeed, many current hardware and software drum machines use samples from these old machines. Although the Rhythm Ace, The Rhythm King, The Sideman and all of these other evocative names from the first age of electronic percussion are now obsolete curiosities, the sounds they made live on, heard on the radio everywhere, everyday.

DOCTOrS AND CAPTAINS

Electronic music on British television in the 1960s

I n the UK in the 1950s and 1960s, some of the most widely heard popular electronic and tape music came not from the pop scene, but from the country's television and radio studios. Experimental techniques, new sounds, and unusual instruments were employed by composers and producers compressing their creativity into, say, a jingle for a local radio station, or the theme music for a children's TV series. On television, both British channels (there were just two then), the BBC and Independent Television, had their own particular sources of creativity: the BBC had a service department called the Radiophonic Workshop; the independent network had a composer and arranger called Barry Gray. Much of the music that emerged from these two sources was never released on record; and if it was, it rarely charted. But so widespread was its use that it became a part of the country's shared musical language. Anyone who listened to the radio or watched television during this time would have heard the strange sounds and music of the Radiophonic Workshop and Barry Gray. Indeed, as many of the programs using this music were exported around the world, much of it was heard internationally, too. Some of it still is.

> The BBC Radiophonic Workshop – Abstract Electronic Sound, Organized

The BBC in the mid 1950s was still characterized by the values of its first director, Lord Reith. Its aims, broadly, were to inform, educate and entertain, although the emphasis often appeared to be on the first two of those functions. The formal, perfectly enunciated, clipped tones of the radio and television presenters reflected the mild stuffiness and establishment nature of the corporation.

Then as now, the BBC was an unwieldy bureaucracy and the repository of a great deal of technical broadcasting knowledge. Despite its superficial conservatism, however, many creative spirits stalked the corridors of its London homes, Broadcasting House and Bush House, bursting with ideas and schemes. One of these was Daphne Oram, who had been working at the BBC since 1943.

Oram was fascinated by the French *musique concrète* experiments and early German electronic music, and recognized the potential of these radical new ideas for enhancing radio drama. In 1950, she composed one of the very earliest orchestral and electronic crossover pieces, the unperformed 30-minute *Still Point*. It was to have combined conventional orchestrations with pre-recorded instrumental sounds and live electronic treatments using then-standard radio equipment.

By early 1957, Oram had gathered together a few like-minded allies in the BBC. Late at night, after broadcasting had stopped, this furtive group of conspirators would gather in BBC studios to make experimental recordings of background music and sound effects, combining the natural recorded sounds and tape editing ethic of the French school of *musique concrète* with the electronic tones and noises favored by the Germans. A number of productions used these recordings to great effect, and the BBC hierarchy was persuaded to formalize the experiments in the form of a new department, the Radiophonic Workshop. Dick Mills, a long-serving Radiophonic Workshop staff member, puts it this way: "They said, 'Why don't we give them a room somewhere, fill it with all of this equipment, and let them get it out of their systems?'"[1]

The department officially came into being in 1958. The omens were not good. It was formally opened on April Fools' day, in Room 13 at the BBC's studio in Maida Vale, west London. It was equipped with substandard, out of date, and sometimes malfunctioning equipment, begged and borrowed from other departments. The term 'radiophonic' was dreamt up to describe what a press release announcing the department's launch called "neither music nor conventional sound effects." The press release went on: "It is a new sound – suggestive of emotion, sensation, mood, rather than the literal meaning of a wind or the opening of a door. Created by mechanical means from basic sounds which may vary from the rustle of paper to a note from an electronic oscillator."[2]

Oram, the workshop's first director, left the new department and the BBC in early 1959, frustrated by what she perceived as the meddlesome and apparently uninterested response to her work by the BBC hierarchy. She set up her own studio in a converted oast house in Kent, and embarked on a freelance career as a composer, inventor, producer, lecturer, and writer. She died in 2003. After Oram left, one of the Radiophonic Workshop's other founders, Desmond Briscoe, was appointed as its head, a position he occupied until the 1980s.

Briscoe was a career BBC man, spending his entire working life in the corporation apart from a period of wartime military service in World War II. Much credit for the subsequent flourishing of the workshop must go to him. Not only was he skilled at navigating the labyrinthine BBC decision-making process to acquire more resources for his department, he was also open-minded and creative, and worked as a sound producer himself.

Right from the start, the work of the BBC Radiophonic Workshop was characterized by several tensions. The first struck at the very heart of the then-current discussions about electronic music and *musique concrète*. Was it music at all, or was it just organized noise? Originally, the official BBC line, as expressed at a press listening session very early in the workshop's life, was conservative: "By radiophonic effects, we mean something very near to what the French have labeled concrete music. Not music at all, really."[3] By contrast, Delia Derbyshire, the workshop's most famous member, was in no doubt: "It was music. It was abstract electronic sound, organized."[4]

Listening to what is currently available of the workshop's output, with the benefit of decades of hindsight, it is quite clear that it produced music in a conventional sense, with melody, chords, and rhythm, and sound effects too. That many people could not recognize this it at the time demonstrates both changing perceptions of music, and the then radical nature of tape and electronic music.

Another tension in the workshop was between a sort of high art seriousness and the more straightforward need to entertain; a fissure, in fact, that seemed to be built into the BBC's very fabric. In the early days of the Workshop, and in the year or so before it was officially formed, but when the formative experiments were being carried out, radiophonic sound was produced for work by playwright Samuel Beckett and comedy group The Goons. Later, local radio time-jingles and children's television themes jostled for attention with radio programs showcasing the work of experimental poets.

And there was one more tension, linked to the previous one, and again typical of the BBC as a whole. The workshop was both a center for innovative free spirits, and a service department for a large corporation. A consistent theme running through its history is of staff eager to join what they saw, rightly, as a hotbed of forward-thinking creativity, and eventually leaving, disillusioned by the bureaucracy and frustrated by the constant pressure of working to unrealistic deadlines. Early descriptions of working practices are alluring. Staff were allowed to work whenever they felt like it, day or night, in a closed world of gadgets and gizmos, and given only the vaguest of briefs. Yet all too often, creative individuals would quickly find this apparent paradise tainted by the mundane need to produce a prosaic piece of work at short notice; a theme, say, for a new regional radio station. Yet from this last tension came the workshop's greatest achievements.

Dr Who was conceived as a short children's science fiction series, the doctor in question being a time traveling righter-of-wrongs who zipped around many dimensions in a machine known as the Tardis. It was to be shown late on Saturday afternoons, in the lull between the afternoon's sports coverage and the evening's mix of light entertainment. No one could have predicted that it would become a long running institution with a capacity for reinvention that mirrored the good doctor's ability to discard one body and acquire another, nor that it would spawn a huge international cult and a whole supporting industry. When it started, it was throwaway light entertainment.

By July of 1963, with transmission due to start in the fall, the need for a theme tune for the new series was pressing. Series producer Verity Lambert briefly considered commissioning French avant-garde composers Jacques Lasry and Bernard Baschet for the job. Working under the name *Les Structures Sonores*, the duo made music with specially built metal and glass sculptures. This idea was soon abandoned, and Lambert found her way to Desmond Briscoe, to discuss whether the Radiophonic Workshop could meet what was becoming an urgent need. The outcome of that meeting was that workshop composer Delia Derbyshire was assigned to produce a

Delia Derbyshire at the BBC Radiophonic Workshop, early 1960s, with Desmond Briscoe in the background.

theme for the new show, assisted by Dick Mills, with Brian Hodgson responsible for sound effects. A popular and experienced theme composer of the time, Ron Grainer, was asked to write the tune. Mills says, "We'd just finished working with Ron on a documentary where we'd provided a lot of mechanical loop rhythms for him to incorporate with his live musicians. That's how Ron got the commission."[5]

Grainer duly wrote his theme on a single sheet of manuscript paper. It was a simple composition, comprising of not much more than a bass line, a melody, and a few written instructions to convey atmosphere, such as "wind bubble" and "cloud."[6]

Armed only with this sheet of paper, vivid imaginations, and a disciplined work ethic, Derbyshire and Mills created the original version of the most widely heard piece of electronic music of the decade in about two weeks in August 1963.

Making electronic music in 1963 was a painstaking business. The rudimentary sound-generating and recording equipment of the Radiophonic Workshop comprised of little more than some test tone oscillators, some equalizers (tone controls), a white noise generator, and a low frequency oscillator dubbed the wobbulator. The oscillators, which were designed to test electrical circuits in conjunction with oscilloscopes, were a mainstay of electronic musicians in the 1950s and early 1960s, and one of the few tools available then for producing pure electronic tones. The Radiophonic Workshop had its oscillators arranged as a very primitive electronic keyboard instrument.

Radiophonic Workshop archivist Mark Ayres says: "They had 12 of these oscillators, usually tuned to a single octave, and they connected them to a very small single octave keyboard they made, and all that keyboard did was that each key turned on and off the output of one oscillator."[7] There was also a magpie's nest of bottles to hit, a homemade one-string 'electric guitar' (a single string stretched between two nails in a piece of wood, with a pickup), a Melodica, an autoharp, a mijwiz (an Arabian pipe), and other assorted junk. There were no synthesizers, no samplers, no sequencers, and not even any usable multi-track tape recorders. These did exist by then,

but the BBC had yet to invest in a professional standard machine for the Radiophonic Workshop.

The various parts in the *Dr Who* theme, so imprinted on the collective memory of generations of viewers, were created using some key elements of this collection of sound sources and recording equipment. The swooping sounds are Derbyshire or Mills turning a dial to adjust the pitch of an oscillator. The hissing sounds are from the white noise generator. The twanging bass line comes from the one string 'guitar.' Many of these basic source sounds were then modified and pitched using the tape composition techniques pioneered by the composers (see chapter 4).

As Ayres explains: "Once each sound had been created, it was modified. Some sounds were created at all the required pitches direct from the oscillators; others had to be repitched later. This was done by taking the piece of tape with the sound on and looping it. The loop was placed on a tape machine and its playback speed varied until the pitch was correct, then the sound was re-recorded onto another machine. This process continued until every sound was available at all the required pitches. To create dynamics, the notes were re-recorded at slightly different levels."[8]

Audio test oscillators simliar to this were widely used in electronic music of the 1950s and 1960s.

Once each sound and note had been made, the process of actually arranging Grainer's theme began. A tape was edited together for each 'instrument' in the arrangement, each note of which was made at the desired length and with the correct degree of attack or decay, by cutting the tape at carefully measured lengths and angles. These individual notes were then stuck together to create the complete part. Most of these bits of tape, with edits as frequently as every inch in places, still survive. At this point, Ayres says, five sub-mixes were made, by recording two or more parts together on to another tape.

When tapes of all the parts were finished, and sub-mixes created, the next stage in the process was to play them all at once. In the absence of a multi-track tape recorder, this involved playing each tape on individual mono tape machines, all of which were manually synchronized and their outputs recorded onto another tape machine. Dick Mills says: "We ended up with reels of tape for differing music lines, all spliced together. We stood at the tape machines and said 'One, two, three, go!' pushed the buttons, and hoped to God it all fitted. Which it didn't. There was a bum note in it. So we took the reels of tape into the corridor and laid them out side by side, and compared where the sticky tape editing joins were, and where one of them didn't coincide with the other two next to it, that was the bum note."[9]

All three of the main players involved in the *Dr Who* theme, Grainer, Mills, and Derbyshire, recognized the conceptual shift in the mechanics of making electronic music, compared to how things worked in conventional studios. In the established professional music studios at that time, roles were clearly and formally delineated.

Engineers and technicians wore white or buff colored work coats with pens in their top pockets. They set up the equipment, producers booked the musicians and gave everybody instructions, arrangers did the charts, musicians played them, and composers were normally nowhere to be seen, their work having been completed long before the session started. In the Radiophonic Workshop, the boundaries between composer, performer, producer, and studio technician became blurred. Composer Grainer, on hearing the first realization of his composition, is said to have

asked, "Did I write this?" Mills was nominally just the level balancer and tape cutter: "I was a technical assistant. What it meant was that these delicate people who were known as studio managers, who were sort of responsible for the creative ideas, always worked with a technical assistant or an engineer, who saw to it that the tape machines were lined up, circuits were plugged in, razor blades and chinagraph pencils were to hand … We always worked as a pair." But he says, "I like to think I did as much towards the *Dr Who* theme tune as Delia did."[10]

Derbyshire, whose role was to creatively interpret Grainer's basic score, was herself no slouch in the technical department that traditionally would have been Mills's domain only. She said: "[Grainer] expected to hire a band to play it, but when he heard what I had done electronically, he never imagined it would be so good. He offered me half the royalties, but the BBC wouldn't allow it. I was just on an assistant studio manager's salary and that was it … and we got a free *Radio Times* [listing magazine]."[11]

The public first heard the *Dr Who* theme on November 21st 1963, at 5.15pm, when the first episode was broadcast. If Derbyshire had looked in her free *Radio Times* that week she would have seen the series described as "an adventure in space and time," with theme music by "Ron Grainer and the BBC Radiophonic Workshop."

Delia Derbyshire and Dick Mills's realization of Grainer's theme was released as a single, although it did not chart. But the *Dr Who* series thrived beyond all expectations, year after year. Several actors in succession took on the central role; filming, which was originally in black and white, moved to color; and the program were exported around the world.

In the wider world of popular music, multi-tracking and synthesizers became commonplace. Yet amidst all of this, the basic *Dr Who* theme created in 1963, although updated several times in the ensuing years with additional parts and different mixes, remained a constant. The theme was eventually replaced by a synthesizer version of Grainer's theme in 1980.

That the *Dr Who* theme was the most widely-heard electronic music composition of the 1960s is unquestionable. Even now it remains one of the best-known electronic hits, instantly recognizable to millions. Its appeal lies in the convergence of good tunes, rhythm, and sound that mark out all great pop recordings: its importance is that it demonstrated that electronic music could do all of the things that conventional music could do. Before *Dr Who*, there was a very broad consensus that electronic music could never quite be the real thing. It was sterile, highbrow, and elitist, interesting to a few, but only in some dry, theoretical, academic sense. But as Ayres says, "An audience that would quite possibly turn its nose up at experimental modern music if they heard it in the concert hall were quite happy to sit down at tea time on Saturdays and listen to it for half an hour."[12] *Dr Who* showed that electronic music could be warm, organic, varied, interesting, and enjoyable.

Over the years a cult has grown up around Delia Derbyshire, which could lead the casual observer into thinking that she was the only musical talent in the Radiophonic Workshop. That is not the case. Many other gifted and original artists served time in Room 13, Maida Vale. Space does not permit examination of all of them, but a brief mention must be made of the late John Baker, whose work, as collected on some of the albums listed in the discography in this book, is worth investigating. He was, says Mills, "the ace performer with the razor blade. He could actually edit in a jazz feel."[13]

But it was Derbyshire whose appeal went further: an exceptional talent; a mercurial, faintly enigmatic nature; refined good looks; the great work followed by a long silence in obscurity. These are the characteristics that make a cult figure.

Derbyshire was born in Coventry in 1937, and remained in the city when it was heavily bombed in WWII. Late in life, she speculated on the effect the wailing sirens and crashing explosions had on her in those formative years: "I was there in the Blitz, and it came to me, relatively recently, that my love for abstract sounds came from the air raid sirens … that was electronic music."[14] She took a maths and music degree at Cambridge University. This combination of a feel for music and the capacity to understand the mathematics of sound stood her in good stead at the BBC Radiophonic Workshop, where she arrived in 1962, having worked as a BBC studio manager since

1960. "She was a mathematician, and she went into it pretty thoroughly on a mathematical and musical basis,"[15] says Mills.

Derbyshire's temperament, her thoroughness and attention to detail, her enthusiasm and her unwillingness to compromise creatively, gave her the mental resources to produce great work, but also exhausted her. Working in a service department at the BBC had its advantages − access to equipment, a regular wage − but there were pressures for someone like Derbyshire, too. Mills recalls, "Delia was a law unto herself. Getting through to her was difficult. She was wildly enthusiastic at the start of any commission, and then it tailed off in direct proportion to the nearness of the deadline."[16] Derbyshire herself recognized this trait: "I think I must have reverse adrenalin. As the deadline gets closer most people speed up − I just get slower."[17] Working constantly on commissions coming in at short notice, which were then often changed at the last moment, she was gradually worn down, and left in 1973. "I didn't want to compromise my integrity any further. I was fed up with having my stuff turned down because it was too sophisticated, and yet it was lapped up when I played it to anyone outside the BBC."[18]

In her 11 years at the workshop, Derbyshire's output for the BBC amounted to music for nearly 200 programs. On top of that there were extra-curricular creative activities, including many working alongside workshop colleague Brian Hodgson. By the time she left she was frustrated and disillusioned, and did little musical work from there on. She died in 2001, age 64, having spent the last 25 years or so of her life working in bookshops and galleries and as a radio operator for a gas company.

Hodgson, her friend and colleague for many years, says, "Delia always said she liked the preparation, the concept, the planning. She just found it very difficult to get those concepts through in a manner she liked. She just thought, 'What's the point in doing all this planning when you can't actually do what's in your mind.' The tragedy was that by the time the sort of equipment came along that Delia would have absolutely reveled in she was no longer capable of picking up the technology. ... She had a wonderful mind, a wonderful talent. She was amazing fun, amazingly annoying and difficult and tiresome and fabulous."[19]

Hodgson's own career in the Radiophonic Workshop spanned several decades. He first joined in 1963, having previously worked in theatre and as a studio manager at the BBC. He left in late 1972 to start Electrophon, an electronic music studio, and returned in 1978 as organizer; then, on Briscoe's retirement in 1984, as head. He had no formal musical training, and concentrated on sound effects, excelling himself in this respect in the *Dr Who* series for many years. Dick Mills took over from Hodgson as primary producer of *Dr Who* sound effects in the early 1970s. He spent most of his working life at the Radiophonic Workshop, from 1958, six months after it opened, until 1993. He had previously worked as a recording engineer with the BBC. Like Hodgson, Mills too had no formal musical training.

The influence of the Radiophonic Workshop on pop music in the 1960s and beyond was substantial, if hard to quantify. In a general sense, its work became a part of the shared musical landscape of a generation. In 1992 *The Wire* magazine speculated whether "[the] secret effect on Britain's ears might not be huge."[20]

More specifically, several luminaries from the pop world actively took an interest in what the workshop was doing. Hodgson and Derbyshire briefly brushed up against some of Britain's biggest bands: The Beatles, The Rolling Stones, and Pink Floyd. Hodgson recalls that Brian Jones of The Rolling Stones visited: "We liked him very much. He promised he would get us access to the Rolling Stones' Moog because we'd never even seen one at that point. He said it was just lying around the studio doing nothing. He died very shortly after."[21]

In 1997 Paul McCartney made an intriguing statement in the pages of Barry Miles's book *Many Years From Now*, saying that in the 1960s he had conceived of the idea of recording his song 'Yesterday' with a radiophonic backing. He talks of looking up the number of the workshop in the phone book, going to Maida Vale and meeting the "woman who ran it" [presumably Delia Derbyshire], and looking in the studio, which was in a shed at the bottom of the garden.[22] McCartney and Derbyshire did meet, but he is confusing his recollection of a visit to the workshop

with another meeting, somewhere else. Hodgson, who worked closely with Derbyshire both at the BBC and on freelance projects, has no recollection of McCartney visiting the workshop or of any talk of there being a radiophonic version of 'Yesterday': "I would have thought Delia would have mentioned it [working on 'Yesterday']. I would have thought Delia would have done it, quite frankly. So many rumors go around, so many legends. Chance meetings turn into long associations which didn't happen."[23]

Mills, who too worked with Derbyshire during this time, also knows nothing about the 'Yesterday' rumor, and suspects there is nothing in it. Finally, just before she died, Derbyshire herself confirmed that, although she met McCartney and he heard her work, the association was fleeting.

She also confirmed where the meeting took place. "He [McCartney] never did come to the workshop. … He came to [Peter] Zinovieff's studio and I played him some of my stuff, that's all."[24] Hodgson, too, confirms that he and Derbyshire met McCartney at Zinovieff's studio.

Synthesizer pioneer Zinovieff was one of the men responsible for the highly regarded early British synthesizer, the EMS VC3. Derbyshire and Hodgson had a brief professional relationship with him as Unit Delta Plus, an organization created in 1966 to promote the cause of electronic music. Perhaps, after meeting Derbyshire at Zinovieff's, McCartney briefly flirted with asking her to collaborate and mentioned the idea to friends before dropping it, nothing more. Whatever happened, by the time Derbyshire met McCartney in Zinovieff's studio, which indeed was in a shed at the bottom of his garden, it was almost certainly in 1966, a year after the recording of 'Yesterday.' So if McCartney did think of a radiophonic version of the song, it would have been a reinterpretation of it, not the original.

Although Derbyshire's contact with McCartney was fleeting, it did prompt a recording fabled amongst Beatles aficionados. Hodgson continues: "How much Delia had to do with Paul after that I don't know. Not a lot, I think. There was a concert at the Roundhouse when Paul sent us a load of stuff, which was all rather a mess. … There seemed to be no coherence to what was on the tape. That is my memory of it, anyway."[25]

The concert Hodgson refers to was actually a two-stage event called The Million Volt Light And Sound Rave, held in early 1967 at the Roundhouse Theatre in Chalk Farm, London. It has a special resonance for hardcore Beatles fans, as the 'mess' that Paul McCartney sent Hodgson and Derbyshire for the event was in fact a sound collage called 'Carnival Of Light.' Having escaped the attentions of the bootleggers for decades, this piece has rarely been heard after the event apart from by a few Abbey Road insiders, and so has acquired the allure of the unobtainable amongst collectors.

The Million Volt Light And Sound Rave was organized by counter-culture designers Binder, Edwards, and Vaughan, already known to Beatles fans as the team that McCartney had hired to decorate a piano in 1966. Their brightly colored Buick, in which they would cruise around London at the time, was featured on the cover of The Kinks' *Sunny Afternoon* album. The three were immersed in a burgeoning London underground scene of artists, pop stars, film makers, and the like, all absorbed with notions of combining pop, the avant garde, and high art, and reveling in the apparently limitless freedom of the Swinging Sixties.

The event, also remembered as the Carnival Of Light Rave, took place over two nights a week apart in 1967, January 28th and February 4th. Various experimental music tapes were played, included 'Carnival Of Light' and work by Unit Delta Plus. It is usually reported that Binder, Edwards, and Vaughan asked McCartney directly to contribute to the event, but in a brief interview with British journalist Mark Ellen, McCartney said that he was asked to chip in by Barry Miles, a 1960s scenester and later McCartney's biographer.[26]

Although 'Carnival Of Light' has never been released, thanks to Beatles researcher Mark Lewisohn something is known of its construction and recording. It was committed to tape on January 5th 1967, during a session that also included the recording of some vocals for 'Penny Lane.' A four-track recording, it was an experimental exercise in overlaying sounds, with elements of *musique concrète*. Track one features organ and drums; track two, distorted electric guitar and sound effects; track three

has more sound effects, a church organ, and John Lennon and Paul McCartney shouting; track four, tape echo, tambourine, and yet more sound effects. The finished piece ran to nearly 14 minutes. McCartney wanted to include the track on the *Anthology* series of albums, but apparently both George Martin and George Harrison thought it was without merit.

Derbyshire may not have seriously discussed collaborating with Paul McCartney, but she did briefly work with Anthony Newley, another British pop star of the time. He had come across Derbyshire's work, and thought the radiophonic style would be a suitably quirky backing for a single. Derbyshire was asked if she could come up with anything, and she duly composed a pretty pop tape composition over which Newley intoned some mildly risqué lyrics. The record was never released, though, because Newley decided to move to Hollywood. In recent years bootlegs of it have surfaced on the internet.

A few years later, Derbyshire had a more fruitful involvement in the world of pop and rock when, with Hodgson, she teamed up with David Vorhaus as White Noise, releasing an album, *An Electric Storm*, on Island Records in 1969. Whereas Derbyshire's collaboration with Newley was very definitely pop, albeit of an oddball variety, White Noise was a much more serious business, best placed in the hinterland between psychedelia and the emerging progressive rock.

Hodgson says: "We were just trying to do something that wasn't *Switched On Bach* [the then popular Moog renditions of Bach tunes performed by Walter/Wendy Carlos]."[27] Although not a chart album, *An Electric Storm* was a steady seller and cult favorite for many years.

Vorhaus met Derbyshire and Hodgson when the two were giving a lecture on electronic music. Vorhaus, a young physicist and musician, found he had many ideas in common with the slightly older workshop duo, and started working with them shortly afterwards. The three completed a couple of tape compositions with added vocals that found their way to Island Records boss Chris Blackwell. To the embryonic band's surprise, Blackwell offered them a deal, and *An Electric Storm* was pieced together over the following year. Although sometimes compared to the roughly contemporaneous work of American bands Silver Apples and The United States Of America, White Noise's work is in a different category. Whereas the American bands created their sounds mainly using primitive homemade electronic instruments, White Noise relied primarily on the tape-manipulation skills of Derbyshire and Hodgson as its main sound source. Indeed, like many Radiophonic Workshop compositions of the period, the White Noise master tapes were an extraordinarily complex and fragile succession of edits.

In recent years, a generation of British electronic musicians, including The Chemical Brothers, Sonic Boom, and Aphex Twin, have referenced Derbyshire's work. This prompted her to tentatively return to music, investigating new computer technology and granting several revealing interviews to fringe electronic-music publications. Sadly, she died before completing any new work.

The BBC Radiophonic Workshop was a unique institution in its day: a boffin's paradise, a refuge for forward thinking electronic composers, a quintessentially eccentric British response to Schaeffer's and Stockhausen's furrowed-brow musings in Paris and Cologne respectively. It was the BBC's own electronic Brill Building hit factory. From science fiction to science, from adult radio drama to children's TV, from flora to fauna, and outer space to the inner mind, the workshop sound tracked them all. But by the 1990s its moment had passed. In the 1970s workshop aficionados and staff alike perceived an artistic downturn.

"The synthesizer made life a little too easy. We went up one of those wonderful blind alleys for about eight or nine years," says Hodgson. But in the 1980s technology finally caught up with the ideals and ideas of the workshop's founders, and computers and sampling "came along and we were able to manipulate real sound again."[28] Under Hodgson's stewardship the workshop was re-equipped as a state of the art MIDI environment and enjoyed a second golden age.

Initially, in the early 1980s, this new MIDI, sampling, and computer equipment was extremely expensive, and only available to well funded professional studios, which by this time the workshop was. But as the decade wore on the equipment got cheaper, smaller, and more readily available, giving rise to a new sort of soundtrack composer – the home studio owner. These people could work cheaply and efficiently, and any advantage a specialist establishment like the Radiophonic Workshop had was eroded to nothing. Its doors were finally closed for good in 1998, although it had been all but dormant for some years before that.

In its 40 years of life, the Radiophonic Workshop was involved in nearly 6,000 separate projects, from five-second jingles to whole 24-part television series. Unusually for a BBC department born in the 1950s, from its inception it kept its own library of listening copies of its work. All too often the radiophonic soundtracks to television programs survive, even though the visual element of the program is long gone. For example, in the 1960s Dr Who was recorded and broadcast in the UK on videotape. After the UK broadcast had been completed, the videotapes were wiped. But before this happened copies were made on 16mm film for possible export. These would be circulated around the world on demand. But once exports dried up, these film prints were destroyed too. So the 1960s Dr Who episodes that survive invariably come from 16mm film copies that were made for export. For those episodes for which no film copy can be found, the visual part of the program has gone forever, although the sounds survive.

Composer and Dr Who enthusiast Mark Ayres has long been fascinated by the Radiophonic Workshop. When the BBC finally pulled the plugs, he was asked by some of the last generation of workshop composers to take on the considerable task of getting this archive in order. This he did, and through a combination of his persistence and BBC inefficiency, much of this unique body of sound and music survives. Ayres has located about 3,500 reels of often fragile tape, many of which are punctuated by frequent, decades-old edits. A large number of these he found forgotten in a BBC anteroom that was the final stopping-off place for items awaiting disposal.

> Barry Gray

Barry Gray's musical career was long, varied, and productive, but because most of it was conducted behind the scenes he was rarely interviewed and written about. Not much is known about his early life, and what has been written in some articles over the years has later been challenged by others who claim to know something different. It is known that he was born in Blackburn, Lancashire, in the north of England in 1908. Apparently Gray was encouraged by his family to learn music from a very early age. He went on to study music formally until his early twenties, before embarking on a wide-ranging career as a writer, arranger, accompanist, and producer.[29]

First securing work with a music publisher in London, Gray worked as a composer, arranger and performer for theatre, variety, and radio, until his career was interrupted by the outbreak of World War II. In 1946, after service in the RAF in Africa, India, and Burma, Gray returned to London to pick up the threads of his career. Despite being well versed in classical music and able to compose for orchestras – his favorite composers were Bach, Mozart, and Beethoven[30] – Gray was not a classical musician or composer in the accepted meaning of those terms. Nor was he a rock'n'roll musician. He was nearly 50 when the first wave of rock hit. Rather, he was a multi-faceted operator in the world of popular music, turning his hand to whatever work came along.

Working freelance, he kept busy in the 1950s writing for publishers, film producers, and the BBC (including a popular Terry-Thomas radio series *To Town With Terry*), and working as an arranger and accompanist with artists as varied as Eartha Kitt, Hoagy Carmichael, and Vera Lynn. He also composed music and jingles for many early television commercials. This mix set the pattern for Gray's subsequent career, which was spent entirely in the world of popular entertainment.

Yet in the midst of this flurry of lightweight work, Gray nurtured a long-held fascination with electronic musical instruments and tape recorders, then the almost exclusive preserve of avant-garde conceptualists and academic institutions. As his commercial success grew, so he was able to fund these more *outré* interests.

Quite where Gray's interest in electronics in music came from is hard to pinpoint. Although obviously very gifted, he was musically quite conservative, favoring conventional orchestral scoring

above all else. It is unlikely that he was directly influenced by the art experiments of the electronic music studios in Paris and Cologne, which had such a bearing on the early life of the Radiophonic Workshop. He was not consciously taking an avant-garde path. His few recorded remarks about his electronic experiments seem to betray ambivalence, as if he was both fascinated by what he was doing and yet didn't think of it as real music. Indeed, late in his life he was still expressing views about electronic music that seem at odds with the groundbreaking work that he did: "I am not partial to actual melody in electronic music, when it's supposed to be creating weird or astral or spacey effects. … Generally most of my electronic music has been what I call electronic effects rather than music."[31] He coined a term to describe the electronic elements in his work, 'musifex,' which appears jotted in many of his surviving manuscripts and notes.

Most likely his interest in electronic musical instruments was born out of a simple fascination for electrical gadgets, combined with his love of music. Both these obsessions Gray shared with Joe Meek, another unlikely figure to be leading the electronic revolution in music in the late 1950s. The two were very different characters, but were probably the only popular musicians/producers investigating electronic music in home studios in Britain at the time. In these studios both would tinker with tape editing and manipulation, coax unearthly sounds from lap steel guitars drenched in reverb, and explore the possibilities of early electronic musical instruments. And in these studios both would create popular music, including pioneering use of electronic elements, that is still widely heard today.

But Gray was in no senses an eccentric, volatile personality like Meek. Short, bespectacled, avuncular, with a broad northern accent, and wide interests pursued with boyish enthusiasm, Gray cuts a likeable figure. He was popular with his musicians and generous to his fans, in the habit of making tapes of his music to send off to enthusiastic children who had written to him.

1956 was a momentous year for popular music in Britain. Two new phenomena, rock'n'roll and skiffle, entered the charts. Both would have far-reaching implications. Barry Gray was untouched by these new developments, but it was a momentous time for him, too, as it was the year he first met Gerry Anderson, the creator of the children's 'Supermarionation' puppet series *Thunderbirds, Captain Scarlet, Joe 90*, and others. For most of the rest of his career Gray was closely associated with Anderson, and his best-known work was born out of this relationship.

Roberta Leigh, a songwriter amongst other things, was instrumental in bringing Gray and Anderson together. She knew Gray through their mutual association with popular singer Vera Lynn, who had recorded several of Leigh's songs, as arranged by Gray. When Leigh proposed to Anderson an idea for a children's television series, *The Adventures Of Twizzle*, it was on the condition that Gray be appointed as musical director. Anderson took up Leigh's proposal, and Gray with it, and the composer was set to work transcribing and arranging tunes hummed into a tape recorder by Leslie Clair, another friend of Leigh's. Anderson was impressed by how Gray developed Clair's simple aural sketches into fully realized music, using a band including Bert Weedon on guitar. The series was produced, broadcast, and two EPs of music and songs were extracted for release by HMV in 1958.

By now, Gray had established his recording studio at his house in Dollis Hill, north London, and it was here, in 1958, that the music for a further Anderson/Leigh collaboration, *Torchy The Battery Boy*, was put together. This time, Leigh sang her own tunes into the tape recorder for Gray to orchestrate into completed musical themes, making use of the Clavioline (see chapter 3). Gray's interest in electronic music led him not only to the Clavioline, one of the few mass-produced electronic instruments then available, but also to the much rarer Ondes Martenot (see chapter 2).

Gray had experimented with a Theremin, but like most people he found the instrument very hard to pitch accurately. The Martenot he saw as a means to getting the sounds of the Theremin but with more control. Gray bought his first Ondes Martenot, a valve model, in 1959, and studied with the instrument's inventor Maurice Martenot in Paris for a month. In 1967, Gray bought a transistor version of the instrument. Even as late as 1982, he was still writing to Martenot ordering spare parts for his instruments.

Gray first recorded the Ondes Martenot on an advert for Mobil oil, broadcast in 1959. This was almost certainly the first time a British audience, apart from a tiny minority interested in modern classical music, would have heard the instrument. Even more people heard it when Gray was invited to compose the title song and all the incidental music for Gerry Anderson's next series, the futuristic *Supercar* (1960). The Ondes Martenot was used on that job, and from then on became a firmly established option in Gray's sound world. He would return to it many times as a composer, sometimes playing the instrument himself, at other times hiring in the virtuoso French ondist Sylvette Allart.

Anderson and Gray's next project was another science-fiction series, *Fireball XL5*. In Gray's mind science fiction was the ideal setting for electronic instruments. Speaking many years later, he said, "Electronic music is mostly suitable only for visuals that are concerned with such things as laboratories, space, very weird and perhaps even strange situations, astral sequences etc."[32] Gray was by now using the Ondes Martenot alongside other electronic instruments, including a Hammond Organ and an English-made Miller Spinetta, a very rare dual keyboard instrument combining a piano and an electronic keyboard. Over the next few years, further Anderson series followed, including *Stingray, Captain Scarlet, Joe 90*, and most famously, *Thunderbirds*. Gray composed and arranged the music for them all, occasionally making use of his electronic arsenal alongside more conventional instrumentation.

While Gray was busy with Anderson he was also doing film work. True to his belief that electronic music was best suited to sci-fi, in 1965 and 1966 Gray produced electronic music and effects for four films. Two of these, *Dr Who And The Daleks* and *Daleks' Invasion Earth 2150 AD* (both 1966), were spin offs from the BBC television series *Dr Who*. Gray's role was to produce electronic effects and interjections alongside conventional scores composed by other people. These films did not feature contributions from the BBC Radiophonic Workshop, which had provided sound and music for the television series.

Barry Gray's Ondes Martenot, which he purchased in 1959. Gray's electronic themes and incidental music graced many science-fiction shows on British television, including Thunderbirds, Fireball XL5, and Stingray.

The other films were *Island Of Terror* (1966) and François Truffaut's *Fahrenheit 451* (1966), where he provided effects alongside a score by Bernard Herrmann. Later in the decade Gray provided the complete score for a Gerry Anderson live-action movie, *Doppelganger* (also known as *Journey To The Far Side Of The Sun*).

Maurice Martenot had always considered that his Ondes Martenot should be an orchestral instrument, a new voice alongside traditional string and wind instruments. The *Doppelganger* music, more than anything else Gray recorded, comes closest to this vision, with Gray making extensive use of the Martenot's eerie tones in an orchestral setting. Up to this point Gray had been in the habit of playing any Martenot parts in his music himself, but for *Doppelganger* he felt he needed a more expert touch, and so hired Sylvette Allart.

In 1967 Gerry Anderson launched *Captain Scarlet And The Mysterons*, a new puppet series. It was a darker concept than previous Anderson series, in which the titular character battles against alien invaders called the Mysterons. The sense of threat is more palpable than in *Thunderbirds*, and the action more violent. Captain Scarlet himself faces all sorts of grave threats, but as he enjoyed the inestimable advantage of being indestructible, things always ended well. Gray matched the darker storylines with tense, suspenseful, often eerie music. And the sci-fi bent of the series meant that it qualified, in Gray's mind, for electronic experimentation.

Throughout the themes and incidental music he composed for the series, electronic instruments, treatments, and sound effects appear regularly. Witness, for example, the 'electronic voice' in the series end-title theme, which is a treatment of Gray's own voice. By this time Gray had added a Baldwin Electronic Harpsichord to his collection, and was very fond of two electric accordions then on the market, the Transicord and the Cordovox.

One of Gray's best compositions for Martenot appeared in *Captain Scarlet*, a short piece called 'Lunarville 7 – Suite,' composed for an episode of that name, set on the moon. As well as the Martenot, played by Gray, the piece uses an electric accordion, played by experienced session accordionist Jack Emblow. (It is unclear which model of accordion Emblow played, as Gray's session notes record the mistaken contraction of both names 'Cordavord'). Tremolo electric guitar and vibes added further color to the piece.[33]

Lasting just under five minutes, 'Lunarville 7 – Suite' opens with a faded-in Martenot vibrato note, before extending into a double-tracked Martenot and accordion rumination, gently punctuated with tremolo guitar and the occasional more abrupt vibes interjection. For about 30 seconds, from 2 minutes 15 seconds, there is a particularly good example of how a Martenot played with the ribbon controller could sound like an in-tune Theremin. 'Lunarville 7' was first broadcast in the UK on December 15th 1967. It would be years before rock groups like Pink Floyd and Tangerine Dream got close to this depth of electronic evocation. Without even knowing the title of the piece, it is impossible to miss the connection with space.

Gray continued to collaborate with Anderson into the 1970s, composing and orchestrating music for a live action series, *UFO*. While he was working on *UFO*, Gray moved to Guernsey, in the Channel Islands, taking his now rather dated collection of electronic instruments with him and setting up his studio 15 feet underground, in a former German bunker.

From then on Gray lived in comfortable semi-retirement, occasionally composing for later Anderson programs, writing children's books, and pursuing his other great passion apart from music, calligraphy. He regularly played piano in the restaurant at the Government House Hotel, and from time to time surprised diners by setting up his Ondes Martenot.

As the Anderson series developed a cult following, in the late 1970s and early 1980s, Gray was occasionally tempted out to attend fan conventions. He also gave a few interviews in which he divulged valuable information about his musical life. He died in Guernsey in 1984. Shortly before his death he had started discussing a new collaboration with Gerry Anderson.

Barry Gray was not a pop star, but his music had, and still has, a vast audience. Much of Gray's output for the Anderson series was released on a run of seven-inch, 33rpm mini-albums from 1965 to 1967, on the Anderson-owned Century 21 label.

Many of these records might well have sold enough to warrant a chart placing. Sales of the first batch of six mini-albums, released for the Christmas market in 1965, sold out their total pressing of 240,000. Subsequent issues in the series also performed well. But the unconventional format of the records, plus the fact that they were often sold through non-standard (for the record industry) retail outlets like toyshops, meant that most sales didn't count in chart terms. Compilations of Gray's Anderson work have been appearing regularly ever since.

Record sales aside, the TV series themselves reached millions in the 1960s. Many are still regularly repeated around the world. At the time of writing, *Captain Scarlet* was showing in a mid-morning weekday slot on BBC2.

Gray's legacy can be seen in several ways. In the simplest terms, he made a major contribution to a run of television programs that have entertained millions of children and adults for decades. But he did more than write popular theme tunes and incidental music. He mixed rousing and evocative conventional orchestration with electronic experimentation – a move that was very rare in television and even film at the time, and predated rock music's fascination with electronics by years.

After Gray's death his collection of tapes, instruments, and papers was stored in a lock-up garage in Chelsea, where it remained for many years. In the early 1990s, Anderson enthusiast Ralph Titterton was contacted by Gray's family after he had written an article about Gray in *Record Collector* magazine.

As a result of this contact, Titterton and his partner Cathy Ford were handed the task of reclaiming Gray's archive and putting it into order. Amongst the damp and dusty collection was Gray's first Ondes Martenot.

This was passed to film composer and Gray enthusiast Francois Evans, who restored it to working order and uses it in his own work.[34] The tapes found in that garage have since been digitally copied, and a reissue program of Barry Gray music is underway on Silva Screen Records.

OSCILLATIONS, OSCILLATIONS, ELECTRONIC EVOCATIONS

American underground electronic rock in the 1960s

I n 1966 a new age in music was quietly ushered in when Robert Moog sold the first production models of his Moog synthesizer. Most early Moogs, expensive, complicated, bulky pieces of equipment, went to well-heeled experimental composers interested in the new instrument's apparently limitless sonic capabilities. It would be a year before Moogs first made their presence felt in the wider world of pop music, and several more years again before they became commonplace. The pivotal event in this gradual emergence was The Monterey International Pop Festival, held from June 16-18th 1967. Not because Moogs were used by any artists performing, but because two early Moog owners and ambassadors for the cause, Paul Beaver and Bernie Krause, set up a stall there to promote Moog products. Beaver had been producing electronic music for films for some time, and owned several early electronic musical instruments, including an Ondes Martenot and a Hammond Novachord. Two months before Monterey, Beaver played Moog on the obscure Elektra album *Zodiac Cosmic Sounds*, a panoply of light orchestral instrumental weirdness and spoken word pseudo-profundities composed and conducted by Mort Garson. This may well be the first ever recording using a Moog.[1]

The rock aristocracy was present at Monterey in strength, both on the festival's bill and mingling backstage, and many of the stars were intrigued when they came across the Moog. Roger McGuinn of The Byrds and Mickey Dolenz of The Monkees were among the first to place orders, taking delivery of their modular systems in the fall of 1967. At the same time, on the cusp of this new era in electronic music, two very different American rock bands were taking a more primitive, homemade approach.

In 1967 and 1968 psychedelia was the prevailing sound of rock'n'roll, either the whimsical British variant or the harder American West Coast acid rock. New York was never such a happening place for psychedelia, but with hindsight what was going on there has had just as significant an influence on rock'n'roll. It was home to The Velvet Underground, a band at their creative peak in 1967/68, whose literary low-life, high art/trash crossover sound has done much more to shape the ensuing decades than the rather florid imaginings of the psychedelic prime movers. And there was another band operating in New York at the time, all but forgotten for 25 years and now only known to a few since a re-emergence of sorts in the mid 1990s. Their sound was as radical in its way as the Velvet Underground's, and although their influence is much harder to identify, they truly were ahead of their time.

The electronic two-piece Silver Apples took their name from a line in the WB Yeats poem, *Song Of Wandering Aengus*. Coincidentally, an experimental classical electronic album called *Silver Apples Of The Moon* (1967), by Morton Subotnick, also took the same Yeats line for its title. The two are not related. Simeon Coxe, the leader of Silver Apples, had no knowledge of the avant garde scene that produced Subotnick's *Silver Apples Of The Moon*.

"I had no background in 'serious' electronic music," said Coxe. "I was strictly a rock and roller who happened to have a friend who had an oscillator that he played along with classical music for fun. One day when he wasn't looking I started jamming along with a Stones record and was hooked."[2]

Coxe made that discovery in 1966 or 1967, when he was singing in a succession of conventional rock bands going nowhere. The last of these, The Overland Stage Electric Band, was a straightforward two guitars, bass, and drums rock covers band playing regularly in Greenwich Village coffee houses when Coxe joined. But within months of his arrival the line up began shrinking. "It started with that same oscillator," says Coxe. "I bought it from [my friend] for $25 and started plugging it into our guitar amps at gigs."[3]

The swoops and howls Coxe coaxed from the oscillator fascinated audiences, but his fellow band members hated it. One by one, the two guitarists and the bassist quit, leaving just Coxe and drummer Danny Taylor. Making a virtue out of necessity, the pair decided to continue, developing a new sound based on Coxe's growing arsenal of oscillators and Taylor's elaborate drum set up. Both would sing. Silver Apples came into being.

The oscillators at the core of the Apples' sound were originally manufactured as electronic test equipment. Similar devices had been adopted by musicians as electronic sound generating tools in the

Simeon Coxe of Silver Apples on-stage in 1968 playing the remarkable Simeon,
made from oscillators, echo machines, hand and foot switches, and much more.

days before synthesizers: Paul Tanner's electro-theremin used one (chapter 1), and Delia Derbyshire had used them when making the *Dr Who* theme (chapter 6). Describing them, Coxe says, "Basically, it's an electronic circuit designed to produce a sine/square wave that is so clean that it can be used to test the integrity of another circuit that has a real-life function, like, say, a submarine's sonar system. What I discovered is that if you hook this box up to a guitar amp you get this infinitely sustainable note with absolutely no distortion. That's a problem. No distortion, no fun. So I routed it through fuzz units, phasers, sound filters, radio circuits, anything I could find that would allow me to manipulate the character of that basic sine wave. Next, I had to have some way to make it go on and off, and since I wasn't a keyboard player, I scrounged a bunch of telegraph keys and routed each oscillator through one. Now I could play some with my feet, some with my fingers, some with my forehead, and get some complexity going, and we started writing songs based on whatever level of accomplishment I had achieved at the time. It was insanity at its purest and most joyous level."[4]

Christened the Simeon by drummer Taylor, Coxe's homemade synth grew to monstrous proportions. A protean beast, at one stage it was made up of nine oscillators (five bass, three rhythm, and one lead), an echo unit, two tone controls, a wah-wah pedal, a radio, three amplifiers, and numerous foot and hand switches. The oscillators themselves could be tuned almost infinitely: "So low that they can only be felt as a sort of throb in your chest, to so high they would be well out of the human range. The pitch is controlled by two things, first a band selector switch that narrows the range of the sweep. This can be thought of as choosing the strings on a violin. Within the range of each string, you can sweep from low to high. And second, the sweep itself, which on most [oscillators] is a large dial right in the middle of the instrument."[5]

Coxe had no formal electronics training, so assembling the Simeon was a process of trial and often error. "I would go to electronic surplus houses and pick up anything that looked interesting, then plug it into the contraption. More than once we had sparks and smoke run us out into the street."[6]

The Simeon's limitations were considerable. For example, bass parts had to use only whatever five notes the bass oscillators were tuned to at the start of a song, as Coxe could not reach to retune them without stopping playing. Yet despite this, it offered Silver Apples a range of tones and sounds unlike virtually anything else in pop music of the time.

The second component of the Silver Apples' sound was Danny Taylor's unique drum setup. Realizing that the Simeon offered limited melodic scope, he assembled a huge kit of tuned drums that enabled him to contribute both rhythm and melody. Pictures show Taylor sitting legs astride a snare drum, with a bass drum at each foot, surrounded by ten tom-toms, two cowbells, four cymbals, and a hi-hat. Taylor was destined to step briefly into pop history twice: as the drummer with Silver Apples, and previously with Jimmy James & The Blue Flames, a band that also counted Jimi Hendrix in its ranks.

Thus uniquely equipped, Silver Apples set about the creative process, with the help of lyricists Stanley Warren and Eileen Lewellen, and bankrolled by a manager named Barry Bryant. He touted the band around New York's record labels, attracting the interest of only one, a waning small independent named Kapp Records. With no other offers to consider, Silver Apples signed with Kapp, and some time in early 1968 went into the label's tiny 4-track studio to record an album.

The recording of the first Silver Apples album could have been disastrous. Coxe, Taylor, and manager Bryant had no studio experience, and when the producer failed to appear, claiming illness, they were left to their own devices to record the album. Taking advice from anyone they could find who'd worked in studios, they gradually mastered a rudimentary method of multi-tracking, recording drums and bass parts onto four tracks, which were then mixed down onto a single track on another machine. The remaining three tracks were then taken up with rhythm and lead oscillator parts, vocals, and sound effects. This accounts for the eccentric final mix of the album, with the rhythm tracks usually panned to one side of the stereo image, vocals somewhere in the middle, and the lead oscillator's shrieks and swoops off on the other side.

The very first Silver Apples gig, with an early version of the Simeon, in front of 30,000 people in Central Park, New York City, May 1968.

The Silver Apples' eponymous debut album starts with one of its most commercial songs, 'Oscillations,' from which the quote used as the title of this chapter is taken. 'Oscillations' became something of a theme tune for Silver Apples, and is emblematic of the band's strengths and weaknesses, demonstrating as it does both the limitations of the Simeon and the band's ingenuity in overcoming them. Starting with an ascending oscillator wobble, the song quickly settles into a one-chord drone from which it never moves. Variety is achieved by Taylor's complex drum patterns and carefully planned stops and starts in the oscillator textures, over which Cox and Taylor chant in harmony. The result is an exercise in hypnotic minimalism with just enough of a tune to make it pop. Released as a single, it received some regional airplay but was hampered, as would be all the band's records, by poor distribution.

The need for greater musical complexity drove the development of the Simeon. Coxe says: "When Stanley Warren showed us his poem 'Lovefingers,' [which became another song on the band's first album] Danny and I both knew immediately that we had to figure out a way to perform the song with a real chord change, just like real bands do."[7]

This led Simeon to buy a few more oscillators, and therefore a few more notes. From then on, Silver Apples did occasionally manage to change chord. The best example of this is heard on the band's second album *Contact*. The three chords of 'I Have Known Love' gave Coxe the basis for Silver Apples' most commercial song, which was an incongruous but happy mix of hippy lyricism, a folksy melody, and The Simeon's drones.

Once the Silver Apples debut album was complete, playing live became a necessity, to earn money to live day to day and to promote the record. But the Simeon was a tangle of dozens of components and leads, and dismantling it, transporting it to a venue, and reassembling it took hours.

At one of Silver Apples' first gigs, a free concert in New York Central Park in front of 30,000 people, Coxe and Taylor had to start setting up the Simeon early in the morning for a show that started at 3pm. Touring was out of the question, until Coxe reformed the Simeon into several modules in custom-built cases, which could be transported and plugged into each other with relative ease.

As far as Coxe was concerned, there were no other bands doing anything remotely close to what Silver Apples were doing, "except that a couple of people kept saying that there was this band called The United States Of America that were classically trained musicians using lab synths, and they were so amazing, but we never heard them play. Still haven't a clue what they were doing."[8] The United States Of America weren't using lab synths, but they were classically trained musicians, and in their way they were amazing.

The leader of the USA, composer, academic, and ethnomusicologist Joseph Byrd, had a background in post-war experimental music. He had spent the late 1950s and early 1960s criss-crossing America, acquiring degrees whilst dipping into various avant-garde scenes. He even spent a spell working with experimental music avatar John Cage: "I 'studied' with Cage at his home in Stony Point ('study' had nothing to do with my showing him my music; I was put to work throwing the I-Ching for the notation of his *Atlas Eclipticalis*)." Byrd was never a big player in avant-garde music, describing himself as "on the periphery of a charmed circle,"[10] and if he had done nothing else his work in such circles would be probably forgotten. But breathing in so rarefied an atmosphere informed his thoughts about his later foray into pop music. It is this later stage in his career that interests us here.

By 1965 Byrd was nominally studying for a doctorate at UCLA, while immersing himself in that institution's New Music Workshop. "We began to attract attention outside UCLA [and] without intending to, I became a celebrity. Rumors about my activities circulated, and for years after I was to be amazed at some of the myths (for example, that I had put a live fish inside a piano – a terrific idea, but it never happened)."

"In 1965, with funding from UCLA Associated Students, we did an elaborate set of concerts and events called 'A Steamed Spring Vegetable Pie.' (The title was randomly chosen from *The Alice B. Toklas Cookbook*.) The final concert of that series closed with [experimental composer] LaMonte Young's piece in which a giant weather balloon is filled on stage (using a vacuum cleaner).

"This takes about half an hour, and I was concerned that I would lose my unsophisticated audience, so I put together a blues band to play during it. Our singer was my friend Linda Ronstadt, who had just moved to Santa Monica, and was living with her folk trio in a six-block area that included The Doors and Frank Zappa. The realization that rock was an access to a larger public came out of that concert, and the idea of forming a band began taking shape."[11]

With these musical activities and a burgeoning political radicalism regarding the Vietnam War occupying his thoughts and time, Byrd left UCLA in 1966. Until this point his musical experiments had involved *musique concrète* and tape manipulation. Now he wanted to go further, into the realms of electronic sound generation. "My first electronic generator was simply four wave-forms that could frequency-modulate each other. This kind of sound is best known today from auto-theft alarms. It had a very 'dead' quality, so I used an Echoplex tape delay to give it depth. It was made by Tom Oberheim [who later manufactured Oberheim synthesizers], and in 1966 he demanded it back. I searched around for an electronics engineer, and came upon Richard Durrett, who was working in aerospace in Orange County."[12] Early in 1967, armed with the Durrett Electronic Music Synthesizer, Byrd put a band together and started his brief and curious journey into the outer limits of pop music, a medium of which he had, at that point, virtually no experience.

But before that new band made a record, the first fruits of Byrd's new direction were heard on a recording by the former folk singer Phil Ochs. Ochs had been one of the generation of singer songwriters to come out of Greenwich Village in Bob Dylan's wake earlier in the decade. He had already recorded three albums for Elektra when, in 1966, on account of his biting topical and protest songs, some sections of the folk community sought to adopt him as savior elect after Bob Dylan's defection into electric rock'n'roll. But like Dylan, Ochs found such expectations restricting. In 1967 he moved to the A&M label, seeking a new musical direction. At this point, Joseph Byrd stepped into the story.

Ochs's first album for A&M was *Pleasures Of The Harbor*, released in August 1967. It shows Ochs the former folk singer reveling in newfound lyrical and musical freedom. This is best expressed in the extraordinary 'Crucifixion,' an allusive allegory about the assassination of John Kennedy, graced with one of the most audacious arrangements in all of pop music. "Phil asked me to arrange the song," says Byrd. "I really didn't think it should be arranged, because its power is in the simplicity of the lyric. But he wanted the kitchen sink: Schoenberg, Stravinsky, Cage, electronic sound."[13] Byrd would give Ochs all of these things, setting a panoramic scene with strings, flutes, brass, backward tapes, organ, electric harpsichord, percussion, and primitive electronic oscillations from the Durrett Electronic Music Synthesizer.

The recording of 'Crucifixion' was drawn out over several fraught sessions. Ochs, used to singing whilst strumming his guitar, found it hard to sing in time without that prop, so Byrd recorded a click track by hitting two drumsticks together. When it came to mixing the song, Byrd, who had fallen out with producer Larry Marks, wasn't invited. The click track was left in the mix, often the only constant factor in the emerging, carefully orchestrated melee, something that has bothered Byrd ever since.

'Crucifixion' closed *Pleasures Of The Harbor*. Nearly nine minutes in length, the swirling concoction cooked up by Byrd gradually overpowers Ochs's tremulous vocal. Although at times in danger of collapsing under its own ambition, it was an extraordinarily adventurous musical statement, a quantum leap from Ochs's previous political folk strumming.

Pleasures Of The Harbor was not a commercial success for Ochs, although it is a good record. His experience of leaving behind the limiting strictures of the folk scene was similar in some respects to that of Dylan's in that he alienated a large proportion of his old audience. Unlike Dylan though, Ochs never managed to establish a substantial new pop fan base. He continued recording into the early 1970s, before political frustration, writer's block, and alcoholism precipitated a decline that ended with his suicide in 1976. Ochs's work has since been compiled and reissued, and he now occupies a secure if modest place in pop history. 'Crucifixion,' with Byrd's spectacular arrangement, stands as one of the great moments of experimentation in all of 1960s pop music.

Never a man to shy away from artistic confrontation and the big statement, Byrd decided to put together a pop band and call it The United States Of America. It did not use conventional instrumentation. After some comings and goings, Byrd settled on a line-up (described as the 'population' on the band's sole album) of his former partner Dorothy Moskowitz as lead singer, and Byrd himself playing organ, calliope, harpsichord, piano, and 'electronic music.' Alongside the pair were classically trained violinist Gordon Mallon, playing his electrified instrument through a ring modulator; Rand Forbes on fretless electric bass; Craig Woodson on 'electric drums' – a conventional drum kit with contact mics on the drum skins that were used to modify the sounds; and occasional member Ed Bogas on additional keyboards. Although the band didn't have a lead guitarist, at the time pop music's primary instrument, they might as well have had, so close to a fuzz tone guitar did the treated electric violin sound at times.

Byrd's contribution of 'electronic music' to the USA meant several things. In the 1950s and early 1960s, in the avant-garde electronic music world that Byrd had moved through, the term electronic music meant experiments with tape as much as it did the use of electronic instruments. Byrd contributed both elements to the USA's sound. Overwhelmingly, though, it is the Durrett Electronic Music Synthesizer that the listener is most conscious of in the band's recorded work.

The United States Of America in 1968. The band's Durrett Electronic Music Synthesizer can just be seen in the bottom left corner.

Like the Simeon, the Durrett Electronic Music Synthesizer was a basic configuration of oscillators, without a piano-style keyboard. It was smaller than the Silver Apples' instrument, and was monophonic. Any multi-layered sounds Byrd created on record were done by multi-tracking sounds on top of each other. Later, when playing live, Byrd's band was able to replicate its studio sound by playing along with two tape recorders containing parts of each song's arrangement. Byrd says: "There was a potentiometer knob for each oscillator, and a selector that changed the interaction between them. Only one waveform could serve as tone generator and one to modulate its pitch. So you could have a saw-tooth wave modifying a square wave tone, as on 'Hard Coming Love.' I guess the art, if there was any in such a primal kind of thing, was in the setting of the tape delays. 'Garden Of Earthly Delights,' for example, was just a reverse saw-tooth modifying a saw-tooth, but it seems to work with tons of delay."[14] The songs Byrd mentions here both feature on the USA's eponymous and only album, which appeared in May 1968. The same month, Silver Apples released their debut album.

The USA were more tangibly linked to the prevailing psychedelic rock scene than were their East Coast counterparts. Although Silver Apples could summon up a trance-inducing repetitive drone that had something in common, in spirit at least, with the output of bands like The Thirteenth Floor Elevators, there was something distinctly *other* about their sound. The musical limitations of the Simeon, with just a few notes being available at any one time, meant that conventional chord structures were hard to pull off. The USA, on the other hand, for all their expressed ignorance of prevailing rock trends, had the knack of composing rock songs and dreamy ballads in the style of many other bands active at the time. The most obvious comparison, enhanced by singer Moskowitz's glacial delivery, is with Jefferson Airplane. Echoes of The Beatles, The Doors, and Country Joe & The Fish can be heard too.

The recording of the USA album was a fractious affair. Byrd and Moskowitz's previous relationship caused tensions, exacerbated by the presence of producer David Rubinson, also a former partner of Moskowitz. There were musical tensions too, with the strong-willed, articulate Byrd propelling the band in an experimental direction, while Marron and Bogus were pushing it towards a more melodic, song-based style. In the end, eight of the ten songs on the album were Byrd's, sometimes written in partnership with Moskowitz, with Marron and Bogus contributing the other two. Actually, the resultant mix — avant-garde sonic experiments, fierce psychedelic rock-outs, and ethereal ballads — was right for the times, with many other British and American acts producing albums with similar combinations of styles.

The two songs already mentioned, 'Hard Coming Love' and 'Garden Of Earthly Delights,' are representative of one extreme of the band's varied sound. Both are Byrd and Moskowitz collaborations. 'Hard Coming Love' is a wild freak out, starting with a lengthy, punishing electric violin solo that is a match for anything by the most excessive of the era's guitar heroes. The band then rein in the intensity for Moskowitz's cool delivery of the verses, each of which ends with a pause filled with Byrd's Durrett noise. Another fast rocker, 'Garden Of Earthly Delights,' more than any other USA song, recalls Jefferson Airplane. Distinguished by virtuoso bass playing by Forbes coupled with fast tom-tom beating by Woodson, the song is frequently swamped in a miasma of Byrd's cacophonous electronics.

In between those two tracks, the wistful 'Cloud Song' shows the band's gentler side. Another Byrd/Moskowitz collaboration, it pulls off the then-fashionable trick of co-opting a character from a children's story — in this case, AA Milne's Winnie The Pooh — as a symbol of peaceful innocence. Marron's violin, thick with reverb and delay, wanders above a muffled percussion pattern, with Byrd contributing restrained background electronic textures.

In contrast, the Marron and Bogus songs, 'Where Is Yesterday' and 'Stranded In Time,' add welcome light relief. After starting with a Latin chant in the manner of The Electric Prunes, the first displays a firm grasp of summery harmony pop in the style of The Mamas And The Papas. 'Stranded In Time' is string quartet balladeering in the manner of 'Eleanor Rigby,' from which Byrd's characteristic electronic assaults are absent. In 'Where Is Yesterday' he restrains himself to two explosive noises, which, used in such moderation, are arresting and effective. This reveals the main weakness of the USA album, which is that the electronic elements are often not properly integrated into the songs. Too often a good psychedelic rock song is swamped by overbearing electronic noise. The effect is impressive occasionally, but after a while it grates, and the listener longs for a more moderate use of the Durrett.

The USA were signed by Columbia, in contrast to Silver Apples, who could only find a failing small label willing to take a chance on them. In terms of commercial success this didn't help – their sole album was only a very minor chart entry. The USA were widely heard, though, thanks to the inclusion of one of their songs on Columbia's big-selling budget sampler album from 1969, *The Rock Machine Turns You On*. Unfortunately the chosen song, 'I Won't Leave My Wooden Wife For You,' was one of the USA's weakest, perhaps selected for its conventionality by whoever compiled the collection. A rather lame boogie, sung by Byrd, it lacked most of the band's appealing distinguishing marks.

The USA and Silver Apples toured in support of their albums in an attempt to bring their music to a wider audience, although commercial success would eventually elude both bands. Byrd recalls that although audiences often appreciated his band, other musicians were less charitable: "Paul Simon once dropped in on one of our sessions, stayed 30 seconds, shook his head, and left. The Velvet Underground played at a hall with us, and – walking off stage – pushed over a tower of our amps. There was a lot of hostility from rock musicians, although some of it was directed toward my politics."[15]

Silver Apples had a much friendlier encounter with one of the biggest stars of the 1960s. In March and April 1969 they were recording at the Record Plant in New York, occupying the same studio as Jimi Hendrix, albeit at different times of the day. Often sessions would overlap, with one act packing up its gear while the other was setting up. On one of those occasions, Silver Apples jammed with Hendrix, an event that was reputedly committed to tape. In 2003 the Hendrix fanzine *Jimpress* published a lengthy examination of this tantalizing encounter, concluding that recorded evidence of it does indeed survive, with

the bass notes of the Simeon being "clearly heard, especially at the end" of Hendrix's version of 'Star Spangled Banner.'[16]

The rise and fall of both Silver Apples and USA, simultaneously but entirely independently of each other, shows that technology can lead art. Both bands were born out of a fascination with the core sounds of early electronic music, and both were quickly overtaken by technological advances. The lives of both would be short. Nothing more was heard of the USA after their sole album. The band spit into two factions, with Moskowitz keeping the band name and carrying on in a more conventional direction, recording some demos before giving up. Byrd released a second album of electronic rock for Columbia in 1969, under the name Joseph Byrd & The Field Hippies. It had little commercial or critical impact. Silver Apples released a second album on Kapp in 1969. By this time the label was in its death throes and distribution of the album was poor. It failed, and Silver Apples split in 1970, managing to record a third album's worth of material that remained unheard until the late 1990s. The truth is that even when both bands were at their respective creative peaks, their moment had already passed. Those early Moog customers, Roger McGuinn of The Byrds and Mickey Dolenz of The Monkees, had completed recordings using their new Moogs by the end of 1967, before either the USA or Silver Apples had even made their albums.

McGuinn's interest in a new electronic instrument could have been predicted. He was fascinated by technological advances, and had a wide-ranging interest in many styles of music, including what was happening in the avant-garde at the time. Indeed, he had already introduced some primitive electronic elements to an earlier Byrds recording, 'CTA-102,' from *Younger Than Yesterday* (1966). Speaking to *Zigzag* magazine, McGuinn said: "We used earphones fed into microphones and talked into them, and then we speeded it up. It was just nonsense but we deliberately tried to make it sound like a backwards tape so people would try and reverse it. ... We were playing a joke really because it was a big fad at the time to play things backwards. We used an oscillator with a telegraph key, and that booming bang that you hear is the sustain pedal of a piano being held down and banged with our fists ... a sort of Stockhausen idea."[17]

On October 20th 1967 The Byrds released the first pop single to use Moog, 'Goin' Back' b/w 'Change Is Now.' The Moog part, performed by Paul Beaver, wasn't included on the version of the song that appeared on the *Notorious Byrd Brothers* album, released in January 1968. Many other tracks on the album featured the instrument, though, most prominently its closing track, 'Space Odyssey.' This is the first example of an established rock band successfully integrating the Moog into its sound, not just as a texture but a significant component of the arrangement.

That Dolenz of The Monkees should have been so interested in the Moog so early is more surprising. The Monkees were a pure pop band, after all, and in 1967 were still trying to shake off the manufactured tag. And Dolenz isn't generally regarded as the most musically adventurous member of the band. Nonetheless, he was one of the very first pop musicians to use a Moog. Session records show that at some point between September 15th and October 4th he played his new toy on 'Daily Nightly,' from *Pisces, Aquarius, Capricorn & Jones Ltd.* Producer Chip Douglas says: "Micky bought a new Moog and he had no idea how to run it or anything. We just kind of turned on the track and turned on Micky's input, plugged him in, and he just kind of fiddled around there on several different tracks. We just put the best little bits in there that we could. After Micky experimented with his synthesizer I thought, 'Well, let's find a real synthesizer player.' I'd heard about Paul Beaver; Micky had told me about him. So I met him through Micky and he was a player, a good player, and he knew what to do."[18]

When they were active, Silver Apples and USA were prophets without honor in their homeland, or any other land for that matter. But over the years their contribution has been recognized by some. The USA album has been reissued on CD several times, most recently on Sundazed Records, when it was rewarded with glowing reviews. Current British band Broadcast have proclaimed the USA as a major influence. Byrd continued a low-profile, intermittent career in music. He has made albums of synthesizer music, and co-

produced Ry Cooder's *Jazz* album. He is currently a teacher.

Coxe gave up music in 1970 after financial pressures forced Silver Apples to split. He worked as an artist for many years. In the mid 1990s he discovered by chance that the Silver Apples albums had a cult following amongst a new generation of musicians. This prompted a re-engagement with music and a subsequent low-profile career performing and recording once again under the Silver Apples name, helped by the enthusiastic endorsement of Damon Albarn from Blur. Despite a serious road accident in 1998 after a reunion gig with drummer Danny Taylor, Coxe remains active. Taylor, however, died in 2005. The Silver Apples albums were reissued on MCA records in 1997.

The two bands' primitive homemade synthesizers are lost. Of the Simeon, Coxe says, "The large sections that are seen in most photos were stashed under a house in Mobile, Alabama, during the 1970s, and then Hurricane Frederick devastated the region in 1979, carrying away the house and the Simeon with it as well. But I still have some of the spare oscillators which I use to this day."[19] After the USA split up Richard Durrett took back his synthesizer. Neither has been heard of since.

MAY THE CIRCUIT BE UNBROKEN

Electronic oddities

> The Stylophone

The Australian light entertainer Rolf Harris has been a fixture on British television for 40 years or so, in which time he has appeared as an artist, singer, and TV presenter. But he features in these pages as an endorser of an unusual electronic musical instrument. This is not as incongruous as it first appears. Harris has often shown a fascination with odd instruments, and has featured in his act both the Aboriginal Australian didgeridoo and the wobble board (a board that he wobbled to produce a wobbly sound).

On Saturday nights in the late 1960s, on BBC1 television, Harris had his own variety show. It was there that he, and the six members of the Young Generation dancing and singing group, first revealed to the public a tiny, hand-held, battery-powered electronic musical gizmo called the Stylophone.

What viewers saw that night was a monophonic instrument, no more than six inches wide, with a built-in speaker. It is played by touching a metal-tipped stylus to a metal dummy keyboard of one-and-

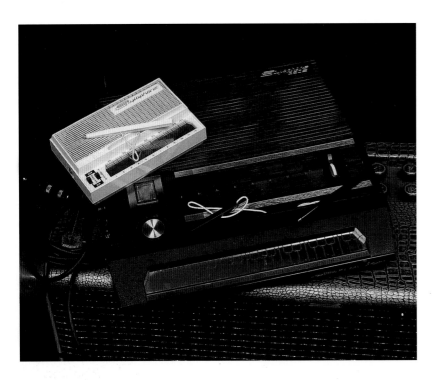

A regular Stylophone is pictured here on top of the deluxe 350S model. Both were made by the British Dubreq company.

a-half octaves. This completes a circuit to produce a shrill electronic tone. There are just two sounds, with or without vibrato. On the back of the device is a tuning knob. That's it, as far as controls for the player go, although, as the Stylophone literature helpfully suggested, a wah-wah effect can be achieved by rhythmically covering and uncovering the speaker with one hand. A mini jack socket lets you plug the instrument into an external amplifier, bypassing the tinny built-in speaker.

Harris's debut with the Stylophone was the start of a long association. He recorded a number of demonstration records, playing popular tunes on the instrument. As he was a big star in Britain, his bearded face featured on much of its packaging and promotional material. Indeed, it was popularly believed that Harris invented the Stylophone, but this wasn't the case. The real inventor was Brian Jarvis; in 1967 he, along with brothers Bert and Ted Coleman, had formed Dubreq, the company that made the instrument.

At first, Stylophones were expensive, costing £8 8s 0d (£8.40/$15, but equivalent to well over £100/$175 today). In time prices came down and sales rose. Helped by Harris's patronage, the Stylophone became a huge success among children. Many a British family Christmas was made that little bit more tense by the angry wasp sound of the little electronic gadget. Thousands were sold before production ceased in 1977. Similar instruments – some of them patent-infringing copies – appeared around the world.

The Stylophone was marketed as a children's toy, although Dubreq tried developing the concept to appeal to professional musicians by producing the bigger 350S model, with a wider range of sounds and two styli (although it is still monophonic). This is an instrument with ideas above its station. It operates with presets only and is not programmable, so it does not compete with monophonic synthesizers of the period. Judged as an instrument in its own right, the 350S has some intriguing features that make it worth investigating. The presets can be combined to build thick-sounding notes with multiple overtones, while dual-setting vibrato and decay switches give further variation. A curious 'photo control' light sensor produces a mild wah-wah effect if you wave your hand directly in front off it. Best of all, though, is the two-speed reiteration control, which breaks the otherwise continuous tone into a series of rapid staccato stabs. Despite these novel features, the 350S didn't catch on as a professional instrument, and sales failed to match those of the basic model. It has turned up on a few records by artists who include Pulp and The Audience. Duran Duran's Nick Rhodes acquired one in the 1970s, when they were still in production, and used it as recently as 2004, on 'Nice,' from the *Astronaut* album.

The basic Stylophone has also been used on pop records, most prominently by David Bowie on his breakthrough hit single, 'Space Oddity.' The Stylophone enters the mix at the same time as the lead vocal, playing a two-note phrase that can be clearly heard in the centre of the stereo image. It continues through most of the song, often buried beneath Mellotron strings played by Rick Wakeman. The Stylophone briefly becomes prominent again at 3:21, playing a melody in a higher register while Bowie sings "Tell my wife I love her very much, she knows."

A perm-haired David Bowie endorsed the Stylophone for Dubreq, and appeared in print adverts proclaiming its virtues, although he didn't use it again for many years. By the late 1990s, those who had grown up with Stylophones rediscovered them, valuing the once ubiquitous toy as a retro-chic reminder of more innocent times. By this time, Bowie's finger was no longer as firmly placed on the cultural pulse as it once had been. Nonetheless, he became aware of the nostalgia invoked by Stylophones and started to use them in concert, sometimes throwing them into the crowd, where they were no doubt caught by middle-aged fans old enough to have owned one the first time around.

> **Casio VL-Tone VL-1**

It is hard to work out what Casio had in mind when it launched the first VL-Tone (VL-1) in 1980. A hybrid of calculator, monophonic synthesizer, and basic sequencer, was it intended for frustrated accountants who needed a creative outlet in between calculations? Or for business-minded musicians

wanting a convenient way both to compose and to calculate royalty statements? Whatever the intention, the VL-1 sold well through electronics stores for several years, retailing at about $70/£30 (about $140/£80 now). It was succeeded by the less successful but similar VL-10, essentially the same instrument in a smaller package, and the VL-5, a four-note polyphonic version that lacks the programmable function but has more presets.

As the VL-Tone combines a calculator and a synthesizer, you could, with a leap of the imagination, see it as a predecessor of later computer-based instruments. But that dignifies it above its station. About a foot long, the VL-1 features a two and a half octave miniature button keyboard, a small digital display on which to do your sums, a built-in speaker, and a mini jack for a line out. Next to the display are various controls for selecting and programming. There are five lead presets – guitar, flute, piano, fantasy, and violin – and one programmable memory function. This is altered by entering numerical values via the calculator. The sounds of a built-in rhythm machine are available in 10 preset rhythms, none of which can be altered, although tempo can be varied. A 100-note sequencer allows one of the lead presets or the

Exploiting the second most famous Stylophone player; Melody Maker advert, 1969.

programmable voice to be recorded along with a rhythm preset. If this option is chosen, a balance control enables the user to alter the relative volumes of the melody and rhythm parts. Tuning can be changed by a screw in the back of the VL-Tone. The machine runs on batteries or mains power.

Claims have been made that the VL-1 was used on recordings by artists as unlikely as Sting and Stevie Wonder, and more plausibly Depeche Mode and The Human League. This might be so, but it is hard to distinguish the sounds of the VL-1 from those of many other instruments Casio produced in the same era, because the same presets are often used. What can't be disputed is that the German band Trio took the humble Casio to the top of many charts around the world in 1982, using the 'Rock 1' rhythm preset as the backing to an engagingly catchy slice of minimalism called 'Da Da Da.' It was produced by Klaus Voormann, a friend of The Beatles, who had illustrated the cover of *Revolver*. Trio main man Stephan Remmler had been given the Casio by a friend of Voorman's, photographer Peter Malz, and played around with it until 'Da Da Da' developed.

In Germany, Trio had several more hits and something resembling a career, but everywhere else

The Japanese-made Casio VL-Tone VL-5 (top) with the company's original calculator / keyboard / sequencer, the VL-Tone VL-1.

they were quickly consigned to history as an archetypal 'one hit wonder' band. But then, in 1997, Volkswagen chose 'Da Da Da' to soundtrack the commercials for its new Jetta car. In the ad, two twentysomething men simply drive around for 30 seconds in a Volkswagen Jetta, nodding their heads in time to the 'Rock 1' rhythm of the Trio record. The ad was popular enough to make the news, and briefly both Jetta and Trio sales increased.

> The Omnichord

A good way of understanding Suzuki's Omnichord, launched in 1981, is to think of it as a stringless electronic autoharp. It's about the same size, and even has a similar shape, albeit with the corners rounded off. And like the autoharp, the Omnichord has a number of chord buttons. There are 27 on the first version: majors, minors, and 7ths, of A, B, C, D, E, F, G, E-flat, and B-flat.

And there the comparison with the autoharp breaks down. Even the basic Omnichord has many more chords than the biggest autoharp, and it has several other features that make it more like an electronic equivalent of the 'easy to play' hybrids of the early 20th century, for instance the Marxophone (see chapter 10). Unlike most of those instruments, though, the Omnichord *is* easy to play. In fact, it is almost impossible to play a 'wrong' note.

The additional features are a rhythm box and an electronic strum plate. The rhythm box is standard cheesy home-organ fare – six presets and variable tempo, nothing else. The metal harmonic strum plate is unique to the Omnichord. About three-quarters of an inch wide and six inches long, it is a set of electronic 'strings' that sound something like a harp when strummed with the flexible rubber plectrum provided. This strum plate is linked to the chord presets, so that when a chord is selected only the notes in the chord can be sounded on the strum plate. So whatever you strum, you will always play the right notes.

The chords themselves can sound in two voices; one a simple organ sound, the other a rhythmic pattern that matches the rhythm preset selected, and includes an organ sound and a bass line. Although the chords only sound if a drum pattern is playing and the strum plate only sounds if a chord is playing, each

An early Suzuki Omnichord, a kind of stringless electronic autoharp, as used by Elvis Costello and Daniel Lanois.

component can be soloed, as all three have their own volume controls. The only other controls are a memory switch that enables you to play a chord continuously without holding down the chord button, and variable sustain for the strum plate. The instrument has a built-in speaker and a jack line out.

As the marketing literature said, the Omnichord is right for you "if you love music but don't know one note from another." An instrument that virtually anyone could play without practice, and that didn't need to be tuned, had obvious appeal, and it quickly became a popular children's toy. It was developed over the years and more features added, including MIDI, which meant that the performer isn't stuck just with the Omnichord's own limited sound palette. Suzuki still produces the instrument, although it is now called the Qchord.

There's a secret history of Omnichord playing in pop, including recordings by Ed Harcourt, Elvis Costello, and The Manic Street Preachers. Daniel Lanois has a collection of Omnichords, and has used them on many of his productions and recordings, including *The Joshua Tree* by U2, and 'Shooting Star,' the last song on Bob Dylan's *Oh Mercy* (1989). For this Lanois uses the harp sound only, not the organ and drum presets, strumming gentle chords to emphasize each change.

> The Optigan

In November 1971 *Billboard* magazine ran an extended feature about new musical instruments. Following a section about synthesizers and the Mellotron, it moved on to the "very inexpensive [$350/£145, worth something like $1,300/£1,300 now] Optigan made by Mattel [which] is potentially even more versatile. Only on the market since September, it is played like a chord-button organ. But the sounds of the Optigan come from interchangeable disks which can be programmed for any kind of accompaniment. Pressing the C-chord button on the Optigan with the 'Blues piano' disk in place will play the recorded sound of an actual blues piano, plus bass and drums doing an accompaniment figure in C major."[1]

What *Billboard* didn't say was that Mattel was a toy manufacturer, and its Optigan was designed for home use, quite unlike the other instruments covered in the feature. Nonetheless, the Optigan does have something in common with the Mellotron, in that both instruments use recordings of 'real' instruments as their sound sources. But unlike the Mellotron, which stores its pre-recorded sounds on tape loops, the Optigan's sounds are located on optically-read, 12-inch LP-sized discs made of transparent celluloid. This gave rise to the instrument's name – a contraction of 'optical' and 'organ.' The Optigan creates its sound by passing a light beam through the transparent discs. The beam is modified by whatever waveform is printed on the disc, 'read' by a photoelectric cell, and translated into an electrical signal. This in turn is amplified and sent to the Optigan's built-in speakers.

In appearance, the Optigan is a typical 1970s home organ: a single manual, three-octave keyboard with an integral speaker and amplifier, in a mock teak case made of a composite material called temporite. It is about three feet wide, a foot and a half deep, and two feet nine inches high.

Next to the three-octave keyboard, are 21 chord buttons – major, minor, and diminished versions of B-flat, F, C, G, D, A, and E. To the right of these chord buttons are two rocker switches, one for tempo and one marked balance, which affect the relative volumes of the chord buttons and the keyboard. To the left of the chord buttons are five 'special effects' switches. The special effects vary, depending on which disc is being used, but they can either be played constantly or as one-off events, depending on the position of the switch. The sound source discs are inserted in a compartment underneath the chord buttons. A volume pedal is mounted underneath the speaker cabinet, to the right hand side. To play the Optigan, the player presses chord buttons with the left hand, and picks out melodies with the right.

Mattel supplied a number of discs for the Optigan, each containing 57 continuous-loop recordings of different instruments, percussion sounds, and sound effects. Discs were usually compiled to represent a particular genre, for example "Nashville Country" or "Latin Fever," and the instruments that appear on each disc are judged appropriate for the type of music. Because the loops played continually, with no beginning or end, each sound has no attack or decay.

The advertising copywriters had this to say about the discs: "The 'soul' of the Optigan is the Music Program Disc. Organs try to mimic or imitate different musical sounds. But with the OPTIGAN you actually play the real sounds of pianos, banjos, guitars, marimbas, drums, and dozens more. The sounds are on the Programs. You choose the sounds you want – to play the songs you want – on our piano-style keyboard and left-hand accompaniment panel. And you choose from Classic guitar to old time Banjo Sing-Along to Nashville Country to Rock and Roll. It all depends on the Program, and there's a Program for every musical taste."[2]

Optigans are unreliable and the sound quality of the recordings on the disks is poor, certainly no match for a Mellotron. Yet the very cheapness of the sounds has an appeal for some; Optigans have turned up on recordings by Blur, Crowded House, Devo, Tom Waits and The Clash.

The Optigan lasted just four years, until 1975. Most were sold in America, although a few made it to Europe. Later in the decade, an unsuccessful professional version of the Optigan was marketed by a company called Vako, under the name Orchestron. This, too, had a brief existence, although one reputed customer was the pioneering German electronic band Kraftwerk.[3]

> Bee Gees Rhythm Machine

Another Mattel product, the Bee Gees Rhythm Machine, was launched at the height of the band's second coming, as a disco act, in 1978. Packaged with the Bee Gees' logo and a photo of the brothers Gibb on the box, it seems like an odd and unnecessary bit of merchandise for a band that couldn't help but sell records. It was sold with a songbook that told you how to reproduce a couple of the Bee Gees big disco hits, and, inexplicably, 'London Bridge' and 'Oh Susannah.'

The Bee Gees Rhythm Machine is defined by its limitations, having just two sound features, which can be played together. The first is a set of three rhythm presets – disco, Latin, and pop – that make a sound somewhere between a bass synth and a very cheap

drum machine. Below these is a one-and-a-half octave monophonic button keyboard with one voice. An integral speaker, volume, and tuning controls, and a mini-jack output complete the package, which is housed in a plastic case about seven inches wide and four inches deep, with the Bee Gees' logo prominently displayed on the top left-hand corner. Kraftwerk made use of this short-lived oddity on 'Pocket Calculator,' from *Computer World*, where it can be heard alongside a Stylophone. Indeed, on the back of the album, the group's Ralf Hütter is shown holding the Rhythm Machine, which is painted black.

The Bee Gees Rhythm Machine – instrument (below, left) and packaging (here) – made by toy company Mattel.

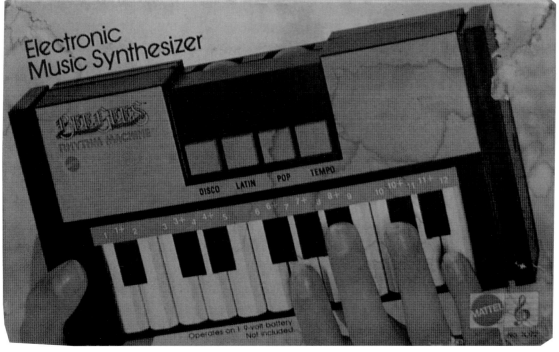

chapter 9

WASHBOARDS AND WHISPERING FOILS

improvised and budget acoustic instruments

The story of unusual acoustic musical instruments in pop is more episodic than that of the electronic sounds we have considered so far. The reason for this is simple. The history of electronic music stretches back only 100 years or so, and for 50 of those it was confined mainly to America, western Europe, and Russia. And although it is a complex, fragmented story, there are lineages that can be traced, with one instrument evolving out of another. It is far harder to make such connections in the case of acoustic instruments, although it is sometimes possible. Often their stories reach back beyond the clutches of history. And often, too, similar instruments existed for centuries in different cultures that didn't overlap at all. Take, for instance, the practice of improvising musical instruments from objects that were not originally intended for musical use. This is an activity that stretches back into antiquity in most cultures.

Improvisation of this sort is sometimes called 'rough music,' where crowds of people bang household utensils like saucepans to express disapproval: maybe to heap disapprobation on an unfaithful wife, or to protest in an industrial dispute. Often the process of improvisation extends beyond the simple use of an object as found, and involves constructing a musical instrument – maybe an approximation of a 'real' instrument like a guitar – from a number of non-musical items. Both phenomena have periodically found their way into pop music, most frequently in connection with a form of homemade musical expression born out of poverty in the southern states of America in the late 19th century.

The original jug bands used domestic implements like spoons and washboards out of financial necessity, alongside other examples of money-saving ingenuity, like home-made banjos constructed with tin plates and broom handles, or one-string bass devices using washtubs or crates for sound-boxes. Cheap instruments like kazoos might feature in a jug band line up, too, alongside more conventional noisemakers like guitars and fiddles. But the term 'jug band' derives from the style's use of domestic jugs, often vessels originally used for carrying alcohol, which generally served as bass instruments. They were played by blowing with lips lightly pursed across the aperture of the jug. This created a buzzing sound that was amplified by the body of the jug, serving as a makeshift acoustic chamber. Using this method, skilled performers could create a sound reminiscent of a tuba.

The jug band style thrived into the early 1930s, particularly in Louisville, Kentucky, and Memphis, Tennessee, eventually falling out of favor during the Depression. The music original jug bands played was not so much a genre in itself, more an accessible style of playing that was applied to popular music of the time by people too poor to afford proper musical instruments. Jug bands absorbed many popular styles, including early jazz, folk, ragtime, and blues. It was a good-time sound, a party music that tended to emphasize the comic potential of its ragbag assortment of improvised instruments and thus drift towards novelty.

The jug band style was revived as a branch of the early 1960s folk revival. By then the term was applied to represent large oddball ensembles that played an assortment of instruments: jugs, spoons, kazoos, harmonicas, banjos, guitars, and more. Almost always these jug bands were not made up of poor people using their instrumentation out of necessity, but young middle class enthusiasts to whom vague ideas of folk authenticity were appealing. Or maybe they just thought the music was good fun. Like the source material it drew on, the music produced in this brief jug band revival was resolutely upbeat and dangerously close to novelty.

Two bands that briefly thrived in this period were The Jim Kweskin Jug Band and The Even Dozen Jug Band, the latter including John Sebastian, later of The Lovin' Spoonful. The jug band revival had little commercial impact in itself, but it did serve as a training ground for musicians who later found fame in the pop world. As author and folk-rock researcher Richie Unterberger says: "Some folk-rock bands grew out of jug bands (The Lovin' Spoonful, The Grateful Dead, Country Joe And The Fish), and the Spoonful at least combined jug band aesthetics with pop to make decent good-time folk-rock."[1]

The jug itself has appeared as a dominant instrument in a rock band just once, played by Tommy Hall in the Texan psychedelic garage punks, The Thirteenth Floor Elevators. The band had tentative

The Thirteenth Floor Elevators on-stage in 1966. Tommy Hall can be seen with jug on the far left.

links to jug music, being an amalgam of two mid-1960s bands active in Austin, The Spades and The Lingsmen. The latter played skiffle, a genre related to jug music. The Spades were fronted by singer, songwriter, and guitarist Roky Erickson; The Lingsmen included in their line up guitarist Stacy Sutherland and jug-blower Tommy Hall. These three became the core of the Elevators.

Hall originated from Tennessee, but had moved to Austin to attend the University of Texas, first studying philosophy, and then psychology. "I knew these guys from Port Aransas who had a skiffle band called The Lingsmen," he says. "I can't remember them all, but Stacy Sutherland was their guitarist. … They didn't really need me, but we became friends, and they let me play the jug, but I wasn't that

accomplished at it." By this time Hall was already experimenting with LSD, and like many early psychedelic explorers saw the drug as a means to expand consciousness and thus change the world, rather than as a recreational tool. He was zealous to the point of religious fervor about his newfound ideas, and saw rock music as a means of expressing them. "I was not a musician in any form," he says. "In fact, I invented my electric jug just so I would have a place onstage with the band."[2]

Once established, Hall set out to do what he really wanted to do, which was to write lyrics. This he did, finding in Erickson a kindred spirit all too willing to embrace his lifestyle and worldview. Many of the Elevators' subsequent songs would be written by the Erickson/Hall team.

The Elevators can justly claim to be the first psychedelic rock band. Their debut album, *The Psychedelic Sounds Of …*, with the 'eye of the pyramid' symbol on its artwork and quasi-mystical sleeve notes from Hall, would have been a perfect encapsulation of 1967's summer of love, except that it appeared in late spring 1966, way before *Sgt Pepper*, Pink Floyd's debut, and the first Grateful Dead album. A fully formed, confident release, with none of the hesitancy often found on first albums by new bands, it included all of the elements of the classic Elevators' sound: the brash punk interpretation of British-invasion rock, raga guitar lines, Erickson's shrieking vocal interjections, and Hall's mesmerizing jug playing.

The band's only hit single, 'You're Gonna Miss Me,' was included on the album. It had originally been issued in late 1965 on Contact, a local Austin label. By the spring of 1966 it was a regional hit, and was picked up for national release by International Artists, the label which dealt with the band from there on. It eventually entered the *Billboard* national chart. From the crunching guitar chord introduction to Erickson's howling fade out, 'You're Gonna Miss Me' is a classic psychedelic garage screamer. But what really sets it apart is the manic chattering of Hall's one-and-a-half-gallon aluminum paraffin jug.

Hall's playing style was unique, bearing little resemblance to the mock tuba parping of the traditional jug bands. Central to his sound is a rhythmic pulsing, which he probably achieved by rapidly moving his hands over the aperture of the jug. He could alter pitch and intensity to suit the music, his sound ranging from lilting waves of gentle undulations to something like the beating wings of a frantic bird trapped in a confined space. Hall describes his instrument as an electric jug, although judging from the photographic evidence this seems to mean simply that he placed a microphone close to the vessel while playing and drenched the amplified sound in reverb.

The Thirteenth Floor Elevators were true counter-culture renegades. Hall's lyrics and sleeve notes openly endorsed psychedelic drug use as a means to enlightenment, which put the band permanently at loggerheads with the conservative establishment in Texas. The inevitable result was a brief career routinely interrupted by drug busts, police searches, imprisonment, and, in the case of Erickson, enforced psychiatric treatment. Yet in its brief existence the band managed four albums, the first two of which, *The Psychedelic Sounds Of …* and *Easter Everywhere*, are excellent examples of early psychedelic rock. By 1968 the band had split. A bogus live album with applause dubbed onto studio recordings was followed in 1969 by a posthumous unfinished studio album, *Bull Of The Woods*. By the time of this last recording, Hall's jug had disappeared from the mix.

After The Thirteenth Floor Elevators' demise, Erickson was tried on drugs charges and given the choice of a prison sentence or treatment in a psychiatric hospital. He chose the latter, emerging three years later exhibiting only some signs of sanity. He has continued an intermittent and eccentric musical career ever since. Guitarist Stacy Sutherland was killed in a domestic violence incident. Hall, meanwhile, lives in San Francisco, where he continues with his drug-fuelled spiritual research. He has been talking for many years about putting his findings into writing. "I'm really not interested in The Thirteenth Floor Elevators at this time in my life," he says. "I'm just way past those times. I'm too busy with my research. I lost my jug long ago. I'm not a musician and will never play the jug again."[3]

That may be so, but his jug playing is still heard. The inclusion of 'You're Gonna Miss Me' on Lenny Kaye's 1972 *Nuggets* compilation ensured that The Thirteenth Floor Elevators were not forgotten. Later in that decade many of their recordings were released in the UK for the first time on the Radar label. In 1990 Primal Scream covered the Hall/Erickson song 'Slip Inside This House' on their *Screamadelica* album. Then, in 2000, 'You're Gonna Miss Me' was used in the film of Nick Hornby's novel *Hi Fidelity*. As millions of people sat comfortably in their seats in cinemas all around the world, waiting for the film to begin, they were greeted by a black screen, Stacy Sutherland's crunching guitar riff, Roky Erickson's screams, and Tommy Hall's electric jug.

Another instrument popular in jug bands that has periodically made an appearance in pop is the kazoo. The sound of kazoos comes from projecting the

The kazoo – without cable – has provided a cheap new voice for artists from The Grateful Dead to Embrace.

human voice against a vibrating membrane. Although instruments of this sort have existed for centuries in cultures around the world, the story of the kazoo as we know it today can be traced back to Macon, Georgia, where, in the 1840s an American named Alabama Vest teamed up with a German clock maker named Thaddeus Von Clegg to make metal kazoos to a design by Vest. Many years later an enterprising traveling salesman called Emil Sorg came across a Vest/Von Clegg kazoo and sensed a business opportunity. In 1912 he joined forces with Michael McIntyre, a Buffalo metal worker, and the two started manufacturing kazoos. Shortly afterwards Sorg disappeared from the story, leaving McIntyre to move to Eden, New York, where he went into business with Harry Richardson, the owner of a metal forming plant. This new venture began large-scale production of metal kazoos in 1914, with McIntyre managing to patent his design in 1923.

In 1916, McIntyre and Richardson christened their company The Original American Kazoo Company. It survives to this day at the same premises, although it has changed ownership several times over the years. It now operates as a working museum, still making kazoos on the same presses installed by

McIntyre and Richardson nearly a century ago.[4] Kazoos come in many different shapes and sizes, including some models designed to look like miniature approximations of brass instruments such as saxophones and trumpets. The classic shape, though, is a hollow tube with one end narrowing to a smaller aperture. About two thirds down this tube is a circular hole with a dish fixed over it. The hole is covered with a wax membrane, attached to the circumference of the hole by a ring. The membrane is free to oscillate and is responsible for the kazoo's sound.

The kazoo is played by humming through the wider of the two apertures. This creates an airflow that makes the membrane vibrate. The sound created is in effect an acoustic treatment of the voice, rather than something created by wind moving through reeds and valves as in woodwind and brass instruments. Simply blowing through a kazoo will not produce any sound at all. This is why some people consider the kazoo not an instrument at all, but a primitive sound-processor.

Because the kazoo's sound is so dependent on the voice it is manipulating, it stands to reason that changing the humming style is the most obvious way to affect the basic sound. It also means that a kazoo player can only play in tune if he or she can hum in tune. Wholly or partially covering up the dish that surrounds the membrane is another way of getting different tones.

Being cheap and easy to play, kazoos quickly caught on with jug bands and folk and blues musicians in the early 1920s. They were widely used while the style flourished, although by the 1930s jug music was falling out of fashion. Most uses of kazoos in pop can be traced back to the jug band revival that was itself a component of a wider folk revival in the late 1950s/early 1960s. The Grateful Dead grew out of a labyrinthine network of folk, bluegrass, and jug combos dating from this time. These influences surface on the band's second album, *Anthem Of The Sun*, on which Jerry Garcia, Bob Weir, and Phil Lesh are all credited with kazoo contributions. (These came alongside, incidentally, other exotic sound sources, including guiro, bells, gong, chimes, crotales, prepared piano, and electronic tape).

Blues-rock guitarist Eric Clapton has never been slow to acknowledge his debt to the folk and blues

thimbles on her fingers for additional percussive attack. Both she and Donegan accepted a session fee only for their work on 'Rock Island Line,' judging that it would be little more than a part of a small album for a limited specialist audience. The single went on to sell an estimated two million copies, and has appeared on numerous compilations ever since. Bryden died at the age of 78 in 1998, continuing to perform and record regularly with her washboard almost until the end.

Because skiffle was such a profound influence on a generation of British rock stars, it is now often thought of as a branch of early rock'n'roll. This is a misunderstanding. When skiffle was a current trend Donegan was often described as a 'jazz sensation' or some other such phrase that rooted him and the movement firmly in the trad jazz revival. But although strictly speaking skiffle and rock'n'roll were rival forms, there is a case to be made that skiffle was at least as important as Elvis Presley, Little Richard et al as a substantial building block of British rock. Try as they might, British teenagers struggled to replicate the swagger of the first generation of American rockers, and most British rock before 1963 is anodyne, timid, and quaint. Perhaps the genres that inspired rock'n'roll were too far removed culturally for British teenagers to either understand or absorb. Then, when the reach of mass media was tiny compared to now, almost the only way for British people to hear the music that made Elvis – electric blues, country, and gospel – was through rare import records or occasional specialist radio broadcasts. Also, rock's primary instrument, the electric guitar, was expensive in Britain in 1956.

Skiffle, on the other hand, was both readily accessible and understandable as a culture, and affordable to take up as a style. The people who made the skiffle records you heard on the radio were not impossibly exotic, glamorous creatures like Elvis or Little Richard. Rather, they were skinny pale youths who looked like you. Everyone knew that Lonnie Donegan came from Scotland, not Memphis. Cheap acoustic guitars and washboards could be obtained; tea-chest basses could be made. And the music was simple and fun. Most skiffle songs required just three chords and a lot of energy. Yet despite its obvious appeal, skiffle was shortlived. It was soon eclipsed in

the tastes of the teenage audience by rock'n'roll, a more sexual, rebellious, stylish, and therefore ultimately more appealing form of music.

In May 1958, less than 18 months after Donegan's first skiffle hit, Melody Maker's front cover was proclaiming that "skiffle is on the skids."[7] Everywhere skiffle bands were folding, or subtly reinventing themselves as jazz or rock'n'roll groups. Skiffle never quite died out, and continues as an underground scene to this day, with its own clubs, festivals, and labels, but it was never again a major commercial force. Its real significance lies not in what survives of it, and not even in the records made when it was at its height. Rather, it is in the fact that skiffle gave a number of British rock musicians their first taste of performing. These included John Lennon, Paul McCartney, and George Harrison of The Beatles, and Brian Jones of The Rolling Stones.

None of Donegan's subsequent hit singles, and there were quite a few, featured a washboard. Rather, he used a bass and drums rhythm section that propelled his music towards the style of contemporary rockers, although he was generally still branded as a skiffle act. Donegan's career outlasted the skiffle craze, and for a few years he remained one of British popular music's biggest solo stars, his fame at the time far exceeding that of most of the first generation of British rockers.

Looking like Woody Guthrie in a suit, Donegan had a verve and energy to his live performances that translated well into his recordings, and he was much admired and imitated. He died in 2002, not long after recording a final album with the help of many of the generation of rock stars he inspired.

Although the skiffle revival in Britain and the jug band craze in America helped inspire a generation of musicians who later found fame and fortune in the rock world, the eclectic low-budget instrumentation favored by the two styles fell out of favor as the 1960s progressed. Only a few later bands who achieved any success in the mainstream felt inspired to pick up a washboard, or hum into a kazoo. One of these was the British experimental folk duo The Incredible String Band, never a group to use one conventional instrument when half a dozen unconventional ones would do.

The Incredible String Band were a band like no other, before or since, a uniquely British amalgam of folk, gospel, jug, blues, jazz, skiffle, and rock styles, combined with optimistically spiritual lyrics. After a first, comparatively conventional, folk album as a trio with banjo player Clive Palmer, the ISB settled into a long career of fluctuating line-ups, based on a nucleus of Mike Heron and Robin Williamson. These two, with their parade of associates, used a huge range of folk and rock instrumentation on their recordings, and pioneered the use of world music instruments in popular music. An ISB arrangement could involve anything from an organ to an oud, a guitar to a gimbri, a sitar to a swanee whistle. Although never big stars, they were a strong draw on the college circuit for years, and released many chart albums.

Heron and Williamson had a fond attachment to skiffle and jug music, and much of the unaffected exuberance of those styles is found in the ISB's music. Williamson says, "My musical background was pretty much straight British folk with skiffle, then into traditional jazz, blues, and then traditional Irish and Scottish music. We did hear a lot of the traditional jug band music, but not until later. Skiffle came out of left field. Lonnie Donegan, Nancy Whisky, Russell Quaye, people like that, who were playing around London, were tremendously hip at the time when I was still at school. After that, real blues singers started to come through, people like Champion Jack Dupree, Sister Rosetta Tharp, Brownie McGee; then we started to get the original jug band records from back in the 1920s."[8]

Not only did the spirit of skiffle and jug music influence the ISB, but the instrumentation of those styles was used in ISB recordings too. Kazoo playing is featured on many albums. A particularly good example, performed by Williamson, can be heard on the 13-minute mini song cycle, 'A Very Cellular Song' from *The Hangman's Beautiful Daughter*. Washboards were often used too. Mike Heron scrapes some syncopation into the old-time gospel style sing-along, 'Log Cabin Home In The Sky,' from *Wee Tam And The Big Huge*.

The ISB thrived in the open-minded culture of the late 1960s. They started to look like an anomaly in the 1970s, although they continued to record well-received albums into the age of glam rock and progressive rock, before drifting apart in the mid 1970s. The ISB were always an albums band first, although they did release singles.

By contrast, active around the same time was another British band that took some of the same sounds into the singles chart. Mungo Jerry was the last British singles chart band to integrate jug and skiffle styles into its sound to the point of actually using washboards and jugs. Led by singer, guitarist, and sometime washboard scraper Ray Dorset, Mungo Jerry scored an international hit with 'In The Summertime' in 1970, and followed it up with a run of good-time jug pop tunes that kept the band in the charts until the mid 1970s.

Mungo Jerry and the ISB, although different sorts of band, shared an unpretentious attitude. This meant that they could use instruments like jugs, kazoos, and washboards without the sense of dislocation that usually accompanies the appearance of such things on pop records. None of these instruments is cool in the rock'n'roll sense of the word, so if you are a rock musician whose appeal is based, in part at least, on a sense of style, then a kazoo solo will always sound incongruous. Mungo Jerry and the ISB escaped this conundrum by not caring about cool; they just took a joy in the music they made.

As with most improvised musical instruments, tracing who first took a violin or cello bow to an ordinary woodcutting handsaw is impossible. But it is clear that the instrument, sometimes called the whispering foil, became popular in the early 20th century in the hands of a number of novelty and music hall acts. In the 1920s, an American team, the Weaver Brothers & Elviry, used a saw in their popular vaudeville show,[9] while an English variety artiste, Joan Stonehewer, performed live and recorded using a saw and sleigh bells, amongst other things, in the middle of the 20th century. There were so many such acts making use of what the French call *la lame musical* (the musical blade), that during the 1920s and 1930s Mussehl & Westphal, the leading musical saw manufacturers, were selling thousands of their products every year. Other companies around the world, including Jedson in the UK, also produced musical saws. But in America, the hardship of the

Depression years, followed by a shortage of steel in the war years, contributed to the saw's decline in popularity. By the time Marlene Dietrich, an accomplished sawist, gripped the saw's handle with her film-star legs and raised the spirits of many an American soldier during morale-boosting tours during World War II, it was already past its heyday.

The saw is played by bowing the smooth side of a handsaw blade – the side without teeth – which the sawist must keep vibrating constantly. Additionally, the sawist must keep the blade curved. It is this curve that affects the saw's pitch: the more squashed the shape, the higher the note, the more elongated, the lower. Most sawists play by holding the blade vertically upright, with the handle of the saw between their knees and one hand holding the top of the blade.

The sawist has a choice between an ordinary woodcutting handsaw and a specially constructed musical saw. Many use a standard length handsaw that you can buy in any hardware store, with a blade of 26 inches. A blade much shorter than this is hard to play because it is difficult to bend. Longer saws, which tend to increase the pitch range, are sometimes used. Specially made musical saws, often with ornate handles and no teeth on either side of the blade, come in different sizes. The sound a skilled sawist can coax from such an unlikely source can range from a piercing shriek to an ethereal, haunting whistle. Pitching notes accurately is hard, which means that many players rely heavily on glissandos to reach notes. This characteristic of playing a saw and the tone of the instrument has led many people to compare its sound to that of the Theremin.

Musical saws are rare in pop music, partly because amplifying them sufficiently to make them a realistic live prospect is very hard. But in 1998, Mercury Rev reclaimed the musical saw from its folksy corner of music history, using it to provide eerie high-end decoration on many tracks on the band's classic *Deserter's Songs* album. The parts were played by Joel Eckhouse. "They gave me a pretty long leash," he says. "I recorded several takes, each a little more daring, so they could mix and match what they thought worked. There was one melody that I learned for a piece, but I was free to improvise and do whatever I felt. I was overdubbing the part, wearing headphones,

which makes perfect intonation a challenge for me, because it's harder to hear the saw directly. It sounds a little off, to my ear, but I guess they were OK with it."[10] They must have been, as Eckhouse's contributions are prominently featured. They can be heard to particularly good effect on 'Holes,' 'Endlessly,' and 'Pick Up If You're There.'

In the words of lead singer/songwriter Jonathon Donahue, Mercury Rev are dedicated to making "music using unconventional instrumentation in the context of rock'n'roll."[11] The band had been attempting this with mixed results for several years by the time their sound finally coalesced on *Deserter's Songs*, their fourth album. A rich blend of wide-screen orchestral psychedelia with strands of rustic Americana, it was the work of a band making a concerted and successful effort to connect to tradition, without being simply revivalist. In this context the musical saw fits so well it seems like an obvious choice of instrument, not a gimmick. Like others before him, including Brian Wilson, Donahue compares the saw to the Theremin: "I love the bowed saw so much more than the Theremin. The Theremin may be space age, but the saw is more organic. It has this uncanny ability to slide into tones, and it has a natural vibrato. And, besides the sarangi from India, it comes the closest to sounding like my favorite instrument: the female human voice. I've been in love with the saw ever since I heard Jack Nitzsche use it on the soundtrack to *One Flew Over The Cuckoo's Nest*."[12]

Deserter's Songs was a huge critical and commercial success. In the years that followed, the band introduced a musical saw slot into live performances. Deployed as a tangential interlude in the main concert, it features guitarist Sean 'Grasshopper' Mackiowiak sitting center stage, picked out of the gloom by a spotlight, with a saw between his knees in the traditional style. He performs a brief instrumental piece backed by very subtle, and quiet, instrumentation from the rest of the band. The saw can't be heard above a full band performance, though, so sometimes they create a sound approximating the saw for the relevant tracks from *Deserter's Songs*, using either a Theremin, or an Alesis air synth or air effects module (optically controlled devices played by waving the hands to interrupt a light beam).

The apparently unlikely combination of Marlene Dietrich and her musical saw, pictured in the 1940s.

Outside of the jug and skiffle tradition, other simple acoustic instruments have found a place in pop music. For example, there is the ancient musical gadget usually sold as the 'jaw's harp', although its traditional name, jew's harp, is still widely used. The origin of the name has been the subject of much debate over the years. Jew's harp is a variant of an earlier term, jew's trump (meaning 'trumpet'). The association with the Jews occurs only in English, but the instrument itself has no obvious connection with either the Jewish people or Judaism. Nor does the name derive from the word 'jaw,' although that is often suggested. A possible source is the medieval English word 'gewgaw,' meaning a toy or trinket.

The jew's harp consists of an oval-shaped frame, usually metal but sometimes wood or bone, from which extend two parallel arms. Between these arms runs a metal tongue that is attached to the frame. Some instruments have two or more tongues. To play the instrument, you hold the oval part of the frame in one hand up to your mouth, so that its arms rest against your parted teeth, with your lips resting lightly on them. You then pluck the metal tongue with your other hand, giving a twanging bass note. Harmonics of this bass note can be sounded simultaneously as you alter the shape of your mouth, which acts as a resonator.

Evidence of similar instruments has been found in cultures dating back thousands of years. Although now often thought of as a novelty device, on account of its cheapness and simplicity, it has a history of real musical use. It is one of 14 featured instruments in a carved minstrel gallery, dating from the 14th century in Exeter Cathedral in southern England. In many other cultures, particularly in Africa and Asia, it used for romantic serenading, and has been banned in the past by missionaries who considered its sound too distracting and seductive.

The percussive twang of the jew's harp has found its way into many rock records, usually the sort that have some sort of debt to folk music. Mike Oldfield's *Amarok* features the instrument, and more recently The Beta Band have integrated it into their eclectic mush of ingredients. Leonard Cohen is fond of it too. His second album, *Songs From A Room,* features a constantly plucked jew's harp through eight of its ten songs, sounding like a cicada in the album's stark, desiccated sonic landscape. Cohen returned to the instrument 35 years later on his recent album *Dear Heather,* where modern recording technology presents it in pristine clarity as the lead instrument on two songs, 'On That Day' and 'Nightingale'.

The kalimba is the currently favored name for an African instrument that makes a sound not dissimilar to that of a jew's harp. It consists of a set of metal tongues attached to a wooden base. It is also known by many other names – sansa, mbira, and thumb piano (even 'Zulu piano' in the past) – and is called a lamellephone by musicologists. Many African countries have a variant of this instrument, the most common with the tongues attached to a flat wooden board. Other versions have the tongues fixed to a gourd sound box, or even a metal drum. The number of tongues may vary, and sometimes they come with loose-fixed shells or bottle tops or the like around their base, to make a jingling sound. The tongues are usually fixed to the base by two metal rods, the second of which acts like a bridge and can be moved to change tuning.

As one of the kalimba's aliases suggests, the traditional way of playing the instrument is to hold it

A couple of jew's harps, ready for twanging.

with both hands and pluck the tongues with both thumbs. Simple to play, and with a pleasing, rubbery twang not unlike that of a jew's harp, the kalimba has often made fleeting appearances on pop records. David Bowie used one on his *Space Oddity* album, as did Tim Buckley on *Goodbye And Hello*, played by Dave Guard, formerly of The Kingston Trio.

The kalimba has found a more permanent home amongst the tightly-drilled horns and massed keyboards of the long-running funk/soul institution Earth Wind & Fire, where it is played by band leader Maurice White. White is devoted to the kalimba, even composing a eulogy to the instrument, 'Kalimba Story,' and naming his production company after it. Whereas most uses of the kalimba in pop are decorative, White uses it as a lead instrument on many songs. The solo at the end of 'Evil,' from *Head To The Sky*, is an incredible feat of dexterity, mixing rapid bursts of staccato arpeggios with brisk, syncopated melodic stabs.

White has now retired from live performance, but when the band was in its heyday in the 1970s and early 1980s, and White was still performing, he would use the kalimba on stage, with a contact pickup attached to the soundboard. "The kalimba represented my link to Africa. It was my way of taking part of that culture and spreading it all over the world," says White.[13]

Any examination of simple improvised musical instruments must include the simplest form of all, which harks back to the ancient tradition of rough music mentioned at the start of this chapter. That is, hitting anything to hand to make a percussive noise. The most famous example of this to appear in the pop charts was in the work of Joe Meek, a man normally associated more with electronic trickery (see chapters 3 and 4).

In 1964 Meek's star was waning in the face of stiff opposition from the new wave of beat groups. He struggled to accommodate this new style into his sound, managing only one big hit in what could be described as the beat style. But a beat record it was, quite literally. 'Have I The Right' was the debut single by The Honeycombs, a band featuring female drummer Honey Lantree. During recording, Meek decreed that the song required a loud stomping beat,

Maurice White of Earth Wind & Fire playing the kalimba on-stage, late 1970s.

particularly to emphasize one phrase, "Come right back," which introduces the choruses. After much experimenting, he decided that the sound he was getting from Lantree's drums was inadequate, so Meek augmented it with various band members lined up on the stairs in his home recording studio in Holloway Road, London. Microphones were then placed underneath the stairs to record the sound of the band stamping in time to Lantree's bass drum. 'Have I The Right,' stamping feet and all, was Meek's last Number One single, reaching the top of the British charts for two weeks in August 1964.

TOY STORIES

Harmonicas, accordions, Melodicas,
ocarinas, and recorders

The harmonica was so widespread in America in the 19th century that it has become an established part of the country's musical heritage and folklore. Tales, possibly apocryphal, identify President Abraham Lincoln as a harmonica player, and suggest that Wyatt Earp slipped one into his waistcoat pocket during the famous gunfight at the OK Corral. The instrument's origins, though, are in Europe. The story starts in Berlin in 1821, when a 16-year-old boy named Christian Buschmann chanced upon the basic design by fixing organ-tuning pitch pipes together. Buschmann called the instrument the *mundäoline*, which combines the German word for 'mouth' with the name of one of the stops on an organ.

Harmonicas were made in small numbers in Germany for several decades, gradually growing in popularity, until in 1857 another German, 24-year-old Matthias Hohner, founded a company in his name that would become synonymous with the instrument.[1] Hohner harmonicas were taken to America by emigrating Germans, and there they became popular amongst travelers because they were small enough to be easily carried. From this derives the popular image of the lonesome cowboy sitting by a campfire in the twilight, blowing a plaintive tune on his harmonica.

The harmonica is still one of the world's most popular and accessible means of playing a tune. Being cheap, durable, and possessing great expressive capacity, it became particularly popular in early 20th century American folk and blues, and, close-miked and distorted, in later electric blues. Pop musicians' enthusiasm for these forms meant that by the 1960s the harmonica had been fully absorbed into the popular music mainstream, with such diverse artists as Bob Dylan, The Rolling Stones, and Stevie Wonder all making distinctive use of it.

Yet despite its enormous popularity the harmonica has struggled to gain acceptance as a 'proper' musical instrument. It wasn't until 1948 that the American Federation Of Musicians recognized it as legitimate. A decade later a new Hohner instrument, the Melodica, which was based in part on the harmonica, would also become popular – yet it too would be seen by many people as more of a toy than a serious instrument.

Hohner's development of the harmonica from its first basic model has established the company on sound financial foundations, and it has thrived for nearly 150 years. In that time many variants of the basic instrument have been produced. One of the more unusual of these turned up on two albums routinely acclaimed as among the greatest of all time, The Beach Boys' *Pet Sounds* and The Beatles' *Sgt Pepper's Lonely Hearts Club Band*.

Bass harmonicas are bigger than standard blues or chromatic harps, the sort most commonly used in pop music, and usually sound 14 bass notes in a chromatic scale from C to C-sharp. They are sometimes combined with chord harmonicas. The Beach Boys used the instrument first, employing session maestro Tommy Morgan, who has racked up appearances with John Barry, Henry Mancini, Randy Newman and Barry Manilow, to name just a few.

Under Brian Wilson's direction, Morgan contributed a rasping part on a song that started as 'Hang On To Your Ego' and was later retitled 'I Know There's An Answer.' Both versions were included on an expanded reissue that first appeared in 1990. Morgan coaxed an unusual sound, a little like a bass sax, from the instrument.

That sound, along with much else on *Pet Sounds*, came to the attention of The Beatles. They were prompted to try out bass harp themselves during the *Sgt Pepper* sessions. The use is less conspicuous than on *Pet Sounds*, emphasizing chord changes on 'Being For The Benefit Of Mr Kite.'

A later record from the pop aristocracy, Simon & Garfunkel's 'The Boxer' from *Bridge Over Troubled Water*, also features a bass harp, a rhythmic part played by Charlie McCoy. It is one of several unusual arrangement touches in an ambitious production that reputedly took 100 hours of studio time. The gliding solo in the middle of the song is a blend of pedal steel guitar and piccolo trumpet (which is, incidentally, recreated live on a Theremin by keyboard player Rob Schwimmer when the duo performs now). The crashing percussion sound that punctuates the wordless chorus was achieved by drummer Hal Blaine hitting his snare drum at the bottom of a lift shaft. Producer Roy Halee captured the cavernous natural reverb effect.

Hohner has produced more than 1,500 different models of harmonica in its 150 years. Yet despite this capacity for getting the most from its core product, it became clear to Matthias Hohner's sons, who inherited the company when their father died in 1893, that there was scope for expansion. So they started to make another Hohner free-reed instrument, the accordion.

The first mention of the accordion is in a Viennese patent by Cyril Demian and his sons in 1829. The name derives from the German word *akkord*, meaning chord, and refers to the new instrument's distinguishing feature: buttons that play full chords. It is this feature that distinguishes accordions from concertinas, the superficially similar reed instruments that are driven by manually operated bellows. The most familiar model of accordion is the piano accordion, which features both a piano style keyboard for playing melodies and an array of chord buttons. Although generally thought of as a folk and popular music instrument, like the harmonica, the accordion has over the years been used in orchestral works by composers as eminent as Tchaikovsky, Prokofiev, and Charles Ives. Hohner's new accordion business flourished alongside its harmonica production, and in 1958 the company took elements from both instruments for its new product, the Melodica.

The Melodica was designed by Rainer Schütze, from an idea by Dr Hans Schere, a Hohner director related by marriage to the Hohner dynasty.[2] Like both the accordion and the harmonica, the Melodica is a free-reed instrument. Like the piano accordion, it can play both notes and chords, and uses a chromatic scale of individual notes, although it does not have an accordion's chord buttons. Like the harmonica it is played by blowing into the reeds, in the Melodica's case through a mouthpiece, although unlike the harmonica it sounds notes *only* when blown, not when sucked (drawn) too.

Initially Hohner introduced two models, a soprano and an alto, both of which are still in production. These remain the most familiar type of Melodica. Color apart – the soprano is green and the alto red – both versions look similar: an elongated rectangular box shape just under a foot long, with rounded edges and corners, a mouthpiece at one end,

De **HOHNER** melodica

soprano en alto

zijn de jongste kinderen van de grote Muziek-instrumentenfamilie uit de Harmonicastad Trossingen. In vorm en speelwijze lijkt de Melodica op de houten blaasinstru-menten de fluit, de schalmei, de klarinet.

Het bespelen is zeer eenvoudig, terwijl ook de ogen de vingers kunnen leiden en corrigeren. Kinderen spelen reeds na korte tijd schoolwijsjes, volksliedjes, populaire melodiën etc. zonder bijzondere leiding of onderricht.

De aangenaam klinkende toon van deze nieuwe muziekinstrumenten verrast alle muziekvrienden.

Alle tonen van de Melodica ontstaan door blazen.

Het gebruik van de Melodica voor het enkel- en voor het samenspel is buitengewoon veelzijdig. De chromatische toon-opbouw en de gunstige toonomvang veroorloven de weergave van alle soorten melodiën, liederen en dansen, zowel één-en meerstemmig, als ook met begeleiding van andere muziekinstrumenten.

Bij het muziek-onderricht zijn deze nieuwe instrumenten zeer nutig als aanschouwelijk materiaal o. a. voor de kinderen, die geen toetseninstrument kunnen bespelen. Bovendien kan in kleine en grote groepen samen gespeeld worden. Ook in samenspel met andere muziekinstrumenten is de mooie klank van de Melodica een aanwinst voor elk instrumentarium. Bij schooluitstapjes, tochtjes en vacantie brengt de Melodica, gelijk haar kleine zuster, de mondharmonica, een zonnige stemming.

Bij het meerstemmig samenspel met beide instrumenten vult de Melodica-Alto de Melodica-Soprano ideaal aan in toon-omvang en klank.

Het bij het spelen niet te vermijden condenswater wordt door een aan de onderzijde aangebracht ventiel verwijderd. (Het knopje van het ventiel indrukken ; dan in het instrument blazen!)

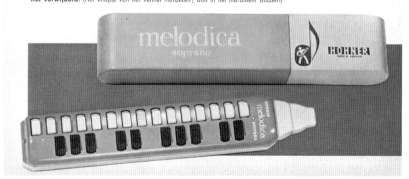

Early promotional literature for the Melodica, which crossed Hohner's accordion and harmonica expertise.

and chromatically-arranged button keys running the length of the top of the instrument. Both instruments have a range of two octaves, the alto f to f'', the soprano c' to c''', with the low notes nearest the mouthpiece. Early Melodicas were constructed of a wood frame covered by a painted metal casing, with keys and mouthpiece in plastic. Hohner abandoned this production method within a couple of years, moving to the now familiar all-plastic design. Despite this difference in materials, the earliest Melodicas look almost identical to current production models.

The word 'Melodica' is a Hohner trade name, although it is now used generically to describe a type of instrument, in the same way that people say 'hoover' when they mean vacuum cleaner. Since the Melodica's introduction, other companies have brought out similar instruments under different names, such as the Angel Melodyhorn and the Suzuki Melodion. The name of another of these derivatives,

the Yamaha Pianica, indicates that it is an example of the second basic type of Melodica, which uses a piano-style keyboard in place of the original button keys. Hohner has made many versions of this instrument, naming them Melodica Piano. Sometimes instruments of this sort come with the option of fitting a long flexible tube in place of the mouthpiece. This allows performers to play the instrument on their lap.

At first Hohner made two types of Melodica, a soprano and an alto. This page from an instruction booklet indicates the musical range of the alto model.

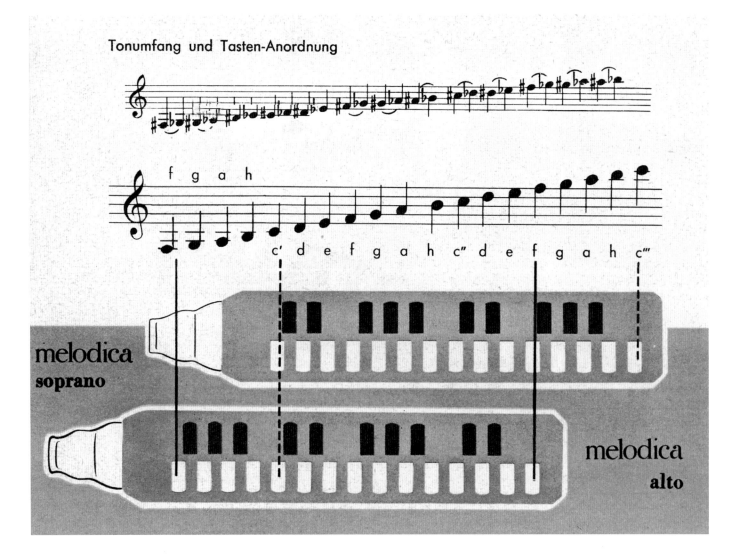

From the start, Hohner recognized that Melodicas had potential as a music education instrument for children, and early promotional literature tends to show children and teenagers playing them. Unlike other simple wind instruments used in schools, like the recorder and ocarina, the Melodica's pitch is not altered by how hard you blow. Blow hard and it simply gets louder. This makes it an encouraging prospect, as virtually anyone can play a simple tune with a little practice. The Melodica, too, offers more scope than many other simple instruments as it can play both melodies and chords. Hohner's early promotion of the Melodica to the children's market was successful, and it remains a popular school instrument. But its success in this area, and maybe, too, the fact that all but the earliest models are plastic, has meant that serious musicians tend to view it as a toy, and not the real thing. This wasn't what Hohner originally hoped for.

Early on in the instrument's life, as well as producing brochures picturing eager children practicing their scales and melodies, the company recruited well-known popular musicians to promote the instrument to a general audience. These included Marvin Kahn, a jazz pianist and author of piano tutor books, who recorded a number of 'introduction to the

A variant on Hohner's Melodica was the Angel Melodyhorn (top), here with extended tube in place of a mouthpiece. Next to it is a Hohner Melodica Piano 26.

Melodica' albums. The pre-rock'n'roll dance band songwriter, singer, flautist, and saxophonist Carmen Lombardo also briefly fronted a Hohner Melodica advertising campaign in the UK, when the instrument was launched there in 1959, priced £3/1/6 (£3.07, or $5.60), a year after its introduction in Germany.

In the 1960s, a further attempt to broaden the Melodica's appeal was made by producing electric models, a move quickly matched by Yamaha, which made an Electric Pianica. Neither instrument lasted long, although recorded evidence of the Hohner model does exist on the title track of John Lee Hooker's *Born In Mississippi, Raised Up In Tennessee*, played by jazz and blues pianist Clifford Coulter. Yet despite all of these efforts to present the Melodica as a 'proper' instrument, it remains to most people a child's toy at worst, and at best a little gadget to add color. This is a shame, as the Melodica has a musical character all of its own, as the few serious musicians who have devoted time to it have proved.

Jazz-rock fusion pioneers Weather Report are an example of an act that used the Melodica as an extra component only. The band were formed in 1971 around keyboard player Joe Zawinul and saxophonist Wayne Shorter, both of whom had served with the experimental jazz-rock line-ups of the Miles Davis band in the 1960s. After a few albums and a flexible line-up, they were joined in 1976 by Jaco Pastorius on bass, whose arrival prodded the group to some of their finest work. Zawinul used the synthesizer as a lead instrument, and, always with an ear cocked for the unusual timbre, played Melodica on two of the band's best known pieces, his own 'Birdland' and Pastorius's 'Teen Town,' both from the 1977 album *Heavy Weather*. But here it is just one strand in an intricate weave of sounds and textures.

Of the very few people to go against the grain and make Melodica their main instrument, nobody has yet eclipsed the late reggae artist and producer Augustus Pablo (born Horace Swaby). Pablo started recording singles as a teenager in 1970, and his early work as a producer and recording artist sold well in Jamaica and in the UK, where reggae had a growing audience in the 1970s.

His Melodica style emphasized the dynamic range of the humble instrument, and dub treatments further broadened its sound, the deep reverb sending it floating over the rhythm track's roomy bass and clipped guitars. Pablo had taught himself piano and clarinet as a child, and you can hear traces of both instruments in his Melodica playing: the rhythmic stabs from the piano; the snaking melodies reminiscent of a clarinet.

Although Pablo was much admired in reggae circles, his own recordings never crossed over boundaries into pop's mainstream. Pablo died in 1999 at the age of 47, but towards the end of his life he contributed to a recording that was heard by a wider audience than he had been granted for most of his work. British indie electronic rockers Primal Scream – a band well versed in dub and reggae – asked him to guest on their *Vanishing Point* album (1997). Pablo appears on one song, 'Star,' also a British hit single, contributing a typically beautiful plaintive melody and short solo passages, with a bed of vintage drum machines and electric piano behind him. To emphasize the contribution, *Vanishing Point's* CD art included a close up picture of Pablo's Hohner soprano

Melodica. Recruiting Pablo placed Primal Scream firmly in a minor tradition of Melodica use in British indie and electronic rock. This can be traced back to the cross pollination of styles encouraged by the doyen of British independent music, radio DJ John Peel, who played Pablo enthusiastically in the late 1970s, alongside the latest post-punk sounds.

Many other Peel favorites of the time took up the instrument, no doubt attracted by its cheapness and the ease with which it can be played, but probably influenced by Pablo too. Andy Gill of Gang Of Four played Melodica on 'Not Great Men' from *Entertainment*. Then New Order used one on 'Truth,' from their debut album *Movement*.

New Order had been formed by the three surviving members of Joy Division after singer Ian Curtis's suicide in 1980. In live performance, the reconstituted band made no effort at all to replace or replicate the compelling and disturbing charisma of their doomed frontman, instead adopting a retiring onstage demeanor.

In the band's very early shows, the sight of guitarist Bernard Sumner picking up what most people considered a toy instrument was a welcome visual curio in what was otherwise a drab presentation. Sumner's playing, coated in reverb, blended well with his band's synthesizer sounds, though, and was no doubt responsible for a surge in Melodica sales amongst the era's earnest young men. A few years later Depeche Mode's Martin Gore used a Melodica on 'Everything Counts,' and he can be seen with the instrument in the band's video for that single. Blur's Damon Albarn is a more recent Melodica enthusiast in the British indie tradition.

But the first big Melodica hit dates back to an earlier age of British pop. A satire on the subject of high taxes, The Kinks' 'Sunny Afternoon,' with its nasal vocal and descending piano line, is one of 1960s pop's most memorable songs, and one of Ray Davies's greatest achievements. The piano part was written by Davies, but played by well-traveled session musician Nicky Hopkins, instructed by Davies to mimic his own rudimentary style. It was Hopkins, too, who performed the Melodica overdub, playing both melodies and chords on a Hohner instrument. It can first be heard at 44 seconds, underneath the vocal line

"Save me, save me, save me from this squeeze," and thereafter through most of the song. Hopkins produced a sound that at times is close to that of an accordion, at others like some muted reed-led jazz band way off in the distance, contributing to the song's peculiarly English mood of indolence, and affluence gone to seed.[3]

'Sunny Afternoon' was a big international hit single in 1966, soundtracking that year's summer from a million transistor radios. It rubbed shoulders in the charts with the debut hit by another British band who, like The Kinks, had a reputation for primitive guitar riffing. That too used a wind instrument much favored in musical education, although this time as a prominent solo voice rather than a part of an ensemble arrangement.

'Wild Thing' by The Troggs is, if nothing else, proof of the value of spontaneity in pop. The song was written by Chip Taylor in a few hours one afternoon and first demo'd in the evening of that same day. The song was originally intended for a long forgotten band called Jordan Christopher & The Wild Ones, whose version sank without trace. But Taylor's original demo found its way over the Atlantic, and into the office of The Troggs' manager Larry Page, who also looked after The Kinks. At this stage in their career, The Troggs were a part-time band fronted by bricklayer turned singer Reg Ball, who had been renamed, with comic audacity, Reg Presley. The band were looking for something decent to record as their debut single, and 'Wild Thing' seemed like it was worth a try.

The recording of 'Wild Thing' would turn out to be the most profitable 45 minutes of work that Presley and his band would ever do. He says: "Larry Page was doing an orchestra session and he said we had to be up there waiting outside the studio in case there was any time left at the end. As it turned out there was three quarters of an hour to get our gear in, get a sound, record it and get out. And we did the b-side as well."[4]

The rendition of 'Wild Thing' that The Troggs took out of the studio after that rushed session flew in the face of prevailing trends when it appeared in the charts in mid 1966. By this stage in its life, pop was becoming more elaborate, more ornate, and more sophisticated. 'Wild Thing,' though, was basic in the extreme, with just a clanging rhythm guitar, a simple root bass part, thumping drums, and Presley's sneering vocal. This was prototype punk rock. Until, that is, the song reaches what must rate as pop's most incongruous solo. It is played on an ocarina, where you might reasonably expect some distorted harmonica or lead guitar.

The ocarina as we know it today is a duct flute that originated in Italy, circa 1865. Traditionally made of terracotta in either an egg or torpedo shape, with a number of finger holes for sounding different notes, ocarinas have more recently been made of plastic especially for schools use. Many cultures have similar instruments in their heritages, and the term ocarina is sometimes used to describe a whole host of simple flute-like instruments.

The inspiration for The Troggs' eccentric arrangement decision was the result of a misunderstanding. What the band were trying to do was develop what they had heard as a simple ocarina part on Taylor's demo. The band's musical director, Colin Fretcher, had worked out an ocarina solo based on this simple part, and what you hear on The Troggs' single is Fretcher playing this solo. But in fact the 'ocarina' on Taylor's demo was the sound of a recording engineer blowing through his cupped hands. The engineer had started to hum along in this way while Taylor was recording 'Wild Thing,' the songwriter liked the sound and decided to add it in to the demo.[5]

The ocarina solo on 'Wild Thing' added a completely unexpected twist to a great rock record, a twist that Presley believes only enhanced the song's appeal. "I always thought you had to get something quirky, any way you could. I think [the ocarina] was so quirky, and the song was so heavy, I think people thought 'Yeah!' It was one of those one-off things that just worked on that particular number."[6] The record-buying public obviously agreed, as the song rose to the top of the charts all over the world. The Troggs went on to score many more substantial hit singles in the late 1960s, and a version of the band fronted by Presley tours to this day. They still play 'Wild Thing,' and still include an ocarina solo, played now by Presley on a specially made resin model. He has tried using terracotta examples but kept chipping them against the microphone stand.

The ocarina has rarely featured in pop music since its moment of glory with The Troggs. Like the Melodica, it is now most popular as an instrument for introducing children to music. In this role, both Melodica and ocarina have gone some way to usurping the recorder, which for decades was the traditional first instrument for a child in most western European countries. About six months after the Melodica and ocarina appeared in the pop charts simultaneously, the recorder made a prominent pop appearance in the hands of Brian Jones, who played it on The Rolling Stones' 'Ruby Tuesday.' This recording came right in the middle of Jones's second phase of great influence over the Stones, after driving the band's early electric blues sound. This was in the period when Jones did more than any other 1960s musician to broaden the instrumental palette of pop.

It is often the fate of pop stars who die young to be remembered for the manner of their passing as much as for their lives and music. Jim Morrison in the Paris bathtub, Buddy Holly in the wreckage of a plane, Mama Cass and the (mythical) ham sandwich. Sometimes a tragic early death eclipses a musical career altogether. Never was this more so than in the case of Brian Jones, the doomed Rolling Stone. So impressed on pop's collective imagination is the image of Jones floating face-down in a swimming pool, in the garden of a house once owned by AA Milne, the creator of Winnie The Pooh, that his musical achievements are all but forgotten.

Yet Jones was a founder member of the self-styled Greatest Rock'n'Roll Band In The World, and, with some justification, saw himself as their leader well into their first flush of commercial success. He was also a revered guitarist on the early 1960s British R&B scene, and was especially admired for his slide-guitar playing.

But for the purpose of this story the most interesting aspect of Jones's musical legacy is the role he adopted in The Rolling Stones when his influence was apparently waning. By late 1965, the balance of power in the band was beginning to shift. Until that point Jones was the musical conscience of the group, and one of two focal points for the fans' interest,

alongside Mick Jagger. Jones was the vaguely sinister pretty boy whom the girls screamed at; Jones did many of the interviews; it was Jones that the TV cameras focused on as he grinned and mugged from behind his lustrous blonde fringe. Keith Richards, by contrast, cut a gauche, toothy figure, as far away from the elegantly wasted chic he later cultivated as Dartford, Kent, was from the Mississippi Delta.

Things began to change when Andrew Loog Oldham began managing the group. Richards and Jagger were packed off and instructed to write songs. After a few derivative early efforts, they established themselves as a songwriting partnership of considerable élan and ability, hitting Number One for the first time with 'The Last Time.' Growing in confidence, the pair honed their arrogant, feral bad-boy image to perfection. Jones, meanwhile, was left looking like just a member of the band, rather than its leader.

Jones was unhappy about being sidelined, and the pain of it eventually contributed greatly to his decline and early death. But at first he responded creatively. During the approximately 18-month period from mid 1966 to late 1967 that encompasses the *Aftermath, Between The Buttons*, and *Their Satanic Majesties Request* albums, and several classic hit singles, Jones found a new lease on musical life.

Seemingly unable to write songs himself, he channeled his energy into exploring new instruments, a facility he had demonstrated as a child in Cheltenham, a genteel English town, where he mastered guitar, harmonica, recorder, clarinet, and piano. By 1966, he rarely touched his guitar or harmonica, until then his main instruments in the Stones. Instead he was turning not only to the already mentioned recorder, but also marimbas, flute, Appalachian dulcimer, Mellotron, tamboura, autoharp, harpsichord, and sitar.

And for those 18 months, the aural colors he added to Stones records did much to define the band's sound in one of its great periods of creativity. At the same time, Jones was showing the world that pop music could accommodate all manner of instruments, from all over the world. Two of the instruments Jones mastered, the dulcimer and sitar, are dealt with in the next two chapters of this book.

STRING-DRIVEN THINGS

from autoharps to zithers

The mountain, lap, or Appalachian dulcimer – or dulcimore as it was sometimes known – is indigenous to Kentucky and Alabama, where it has been used to accompany folk song since the 18th century. Dulcimer player, writer, and recording artist Jean Ritchie believes that its origins can be traced back to several northern European stringed instruments bought over by settlers, including the German scheitholt, the Norwegian langeleiks, and the Swedish humle.[1] The instrument was particularly popular locally in the late 19th and early 20th century, but credit for its spread into the international community of folk musicians must go to Ritchie, who since the 1950s has been playing and writing about the instrument with a passion.

Ritchie was born in Kentucky in 1922 into a family of dulcimer players and makers. Now in her eighties, she remains active as a performer and recording artist. In 1952 she released what amounted to a recorded tribute to her musical heritage on a ten-inch album, *Jean Ritchie Singing The Traditional Songs Of Her Kentucky Mountain Family*. It was only the second release on Elektra, a label that in the 1960s released many albums in the emerging folk-rock style, which took the traditional songs, styles, and instrumentation of artists like Ritchie and blended them with rock.

The use of the word 'dulcimer' to describe Ritchie's favorite instrument has sometimes led to confusion in the pop world. For many, the word conjures up an image of a hammered dulcimer or a plucked zither, of which there are many variants in the traditions of most world cultures. We will look briefly at some of these later. The mountain dulcimer is very different, though. It has what looks more like an elongated violin body, with a fretboard running down the middle. About three feet long, usually with a narrow, curvaceous hourglass-shaped soundbox and a small headstock, the dulcimer has three courses (strings): one is traditionally used as the melody string, with the other two as drones. Many modern models have the main melody string doubled up, as on a 12-string guitar or mandolin. A two-octave fretboard runs the length of the soundbox, with frets spaced diatonically (including only the notes of the major scale). The melody string is tuned to the dominant, or fifth, of the scale, while the tonic or key-note of the

scale is on the third fret. So, if the unfretted melody string is tuned to a G, the first to seventh frets play the following notes: A, B, C, D, E, F, and G.

This arrangement of frets means that is necessary to retune the dulcimer to play in different keys. Conveniently, much can be achieved by retuning the melody string only. A typical major tuning would have the melody string tuned to a G, the first drone to a G also, and the second drone to a C. Fretting the melody string at the third fret would thus give a simple C chord. To play in C minor, the melody string is tuned up to a B-flat, making the key-note on the third fret E-flat: E-flat is the relative major of C minor and uses the same notes. Since C and G are the root and fifth of both C major and C minor, the drones are left the same.

The time-honored Appalachian method is to play seated, with the dulcimer on your lap with the headstock to the left. This means that the melody string (or double string) is the one nearest to you. This you fret with a 'noter' (a small piece of wood held between the finger and thumb of the left hand), while strumming away from your body, either with your thumb or a feather quill (goose or turkey preferably).

Harmonically, the shifting melody note against a background of constant drones is reminiscent of bagpipes, while the actual sound of the dulcimer's strings is bright and clean, something like a mandolin or banjo. Traditional players like Ritchie will almost always play in this way, with the occasional variation, for instance using a violin bow to sound notes. Having a small soundbox, the mountain dulcimer is a quiet instrument, and played in the traditional style it is most effective as a haunting, crystalline accompaniment to a ballad.

Ritchie popularized the mountain dulcimer to the extent that by the folk revival of the late 1950s it was being used by musicians beyond the geographical boundaries of its traditional home. Indeed, by the early 1960s the instrument was being made and played by English folkies. But it would take another, younger player to bridge the gap between folk and pop, and introduce the instrument to the rock world.

Richard Fariña was a man prone to cultivating around himself an aura of mystery. Born in 1936 in Brooklyn, he had Irish and Cuban blood, and

A typical mountain dulcimer, with its long fretboard running almost the entire length of the body.

sister Mimi. The new couple started to perform as a folk duo, eventually recording two albums for Vanguard, *Celebrations For A Grey Day* and *Reflections In A Crystal Wind*.

Ritchie met Fariña at a party in New York City in the early 1960s. He was then not active as a musician, but, Ritchie recalls, was fascinated by her dulcimer: "He got quite excited ... examining it and trying a few strums on it, saying he would like to learn to play one."[2] And this he did, picking up tips from other players, including Hester, initially using a dulcimer she gave him. Shortly afterwards, during a trip to Britain, British luthier Terry Hennessy built a dulcimer for Fariña. It was made from mahogany, with a walnut fretboard and spruce top, stained dark, and finished with a plastic pickguard.[3]

This was the instrument that Fariña would use on all of his recordings with Mimi. These, although more folk than rock, can be seen alongside Dylan's and The Byrds' efforts of the same period as part of a movement that introduced the styles of traditional American and British Isles music into electric rock. From folk the Fariñas took unadorned, stark harmonies and a stringed instrument ensemble comprising mountain dulcimer, autoharp, and guitar. From rock they sometimes took an electric rhythm section, but more importantly a pop songwriting sensibility that grasped the importance of melodic hooks. Richard Fariña was not only the duo's dulcimer player, but also the main songwriter, while Mimi played guitar and autoharp. Both sang.

Although clearly versed in Appalachian music, Fariña approached his dulcimer free from the constraints of any tradition. He often strummed it aggressively like a rhythm guitar – sometimes even holding it across his chest – and thus exploited the instrument's percussive possibilities. "His playing," Mimi said, "was very wild, like his spirit." Neal Hellman, author of *The Richard Fariña Dulcimer Book*, adds: "His style ...was contemporary, and it took the dulcimer in an entirely new direction. For many people who didn't grow up with Appalachian music, that was the first dulcimer they ever heard."[4] Blended with Mimi Fariña's tinkling autoharp or picked acoustic guitar, the duo made a brash, bright, eerie noise – somehow sounding both ancient and modern.

flamboyantly colored his early adulthood with stories, possibly apocryphal, of revolutionary derring-do in both countries. The aspects of his life for which there exist solid evidence are hardly less romantic. In the late 1950s he had shared a college room with enigmatic novelist Thomas Pynchon; by the early 1960s he was hanging around with Bob Dylan and Joan Baez. Then, after a whirlwind romance that started in Paris, Fariña split with his first wife, folk singer Carolyn Hester, and married Baez's younger

**Brian Jones of The Rolling Stones in the 1960s with the
rare Vox Bijou electric dulcimer.**

A track called 'V.' on the duo's first album, titled after the Pynchon novel of the same name, is a showcase for Fariña's frenetic and almost Eastern playing. The same album's 'Reno Nevada' showed how the same sound could be incorporated into a pop song, with the dulcimer adding sweet counter-melodies to a loping, insistent chord progression.

By the spring of 1966, the darkly handsome, hip, and clever Fariña looked set for stardom. With Mimi he was making respected, interesting records that were received well, although they sold modestly. As a writer he was on the verge of success, with his debut novel *Been Down So Long, It Looks Like Up To Me* ready to be published after a lengthy gestation. But it wasn't to be. He died riding pillion on a red Harley Davidson on April 30th 1966, his death an abrupt full stop to all his promise. It was Mimi's birthday, and his novel had been published two days before.

Excepting a posthumous collection of live recordings and outtakes, *Memories*, nothing more was heard of Fariña's dulcimer, a four-string model that now resides in the collection of the Smithsonian Institution in Washington DC. It is reasonable to speculate that, had he lived, Fariña would have moved further into electric music, given the drift in that direction over the duo's two albums. Shortly before his death, Fariña approached Hennessy with a request for a new dulcimer, with a pickup fitted. That dulcimer was never made, but just two months after his death a much bigger audience than Fariña ever commanded would get to hear a mountain dulcimer, with a pickup, on a pop record.

Quite how Brian Jones of The Rolling Stones came across the instrument remains a matter for conjecture. But come across it he did, and he became the first rock guitarist to use this rural American instrument in true electric rock. Jones was a student of world music decades before the term was invented, and by 1966 was already investigating instruments as culturally diverse as the sitar (India), the koto (Japan), and the marimba (Africa), as well as tinkering with electronics. In the press at the time he talked about an interest in Appalachian music, although he seemed uncertain about the mountain dulcimer's origin, saying: "It's an old English instrument used at the beginning of the century."[5] But whether, as some claim, Jones was introduced to the instrument by Fariña himself remains unclear. Stones biographer Philip Norman even says that Fariña *gave* Jones his first dulcimer.[6] It is certainly possible that the two met, as the Stones guitarist knew Dylan, and Fariña was for a while a part of Dylan's inner circle. But this intriguing possibility doesn't feature in other tellings of either Jones's or Fariña's stories, so it seems more likely that Jones simply heard Fariña's recordings. But however Jones first came across the instrument, by March 1966, just a month before Fariña's death, he was using it in sessions for The Rolling Stones' album *Aftermath*, which was released in June of that year.

Aftermath was a pivotal moment in the Stones' career. As the first album to be comprised entirely of Jagger/Richards originals, it marked the point at which erstwhile leader Jones finally lost all vestiges of control over the band. But it was also the start of a period of about 18 months that saw the release of three albums and several classic hit singles, in which Jones pioneered the use of world music instrumentation in pop. He played sitar on *Aftermath*, an event that is discussed later. He also played mountain dulcimer on two songs, the best known of which is 'Lady Jane.'

The baroque pop of 'Lady Jane' pits Mick Jagger's carefully enunciated paean to 'my sweet lady Jane' against a delicate backing track covered with Jones's fingerprints. His dulcimer part – alternating between a reinforcing counter-melody to and a call and response with Jagger's vocal – blends with a picked acoustic guitar. Jones played a dulcimer with a doubled melody string (in other words, a four-string like Fariña's). Heard in this context, along with an acoustic guitar, it has persuaded some people to think that a single 12-string guitar is being used, rather than the two distinct string instruments. Jones played his dulcimer in the traditional style, with the instrument on his knees, fretted with a noter and plucked with a quill. You can clearly hear Jones sliding the noter between frets. The effect of the song is studiously 'olde worlde,' an impression only heightened when a harpsichord joins in halfway through. 'Lady Jane' was a chart single in America. In Britain it was released as an album track only, but remains a well-known Stones song. *Aftermath's* other dulcimer song, 'I Am Waiting,'

is much more obscure, but still deserves a listen. Here, Jones uses a style that has more in common with Fariña's – strumming insistently on the beat.

The Stones have always been a touring band, and Jones took many of his unusual instruments out on the road with him, including his dulcimer. The instrument he used on stage was an electric model with a pickup fitted by Vox, the manufacturer of the white 'Teardrop' guitar with which Jones is commonly associated. This made playing the dulcimer with a rock band a more realistic prospect: it is a quiet instrument, and miking up an acoustic model would never create sufficient volume, even allowing for the modest backline amplification used by bands of the time. Thus equipped, Jones made an impact on at least one fan, with Chrissie Hynde, later of The Pretenders, reminiscing: "I saw them playing in Detroit in 1966. I remember Brian playing the dulcimer on 'Lady Jane.' I even made a dulcimer when I got to university, I was so impressed."[7]

So keen were Vox to capitalize on the association with The Stones that they even advertised an electric dulcimer, the Bijou, later in 1966. In advertising copy riddled with ethno-musicological confusion, Vox claimed that "together with the Vox research team, Brian created the Vox Bijou Guitar, responsible for that sitar sound of the Stones' latest recording."[8] (Meaning 'Paint It Black,' also on *Aftermath*, presumably.) It never went into production, although a few were made: Jones had at least two (one was stolen while the band were on tour in the States, and Vox flew in a replacement), and an example was displayed at music fairs in October 1966. These are probably all now lost forever. Jones's own instrument – if he still had it at the time of his death – might well have gone missing then, as many of his possessions were lost in the confusion of the immediate aftermath.

Mountain dulcimers have turned up in rock from time to time since Jones's demise, almost always in a musical setting that either refers to some sort of traditional folk music, or indeed *is* traditional folk music performed with rock instrumentation. But it tends to be an instrument that rock musicians pick up occasionally, as Jones did, and only one person so far has made it one of his main instruments.

Like Brian Jones, Tim Hart of British folk-rock innovators Steeleye Span was a guitarist before he was a dulcimer player. He came to the mountain dulcimer through an American folk performer – not Jean Ritchie or Richard Fariña, but Peggy Seeger, the half sister of Pete Seeger and the widow of the late Ewan MacColl. Seeger was born in New York but relocated to London in the late 1950s, where she quickly became a fixture, with MacColl, on the British folk circuit (playing, incidentally, a Hennessy dulcimer like Richard Fariña's). Hart saw her playing dulcimer in London's folk clubs, the instrument appealing to the traditional folkie in him because "a lot of folk songs don't have chords, they have drones, and playing a dulcimer you can play drones and a counter melody."[9] Future Steeleye Span singer Maddy Prior bought Hart his first dulcimer as a birthday present, some time in the mid 1960s.

Initially Hart played a standard acoustic mountain dulcimer, but in 1969 he had four adapted models specially made, paid for by an advance given to the newly-formed Steeleye Span. These new dulcimers, two of which were acoustic and two solidbody electric, had an extra fret added for great harmonic flexibility. "It started off as an Appalachian mountain dulcimer, which I adapted," says Hart, "a three-string instrument with one of the strings doubled. If the open string was [tuned to play a melody in] C, what would be the note of B-flat was added. That one little fret didn't change the character of the instrument a lot, but it broadened its scope."[10]

It was the electric models that Hart used on all subsequent Steeleye Span records and when performing live, although he is only credited with 'electric dulcimer' on the band's first album.

Hart's playing was a mixture of the traditional and the new. He sometimes fretted with a noter, and sometimes with his fingers, "with my thumb on the first string, and fingertips over the other strings, like a spider over it." He strummed with plectrums. "I started off with quills, but they were a bit impractical; they'd break halfway through a song."[11]

Along with Fairport Convention, with whom they had much in common, Steeleye Span were the most successful of the British folk-rock bands to appear at the end of the 1960s. Initially concentrating on interpretations of traditional song, the band mixed electric guitars with folk instruments, including autoharp, concertina, mandolin, and banjo, with Hart's electric dulcimer forming the bridge between the two styles. Although the band had deep roots in traditional folk music, they played loud and were capable of kicking up a rocky din, even without a drummer.

Hart's dulcimer playing can be heard on Steeleye Span records right through his tenure with the band, which lasted until 1982. It isn't always possible to identify when the dulcimer is playing, though: often it provides a background droning texture, which can be hard to isolate from the rest of the arrangement, and when Hart plays melody lines the dulcimer can sound like an electric guitar. But a particularly effective and prominent use of the instrument can be heard on 'The Lark In The Morning' from the band's second album, *Please To See The King* (1970). Here Hart provides a constant bright, distorted dulcimer backdrop for the band's interwoven harmony singing, sliding up and down the doubled melody string with the drones filling out the sound.

Even now the odd magazine article about Brian Jones erroneously insists that the instrument he played on 'Lady Jane' was a hammered dulcimer, which is actually a very different instrument to the mountain dulcimer. The confusion arises because the generic term 'dulcimer' is usually used to describe any number of instruments from around the world that are played using hammers or beaters, while the mountain dulcimer is much more obscure. Typically these hammered dulcimers have a trapezoidal sound box over which many light strings are stretched, usually at least doubled to give sufficient volume to each note. The instrument is placed either on a stand, a table, or on the player's knees, depending on its size. It is played with two hammers like a glockenspiel, although some people use their fingers to pluck the strings. Such instruments turn up sometimes in pop music, recently on the Wilco album *A Ghost Is Born*. The instrument appears on three songs, most prominently on 'Company In My Back.' Here it is played by drummer Glenn Kotche, whose coordination with two drumsticks equips him to use the dulcimer's hammers to pick out the strict arpeggio pattern that occurs after the songs' choruses. In ethno-musicological terms, all dulcimers, hammered or otherwise, are a form of zither, a broad classification that includes the Japanese koto and many other similar instruments from Africa and the Far East.

In popular Western understanding, though, a zither is a similar looking (and sounding) instrument to the hammered dulcimer – although generally played by plucking the strings rather than hitting them with a hammer – and comes from Europe. These European zithers are Austrian and Bavarian in origin, and were developed during the 19th century. There are many variants, but the most common has 34 strings stretched over a slim rectangular soundbox with a curved appendage on one of the long sides. The most obvious difference to the dulcimer is that this sort of zither has a fretboard over which five of the strings pass. These are used for melodies, the player plucking the strings with fingers or fingerpicks, while the unfretted strings are used for chords and bass notes. Although zithers occasionally turn up in classical music, they are generally used as folk instruments.

Variants of the plucked zither and hammered dulcimer types are popular in central and eastern Europe in particular, and have been sometimes used to create an evocation of this part of the world in film music. In the 1960s spy film, *The Ipcress File*, composer John Barry achieves this by using the cimbalom, a Hungarian instrument. The cimbalom is a large hammered dulcimer standing on fixed legs and played with beaters, designed in the late 19th century for use in concert halls. The melody Barry wrote for the cimbalom, backed by rhythmically insistent flutes, brushed drums, and muted brass, established a style that was jumped on by composers for any number of subsequent spy films and TV series – part smoky jazz, part minor key mystery. Actually titled 'A Man Alone,' Barry's theme was inspired by an earlier movie theme that also conjures up sinister images of dark, misty European streets: "*The Ipcress File* was like my homage to *The Third Man*," said Barry. "I knew that was how I wanted to do it from the start."[12]

Director Carol Reed's *Third Man*, about corruption in Vienna immediately after World War II, starred Orson Welles and was written by British novelist Graham Greene. It is routinely hailed as one of the great movies of all time. Anton Karas's zither soundtrack is as crucial to the film's success as Greene's story, Welles's super-sized charisma, or Reed's directorial skill. Karas was an unknown amateur musician when Reed found him playing at a party in a local tavern in Vienna, just before the film went into production. Undeterred, Reed hired him to compose the film's musical score – a brave move, as Karas had no experience of recording, let alone composing a movie score.

But Reed's hunch paid off, with Karas coming up with simple zither music – no other instruments were used – which, although pretty in itself, sounds unsettling in context, when associated with the amoral character played by Welles.

The main theme made a star of Karas, and was released as a single in 1950, lodging in the US Top 40 for three months. With the proceeds Karas bought a bar in Vienna (which of course he named 'The Third Man'), where he returned to what he knew best, playing his zither to patrons, and occasionally venturing out to record for the German and Austrian market. So closely did Karas's theme tune come to be associated with the film and its star, Orson Welles, that later, when the actor walked into restaurants, house musicians would often strike up the theme, to his considerable annoyance.

Hammered dulcimers and zithers are complex instruments, requiring much skill to play them well. The autoharp, though, with its ready-made chords, is a much easier way to a similar sound. Designed in Germany in the 1880s as a home instrument, the autoharp looks something like a Bavarian zither, with a number of metal strings – usually 36 – stretched over a shallow soundbox and wound around pegs at one end, with a key that fits these pegs tuning the strings to a chromatic scale. The sound box is five-sided, a rectangle with one corner sliced off. A number of chord bars, at least six, run transversely across the sound box, held above the strings by springs at each end. Each bar has felt pads that dampen some strings when the bar is pressed down – those not required for the given chord – while the remaining undampened strings sound the correct notes. The autoharp is usually played either upright, against the

The autoharp originated in Germany in the 1880s as an easy-to-play instrument.

player's chest, or flat on the lap, the left hand pressing down chord bars while the right hand strums or picks the strings.

Although originally European, autoharps were taken up enthusiastically in rural America from the 1920s onwards, and continue to be widely used in folk and bluegrass music. Both German and American manufacturers still produce them. The appeal of the instrument is two-fold. Firstly, even in the hands of a player with very limited technique, the many strings of an autoharp can provide a rich, full sound, particularly effective as an accompaniment for a ballad singer. Secondly, the instrument is easy to play with virtually no practice. Simple chord progressions can be strummed by anyone with two working hands. The only challenge an autoharp presents to a novice player is that it can be hard to tune.

The American country music dynasty The Carter Family popularized the autoharp on their many recordings from the 1930s onwards. That group's most famous member, June Carter Cash, wife of Johnny Cash, continued to play the instrument on her own

recordings until her death in 2003. Given the instrument's strong association with what is now called American roots music, it is not surprising that it first started to appear in rock and pop music in the hands of musicians with a clear debt to traditional folk, country, bluegrass, and Appalachian forms.

The most committed autoharpist in pop was The Lovin' Spoonful's John Sebastian, who used the instrument on many songs during the band's brief but productive career.

Bob Dylan and The Band had one lying around in the basement of Big Pink, their house in Woodstock, in 1967. Julie Dyble, singer with the first incarnation of Fairport Convention, played an electric autoharp (which she believed was the only such instrument in Britain at the time) on the band's debut album (1968). She later took it to her next band, Trader Horne. The Electric Prunes singer James Lowe used one to eerie effect, picking out heavily reverbed notes and sweeping chords on 'Big City,' from the band's second album, *Underground*. Even the BBC Radiophonic Workshop had one amidst its collection of test oscillators and broken pianos.

Although autoharps have appeared frequently on pop records since the 1960s, more often than not the instrument shows up as a peripheral texture, rather than a dominant instrument. Because it is so easy to play it often seems like a last refuge for someone wanting to get in on a session but not being able to contribute anything else. Brian Jones's recording career with The Rolling Stones ended rather forlornly in this manner, with an inconsequential autoharp strum on 'You Got The Silver' from *Let It Bleed*. It's the bright, metallic sound on the right hand of the stereo that appears about 50 seconds into the song, mixed low.

Another attempt to make the zither/dulcimer concept accessible was the Marxophone, one of many quaint hybrid instruments produced in America in the late 19th and early 20th century, glorying in names like the Banjolin, the Ukelin, the Mandolin-uke, the Marx Piano Harp, the Marxolin, the Pianoette, the Pianolin and the Tremoloa. The idea behind these oddities was to combine characteristics

The Carter Family in 1928; Sara (right) holds an autoharp, alongside Alvin and Maybelle.

of two or more existing instruments into an accessible package. In the days when most people made their own musical entertainment at home, they were sold to innocent non-musicians on the alluring promise that you too could make beautiful music with hardly any effort at all. One that has stood the test of time is the banjulele, or the banjo-uke, with a body like a small banjo, strung like a ukulele. Most failed and are long out of production, but they sold in large numbers for a while, being marketed enthusiastically by door to door salesmen and in catalogues.

The Marxophone (sometimes mis-spelt 'Marxaphone' on record credits) was invented by Henry Charles Marx (1875-1947) and was patented in 1912. Marx was the Dr Frankenstein who created many of the hybrid musical monsters. His business thrived for a while, to the extent that he was able to found the Marxochime Colony in New Troy, Michigan, in 1927. This included not only a factory for making instruments, but a large house for the Marx family and cottages for workers.

The Marxophone was one of the colony's better efforts. It has a similarly shaped and sized soundboard to that of the autoharp. The string arrangement, however, combines elements of the hammered

Henry Charles Marx's Marxophone was like a cross between autoharp, hammered dulcimer, and zither.

dulcimer and the zither. Two octaves of melody double-strings are sounded with a set of weighted hammers, mounted above the strings. These hammers are operated with the fingers of the right hand hitting typewriter-like keys. When plucked, these bounce on the strings, giving an effect similar to a rapidly played hammered dulcimer or a double-picked mandolin. To the left of these hammered strings, when looking down on top of the instrument with the hammers nearest to you, are four sets of chord strings, similar to those on a zither, that give G, F, C, and D7. The Marxophone is usually played on the lap or a table top, with the hammers nearest the body. The left hand strums chords, the right operates the hammers.

The best use of the Marxophone in pop came in the hands of Ray Manzarek of *The Doors*. The band recorded a reading of Bertolt Brecht and Kurt Weil's 'Alabama Song' on their first album *The Doors*. Manzarek added a Marxophone response to each of Morrison's vocal lines. Although it was an American instrument playing on a song nominally about America, the closeness of the sound to both the zither and hammered dulcimer immediately suggests drunken menace in the mean streets of a nameless central European city, particularly as it twangs its circus melody in response to Morrison's stentorian delivery of the line "show me the way to the next whisky bar." At about the same time another very different American band, The Monkees, added Marxophone to 'PO Box 9847' from their 1967 album *The Birds, The Bees & The Monkees*.

Pounced on by latter-day bargain hunters, Marxophones still crop up on recordings from time to time. Aimee Mann's album from 2002, *Lost In Space*, features the instrument, alongside a host of other oddities played by guitarist Michael Lockwood. He says, "I spend half of my time trying to make a guitar sound anything other than what it is supposed to sound like! For me it all comes down to the song and if the mood of the song calls for the sound then you can get away with it. It is about supporting the melody and setting a mood for the lyric."[13] This he does with the Marxophone on 'The Moth,' using the distinctive bouncing hammers to play a descending melody line in answer to Mann's simple chorus refrain. You can also hear an example on The

Magnetic Fields' album, *i*, along with something described as the Violin-uke, another American hybrid from the early 20th century which, as the name implies, was meant to combine the characteristics of the violin and the ukulele. There were actually several instruments that tried this particular trick, the most successful being the Ukelin.

The Ukelin is the musical equivalent of a fairground freak-show curiosity. The body of the instrument, shaped like a ukulele and with a soundhole, extends into a broad, hollow neck that has another soundhole. Sixteen melody strings are stretched over the 'neck' hole, while another set of strings is mounted over the body hole, providing four accompanying bass chords. The accompanying instruction booklet says that the instrument is to be placed on a table in front of the player, with the body closest to him. The melody strings are then played with a short bow held in the right hand, while the chord strings are strummed with the left hand. As

with the Marxophone and most other hybrids of this type, special numerically-coded Ukelin music guided people how to play the popular tunes of the day. Ukelins were made in very big numbers by Oscar Schmidt, a company best known for its autoharps. They were manufactured for far longer than most similar hybrids, too, only going out of production in the early 1960s. k.d. lang reputedly performed a brief Ukelin cameo on *All You Can Eat* (1995).

Although marketed as 'easy to play' instruments, Ukelins, Marxophones and the whole mutant family of hybrids were hard to master. For most buyers, the promise of easy home music was never realized, and the instruments were quickly consigned to closets, attics, and cellars, from which they are now emerging, strings rusty from decades of idleness, to be snapped up by the eBay generation.

FULL OF EASTERN PROMISE

the sitar in 1960s pop

I n the summer on 1966 the British music press worked itself into a frenzy about the latest craze to consume Britain's guitar heroes. "The top boys are going through a new stage," *Beat Instrumental* breathlessly announced. "The immortal blues artistes who they were raving about a short while back have been eclipsed almost completely by the weird and wonderful works of Ravi Shankar."[1] Shankar's name, at least, is now familiar to the pop audience, thanks to his association with The Beatles. But back then he was known only as an Indian classical musician, albeit to an international audience. And the "weird and wonderful works" that so inspired a generation of pop guitarists were, for the best part, mainstream selections from the classical and traditional sitar repertoire, and Shankar's own compositions in that style.

The sitar is one of the principal instruments in Indian classical music. A long-necked stringed instrument, it is thought to have evolved from an ancient form of Iranian lute, and incorporates features of the vina, an earlier Indian stringed instrument. The body of the sitar is usually called a gourd. It originally *was* a gourd, but is now more likely to be made of wood. From this a long, broad, hollow neck extends to a head holding tuning pegs, behind which there is often a second, smaller gourd. Movable frets, usually 21 in number, extend down the length of the neck. These arch above the fretboard rather than being embedded in it, as they would be in a western fretted instrument. The player can move the frets to set the intervals between notes required for different scales.

The string set-up varies, but generally there are three groups of strings: the four main playing strings, three drone strings, and 11 or more sympathetic strings, the last of which run underneath the frets. Two of the drone strings and the sympathetic strings have tuning pegs running down the side of the neck. The broad bridge on which the main strings and drones rest is derived from that of the vina, and gives the sitar much of its distinctive ringing sound. The sympathetic strings have their own smaller bridge in front of the main one.

One noticeable feature of the sitar is that the strings run down one side of the neck, leaving a part of it apparently redundant. This is to allow for the bending of notes, an integral feature of Indian music and one that appealed to the 1960s generation of rock guitarists raised on the blues – another form that relies on string bending for much of its expressive power.

Conventional wisdom has it that George Harrison was responsible for Western pop's infatuation with the sitar, starting it all when he recorded a brief lick on 'Norwegian Wood,' from *Rubber Soul*. That is true, but not the whole story.

The Beatles recording was the first pop record to feature sitar, and it inspired many others to try out the new sound. But as often happens in the process of musical evolution, a number of people had the same idea at the same time, often independently of each other. The sitar craze was kept going by other big names and big records, particularly Brian Jones on the Rolling Stones' single 'Paint it Black.'

Indeed, rock guitarists had been experimenting with the instrument *before* Harrison. His hesitant efforts on 'Norwegian Wood' were the first the world heard of sitar pop, but if he hadn't committed that fateful overdub to tape, someone else would have used the instrument on another record shortly afterwards. The popularity of the sitar might not have spread as widely without Harrison's endorsement, and it might not have lasted as long as it did, but the craze would still have happened.

Although American guitarists did take up the sitar, this was originally a British phenomenon. It took root and flourished in London in 1965/66, when the city could justly claim to be the international capital of pop. It was a close-knit scene, with members of The Beatles, The Rolling Stones, The Who, The Kinks, and many lesser bands and session players mixing freely, professionally and socially. There was competition, but also camaraderie, and ideas were freely exchanged. Internationally, too, there was a sense of musical adventure, with Dylan, The Beach Boys, and The Byrds doing things that would have been unimaginable just 18 months before. In London, one aspect of that same attitude was the number of British musicians experimenting with Indian influences without using Indian instrumentation. Folk guitarist Davey Graham was dipping into this particular well of inspiration as early as 1964, on his *Folk Blues And Beyond* album. Then, in April/May 1965, The Kinks recorded a single, 'See My Friends,' which

full of eastern promise

incorporated a sitar-like drone, albeit recorded on guitar. "It's feedback by accident, playing above my guitar," says Ray Davies. "We compressed it and it sounded really unique. We'd traveled to India a year before and that had stayed with me."[2] At about the same time that Davies was conducting this Eastern-inspired experiment, two more British bands, The Yardbirds and The Beatles, were having similar ideas. More of them shortly.

The sitar craze wasn't the first time pop had crossed national boundaries in the search for inspiration. In 1951, a pianist, saxophonist, conductor, composer, and arranger called Les Baxter recorded an album on Capitol called *Le Sacre Du Sauvage* (Ritual Of The Savage), which marked the beginning of the 'exotica' genre. It included what would become exotica's theme song, 'Quiet Village,' later a big American hit for Martin Denny. *Le Sacre Du Sauvage* was the first of a run of albums for Capitol that lasted until 1962, during which time many other artists, including Denny, added dozens more.

Like all genres, exotica resists easy definition. Its portrayal of various foreign forms of music (predominantly Polynesian, Afro-Caribbean, and Hawaiian) owed a debt to the Hollywood stereotypes of the time – all rustling grass skirts and whooping Tarzan cries. It was not in any sense the real thing, but an imagined idea of what that music might sound like. Its chord progressions and grooves owed something to jazz, but without such artistic gravity. Sometimes it was meant to serve as light background music, at others it was showy and attention-grabbing. Perhaps it is best to think of exotica as the music of an imaginary country: part Hawaii, part Africa, part West Coast technological paradise, a place where seasoned musicians who had already worked extensively in jazz, light classical, soundtrack music, and pop were served endless cocktails by dusky maidens (who were usually photographed in a state of mildly risqué disarray for the album sleeves).

Exotica conjured up an alternative fantasy world to the harsh urban sounds of the newly emerging rock'n'roll. It petered out in the 1960s, consigned to bargain-bin obscurity for decades before being rediscovered as kitsch chic in the early 1990s. Some exotica albums did make use of unusual ethnic

instruments, particularly percussion, but not the sitar, at least not until after rock had introduced it into Western music. Exotica also used early electronic instruments. In that respect at least it is important music, opening up pop to the possibility of combining what are now called 'world music' instruments with more conventional sound sources.

But back to the sitar. George Harrison's first encounter with the instrument is well documented, not least in his autobiography *I Me Mine*. It happened on April 5th and 6th 1965, during the filming of *Help!*, when the action moves briefly to a restaurant where Indian musicians are performing in the background; one is playing a sitar. Harrison was

The leading Indian sitar master Ravi Shankar pictured with George Harrison in the late 1960s.

fascinated. Investigating further, he bought a Ravi Shankar album, and then his first sitar.[3] In time he made contact with The Asian Music Circle, a group formed in the 1950s in London to promote Asian music. There he met Ravi Shankar and other Indian musicians. Shankar would go on to give Harrison lessons, with the Beatle becoming a serious student for a while. Although Harrison stopped concentrating on the sitar in 1968, his interest in Indian music ran deeper than the fashion he inadvertently helped to inspire, staying with him until his death. But he owned a sitar for several months before using it. It would not be until the recording of 'Norwegian Wood,' on October 12th 1965, that he first tried it in the studio.

The song hadn't been written with a sitar in mind, and nor was the sitar part particularly striking. But it started something, for Harrison and others. "On 'Norwegian Wood' it wasn't much," he said later. "It was just an attempt, an introduction. My real love of the sitar came *after* 'Norwegian Wood.'"[4] 'Norwegian Wood' was included on *Rubber Soul*,

released in December 1965. Within months many other major artists would have sitar records in the works, and Ravi Shankar found himself courted by a media eager for his knowledge of the 'weird new instrument.' The pop world's ignorance was striking.

In a debate that filled pages for several months, *Melody Maker* described the sitar as a "guitar-like instrument," and the tabla as "a sort of Indian conga drum."[5] Shankar's response to all of this was ambivalent. "It is good if it is going to encourage a serious interest in the music. But if it is going to be like so many things, just a passing fancy, then it is not going to be much good."[6] Harrison agreed: "What I dislike about the sitar is the way it's become the 'in thing.' I never wanted this. It's just become a part of the bandwagon, with too many people having a go with it, just to be considered 'in.'"[7]

Born in 1920, Shankar has enjoyed a career of more than 65 years. He began to study sitar seriously at age 18. After a decade of concerts and recording in India, Shankar was performing internationally by the 1950s. He played in the Soviet Union in 1954 and

Ravi Shankar playing sitar on-stage with fellow Indian musicians during a concert in the late 1960s.

Europe and America two years later. Ten years after that, his association with Harrison propelled him into pop consciousness, his position cemented by appearances at the Monterey Pop Festival, Woodstock, and the Concert For Bangla Desh. Such dalliances offended purists, of course, and Shankar himself came to rue the lazy, inaccurate association between Indian music, drugs, and psychedelia that was routinely made in the pop world in the 1960s.

In fact, the Indian classical tradition from which Shankar comes is characterized by rigorous, almost devotional discipline, and a formal respect for the music and its instruments. The cultural gulf is illustrated by a story about Shankar told by Harihar Rao, his student and sometime manager. Shankar and Jimi Hendrix were backstage at an event, probably the Monterey Pop Festival. "Indians do not even step over their instruments, they are considered sacred, and so they always make sure they keep their instruments on a table or on a higher level … and here was Jimi Hendrix, who had tuned his guitar, and put it in a case, and was standing with one foot on the case and was smoking. … It really bugged Ravi Shankar; he said very nicely, 'It's your music, whatever you want to do is fine, but it breaks my heart to see someone stepping on a musical instrument.'"[8]

Yet despite these tensions, Shankar's involvement with Western pop pioneered the breaking down of musical boundaries between different cultures. As well as working with Harrison, he went on to work with figures as varied as Yehudi Menuhin and Phillip Glass. In a long career as a performer and composer, he has experimented with electronics, written for film, and composed ballets. Perhaps he has felt some regret at the cheapening of the sitar during the pop craze of the 1960s, but at least he can take comfort from the fact that it was an expression, albeit flawed and commercialized, of the idea of music as an international language, a notion he endorses.

'Norwegian Wood' might have been the first pop record released to feature sitar, but Harrison was not the first pop guitarist to take an interest in the instrument, nor were The Beatles the first band to attempt to use it on a recording. So who got there first? There are three complications: first, the understandable competitiveness of the musicians involved; second, the fact that a lot of people had the same idea at almost the same time; third, the fact that memories of precise dates fade with time. But establishing who got their first is less interesting than discovering that several people were traveling towards the same destination independently, with Harrison's recording being the catalyst that prompted their eventual coming together.

Well-traveled instrumentalist Shawn Phillips claims to be the first rock guitarist to play sitar. Phillips is associated with the early 1970s singer-songwriter boom, although his career started way before that. A singer, songwriter, and musician whose work encompasses folk-rock, jazz, progressive, pop, and classical influences, and he has been admired for decades without ever becoming a big star. The son of spy novelist Philip Atlee, Phillips lived in many countries around the world as a child, an experience that gave him a taste for world music. His peripatetic career took him to England for several years in the mid 1960s, where he worked with Donovan.

It was with Donovan that Phillips first recorded sitar, although he says he had already been experimenting for some years by that time. "I started playing the instrument in 1962. I was gigging in Toronto, at a club called The Purple Onion, and I had a night off. Someone said I should go see this concert by a guy named Ravi Shankar, so I did, and was completely blown away by what he did with the sitar, and was hooked. I went backstage, after the concert, and asked him to explain the instrument to me. He was extremely kind, and showed me how to hold it, and sit with it, and what the basic parameters of it were."[9]

But although Phillips's introduction to the sitar pre-date Harrison's, his recording debut with it does not. Session records show that Phillips's first sitar recording with Donovan was 'Sunny South Kensington' committed to tape at studio 3, Abbey Road, on December 19th 1965, just over two months after Harrison recorded the 'Norwegian Wood' part. Several other sitar sessions with Donovan followed in the ensuing months. At this point in his career, Donovan's release schedule was disturbed by all sorts of contractual shenanigans, which meant that 'Sunny South Kensington' didn't actually appear on record until March 1967, on the US-only *Mellow Yellow* album. The first Donovan recording with sitar to be released was 'Ferris Wheel,' recorded April 4th 1966 and released on the American version of *Sunshine Superman* in September of that year.[10]

Big Jim Sullivan started the 1960s as guitarist for English rock'n'roll singer Marty Wilde and ended the decade as guitarist for Welsh balladeer Tom Jones. In between, he worked the London session circuit,

British session musician Big Jim Sullivan in 1967 with his sitar, which he played on many records of the time.

playing on thousands of recordings and hundreds of hits. "I was doing three sessions a day, and playing on anything from three to six numbers per session."[11] Given that work rate, it is not surprising that Sullivan can't remember what records he played on. He does remember, though, that he did many sitar sessions.

His interest had been fired when he saw Indian master Vilayat Khan the with a sitar, recording at EMI, probably in 1964. "I was doing a session and I heard these incredible sounds and I just stayed there watching them. It was so beautifully melodic. ... Vilayat Khan's technique with bending strings was so incredible and so in tune that I was totally amazed."[12]

Inspired, Sullivan immediately purchased the first sitar he could find, and set about studying the instrument with some resolve. He knocked on the door of Nazir Jairazbhoy, a music lecturer at the University Of London's School Of Oriental And African Studies (SOAS), and asked for lessons. Jairazbhoy obliged. He came from Bombay but had been at SOAS, first as a student and then as a lecturer, since 1954. He must have been surprised to have a rock guitarist earnestly questioning him about Indian music, but he was musically broadminded, interested in jazz and some pop as well as Indian classical music.

Jairazbhoy was one of several Indian musicians apart from Shankar to play an important part in the pop sitar story. The musical quick-thinking that served Sullivan so well on the session circuit, when tracks were often cut on the first take with no rehearsal, helped him as he learnt the sitar. Jairazbhoy remembers: "He had a knack. He was a real musician. Just his guitar skills would not help, but he could catch anything very quickly. He had a musical mind and a musical touch. Jim was very quick at catching on."[13]

Like Harrison, Sullivan dedicated himself to sitar at the expense of guitar for several years, returning to his original instrument in 1969 when he signed up with Tom Jones. Because he played on so many records, he doesn't remember which ones featured his sitar playing. But there's an even chance that it is Sullivan providing the Eastern flourishes on most British pop recordings of the era that feature the instrument.

By 1966 there was a community of rock sitarists in London. Both Big Jim Sullivan and Shawn Phillips talk of getting together with the two best-known players, George Harrison and Brian Jones, to swap tips. Phillips recalls: "I was working with Donovan, at the time, and he was instrumental in the introduction to both The Beatles and The Moody Blues. Very shortly thereafter, George invited me to have dinner with him, and asked if I would give him some pointers on the sitar. I think we got together five or six times. I had met Brian long before that, and we experimented with not only sitar, but oud and other Middle Eastern instruments."[14]

Quite where Jimmy Page fits into all of this is unclear. Page is now known firstly as Led Zeppelin's guitarist, and secondly for his brief association with The Yardbirds. Before that he worked the session circuit as a teenager, often teaming up with Big Jim Sullivan. Page was then known as Little Jim. It was during this first phase of his career that he too experimented with sitar. Exactly when he started playing the instrument isn't certain, but there are pointers indicating that it pre-dated Harrison's first recording. On balance, Page probably wasn't the first rock guitarist to play the sitar. But he was present when a rock band first attempted to record with a sitar. Indeed, some accounts say that his interest in the instrument started at that point.

The Yardbirds has started out as an electric blues band cut from the same cloth as The Pretty Things and The Rolling Stones. Their version of Graham Gouldman's 'For Your Love' was a departure, an ornate chamber-pop arrangement driven by a jangling harpsichord. It was a big hit in spring 1965, and with that came the pressing need for a follow-up. That would come in the form of another Gouldman song, 'Heart Full Of Soul,' recorded in March/April 1965. The single that came out of those sessions was distinguished by a spidery Jeff Beck guitar motif, but it could have turned out very differently.

According to The Yardbirds' then manager, Giorgio Gomelsky, what happened at Advision Studios, London, where the band worked, was the first attempt to record a pop record with sitar. Gomelsky's story, the thrust of which is confirmed by Yardbirds drummer Jim McCarty and Jeff Beck biographer Annette Carson, is that he had nurtured an interest in what is now called world music for some time, "and

when I heard the demo of 'Heart Full' it was absolutely evident that the intro riff was eminently suited for sitar and tabla. … I convinced the owner of my favorite Indian restaurant in London to look for Indian musicians (sitar and tabla) if there were any in the Indian community in London at the time, and book them into his joint, a good idea by itself but also so we could hear them. He did find some, from Kenya of all places [where there was a large Asian community], and I was able to check them out and subsequently book them for a session a few days later. … We weren't at all sure how to record these instruments. So we set the two Indian gentlemen up in the middle of the floor, sitting on an (oriental, of course) carpet under a couple of cardioid mikes hanging from overhead booms."[15]

It was then that the problems started. The sound of the recorded instruments was fine, but the musicians struggled with the timing and feel of the rock beat. Studio time was limited by funds and another band was due to come in later in the day, so guitarist Jeff Beck was given the job of finding a guitar sound to replace what looked like being an unsuccessful sitar part.

Gomelsky continues: "Our friend Jimmy Page was visiting us … so he and Jeff got an amp set up in the bathroom of the studio, the only place available, in an attempt to come up with some trickery to imitate the sitar sound on a guitar, and every ten minutes or so I would check up how they were doing. Time was running out, we needed a bit of luck. Miraculously, Jeff came up with something we could use, and we politely parted company with the rather puzzled Indian musicians – who had never been in a studio before – but not before Jimmy, wildly enthusiastic about the sounds emanating from it, bought the sitar (and the cloth it was wrapped in) from them for £25! I shall never forget watching him walking down the street with that strange shape under his arm."[16]

Beck, for his part, remembers that the Indian musicians "couldn't understand the timing, which was 4/4. They were playing all over the place. When they'd gone, I had the riff going through my head and I just picked out the notes, playing octaves on the middle G-string. By bending the notes slightly off key, it sounded like a sitar."[17] Many years later the aborted

sitar version of 'Heart Full of Soul' appeared on the CD boxed set *Train Kept A-Rollin'*, its awkwardness and hesitancy matching Gomelsky's description of the session. Beck's biographer Carson confirms that Page attended The Yardbirds' 'Heart Full Of Soul' session and bought the sitarist's instrument, but adds the detail that Page already owned another.[18] This might well be true. A year or so later Page was giving the *Melody Maker* an anecdote about buying his first sitar for £65 ($180), claiming at the same time that he was the first British guitarist to own one.[19] By 1967 he was saying, "I had a sitar years ago. I take Indian music very seriously."[20]

Another British pop sitarist, Brian Jones of The Rolling Stones, responded with a testy "What utter rubbish!" when it was put to him that he was copying The Beatles by using the sitar on the *Aftermath* album and 'Paint It Black' single.[21] Nevertheless, it seems that he did pick up the instrument a little later than Harrison, Phillips, Sullivan, and Page, although there are reports of him listening to Indian music as early as 1961. Jones took the sitar seriously, and could talk at length about the musical technicalities of playing the instrument. He was a natural multi-instrumentalist, someone with a knack for picking up an instrument and getting a tune out of it immediately. This facility he put to good use with the sitar, quickly developing a degree of competence that enabled him to exploit the instrument's sounds without resorting to the sort of cod-raga exercises that many pop sitarists favored. His double-tracked part on 'Mother's Little Helper,' from *Aftermath*, is executed with some brio. And his playing on the classic 'Paint It Black' is the era's best pop use of the instrument.

Much has been written about The Beatles' innovations at this time, less about those of The Rolling Stones. But 'Paint It Black' is a highly original record, one of many the band made after shrugging off their early derivative electric blues style. If it sounds less original today that is down to its familiarity, and the fact that it spawned a whole subgenre of minor-key psychedelia. A lilting opening sitar flourish rouses suspicions that the song will be

Brian Jones of The Rolling Stones plays sitar on the group's 'Paint It Black' in a 1966 television appearance.

another of the Eastern pastiches beloved of pop musicians of the time. Such concerns are wiped away by Charlie Watts's pounding drum intro, though, which hurls the song into a series of tense, claustrophobic sitar-driven verses, with relief coming in the guitar-dominated chorus sections. The sitar wasn't the only unusual arrangement feature on the record. Bassist Bill Wyman doubled up his own original bass guitar part with a second part played on the bass pedals of a Hammond organ, which he performed with his fist while lying on the floor.

The genius of the sitar part lies in its combination of pop accessibility – it's a tune you remember after hearing it once – and its evocation of doom and mystery. The lyrics of the song leave you in no doubt that something dark is happening, but quite what you never know. Their vague impression of menace and impending catastrophe is darkly underscored by the mesmerizing sitar line.

Brian Jones's debut recordings as a sitarist on 'Paint It Black' and 'Mother's Little Helper' on *Aftermath* were recorded in Hollywood in the spring of 1966. Shortly afterwards, when both single and album had been released, Jones explained that he had been taught the rudiments of the instrument and a little about its history by an Indian musician, a student of Ravi Shankar, whom Jones referred to as "Hari-Hari."[22] At the same time Mick Jagger, in another interview, said, "We just stuck the sitar on ['Paint It Black'] because some geezer came in. He was in a jazz group and played sitar … and we said, 'Oh, that'll sound good.'"[23] These two statements add up to the near-certainty that the person who taught Jones and was present at the 'Paint It Black' sessions was the same man, sitarist and Indian music teacher Harihar Rao. At the time he was teaching at UCLA, had been a student of Shankar's since 1945, and was playing sitar in a jazz group called the Hindustani Jazz Sextet.

He tended to just use the name Harihar, and it easy to see how a journalist or Jones himself, unfamiliar with Indian names, could make the mistake. Harihar doesn't remember any specific connection with The Rolling Stones, but thinks he must have been the person Jones and Jagger were referring to, saying: "This was the time when the sitar was the most popular non-Western instrument …

and any Western musician who wanted to play sitar and was in the proximity of Los Angeles came to me. It was kind of a flood all of a sudden. There was no other sitar teacher or Indian music teacher that was working with Western musicians. … I was never really interested in the [pop] scene so I never asked them 'What do you do?'"[24]

Along with Ravi Shankar and Nazir Jairazbhoy, Harihar Rao was one of a handful of Indian musicians who not only directly influenced Western pop, but also pioneered the fusion of music from the East and West. Apart from Jones, Rao often came into contact with pop/rock musicians in the ensuing years. Through his association with Ravi Shankar he played tambura on George Harrison's Dark Horse tour. He also taught Indian music concepts to figures as diverse as guitarist Ry Cooder and Moog pioneer Paul Beaver, and played sitar on one of the first sitar pop albums, *Raga Rock*, credited to The Folkswingers. It is worth noting, too, that although Rao's Hindustani Jazz Sextet never recorded, they were experimenting with their particular blend of East and West before the pop sitar era. Similarly, Jairazbhoy recalls playing sitar in a scratch jazz band as far back as the early 1950s.

In 1966, anything The Beatles and The Rolling Stones did was bound to be copied by just about everyone else in pop. So as the year wore on, and then into 1967, literally hundreds of sitar pop records were released. Some of these featured little more than pseudo-Indian decorations, a solo or riff on an otherwise conventional pop record. There was also a rash of instrumental 'sitarploitation' albums, full of sitar interpretations of current pop hits. Many of these actually featured electric sitars, not the real thing, of which more later. But amidst these cash-ins there were many good records that made interesting and accomplished use of sitar. Big Jim Sullivan's *Sitar Beat* album, a set of instrumental sitar interpretations of pop hits of the time interspersed with a few originals, is much better than it sounds, an excellent showcase for Sullivan's talents.

Those doyennes of eclecticism, The Incredible String Band, used sitar on many recordings, mostly in the hands of guitarist Mike Heron. Like Sullivan, Heron was taught by Nazir Jairazbhoy, taking up the instrument "to illustrate or color"[25] songs by Robin Williamson, his partner in the band. But Jairazbhoy himself added the deft licks when the band first used sitar, on *5000 Spirits*, making the album one of the first true East/West world music collaborations. You can hear him to particularly good effect on 'The Mad Hatter's Song.' In a comment on the fleeting nature of pop fashion, Heron sold his sitar through classified ad magazine *Exchange & Mart* when The Incredible String Band spilt up in 1974, and hasn't played one since. Sullivan and Heron weren't the only rock guitarists Jairazbhoy tutored. He also taught Andy Summers, later of The Police, but at the time a member of Zoot Money's Big Roll Band. The pair recorded a sitar duet called 'Soma,' a Summers composition, for the Zoot Money album *Transition*.

Although the sitar craze started in London, it wasn't long before it had made the transatlantic journey that, one way or the other, is such a feature of pop's evolution. One of the first American musicians to experiment with the instrument was Lowell George, in 1968. Ravi Shankar was living in Los Angeles at the time, and George later made reference to studying Indian music under Shankar for a year. The extent and exact nature of this tuition, and how far George went with his studies, is hard to quantify, but Elizabeth George, whom Lowell married in 1976, recalls: "[George and Shankar] knew each other quite well and Ravi was very supportive of Lowell. It was all about learning different aspects of music."[26]

George, later of Little Feat, was then just emerging from a spell with an obscure band called The Factory and joining garage punks The Standells, as singer, guitarist, and sitarist. George's spell with the band was brief. According to organist Larry Tamblyn, George played just a handful of dates. "The only one I remember," he says, "was at Pierce College in Canoga Park, California. It was an afternoon concert, outdoors. As part of the show, Lowell sat on the floor and played the sitar and sang. It was quite a departure from the group's sound."[27]

It was George's sitar that, indirectly, became the catalyst for a deterioration in his relationships with his new bandmates. Tamblyn remembers traveling to a particular concert in George's VW bus. "Lowell was driving. I was in the back seat with three other members of the group and Lowell's sitar, which he propped up on the seat back. Going around a curve, I accidentally leaned on the sitar, and the gourd [body] broke completely off. Even though I apologized, I think that began our adversarial relationship."[28]

> Electric Sitar

The unfortunate demise of Lowell George's sitar hints at a problem with using the instrument in rock music. While it was possible to record a sitar and integrate the sound into an electric band, taking one on the road for live use was another matter. The sitar is big and fragile, and although some experimented with fitting pickups, getting it heard above a drum kit and a couple of electric guitars was always a challenge. Add to that the fact that although it was possible for most guitarists to get a simple tune from a sitar easily, playing the instrument properly was another matter. In Indian music, years of study are necessary before a player is considered competent to perform. In 1967 these problems began to exercise the mind of Vincent Gambella, better known as the American session guitarist Vinnie Bell.

Bell had noticed an increasing number of bands trying to work with sitars, wanting the sound but struggling with the practicalities. In response he devised an electric guitar-based instrument that would be immediately familiar to any guitarist, yet would sound like a sitar. With Nathan Daniel of the Danelectro Corporation, Bell submitted a patent application in July 1967 for an electric sitar that would carry a Danelectro-related brand, Coral. Early models began to appear shortly afterwards, although a patent wasn't awarded until late 1968.

The Coral is the most familiar of several electric sitars that came on the market around this time. It has two features: a large flat bridge and a set of sympathetic strings that are intended to mimic a real sitar. An unusual asymmetrical curved body, from which protrudes a standard guitar neck and headstock, makes room for the conventional six guitar strings, amplified by two pickups, plus 13 sympathetic strings with one pickup of their own. The guitar strings run over the flat plastic bridge, and it is this that is mainly responsible for the Coral's sound. The sympathetic strings are all but inaudible unless a careful balancing act is performed with the volumes

of the respective pickups for both sympathetic and guitar strings. The buzzing tone this bridge produces, in the context of a pop record, sounds something like a sitar. But it comes with a high price. Accurate intonation is almost impossible because the strings aren't fixed at a single point, but rather rest flat on an area an inch or more in length.

The same flawed flat bridge appeared on another Danelectro electric sitar, a simple one pickup model with an oval-shaped body designed to mimic that of a sitar's gourd. Danelectro dispensed with the Coral's sympathetic strings for this 'baby' model – a decision that in fact had virtually no impact on the instrument's sound.

The Coral electric sitar was a late-1960s instrument aimed at pop guitarists.

Despite the design flaw in the bridge, both Danelectro electric sitars were popular for a while. This despite Bell appearing in an advert for the Coral in an absurd turban get-up, appealing to puerile racial stereotypes with the slogan 'You Don't Have To Be Hindu To Play Coral Electric Sitar.' In a straight comparison the electric sitars couldn't match real sitars for tonal depth, but their tinny approximation has a charm in itself, and they became a quick fix for any pop musician looking for the 'in' sound. From 1967 onwards many of the 'sitar' sounds on pop hits, particularly those recorded in America, are actually made by Danelectro electric sitars. These include 'Green Tambourine' by The Lemon Pipers (Bell himself played the part), 'Cry Like A Baby' by The Box Tops, and 'The Games People Play' by Joe South.

If the Danelectro electric sitars were little more than guitars modified to sound like sitars, the third electric sitar on the market at the time, the Rajah Zeetar, at least looked a bit like a real sitar. The gourd-shaped papier-maché body, broad neck, raised frets,

and sympathetic strings were all plausible enough imitations of the real thing. But the instrument, with two pickups and a stereo output, was tuned like a guitar and claimed to be playable by "anyone who plays a guitar." Launched at $319.50 (£116), it was also very expensive, more than double the price of the baby Danelectro, which no doubt contributed to its failure.

The sitar wasn't the only Indian instrument to attract the attention of rock musicians in the mid-1960s. George Harrison also used a surmandal (sometimes spelt 'swarmandal') on 'Strawberry Fields Forever.' A zither with 30 or more strings, it is usually used as a vocal accompaniment. It turned up again on 'Within You Without You' on *Sgt Pepper*, Harrison's most fully realized excursion into Eastern sounds, where it appears alongside several other Indian instruments, including the tambura (or 'tamboura'). This is superficially similar in appearance to the sitar, with a gourd-shaped body and long neck. It has four strings, which are played open, without any fingering, in a constant pattern. This provides a droning background accompaniment for other stringed instruments or the voice.

'Nobody's Fault But My Own' from Beck's *Mutations* features both sitar and tambura (played, incidentally, by Warren Klein, previously a member of The Factory with Lowell George). Simple electronic instruments have existed since the late 1960s that replicate the tambura's mesmeric repetitions. Now many of these are sample based, but initially they utilized electronically generated tones sculpted to resemble the real tambura's twang. An instrument like this forms the backbone of Primal Scream's 'Long Life,' the last song on *Vanishing Point*.

Ravi Shankar's great fear about pop's adoption of the sitar was that it would prove to be nothing more than a shallow, passing fancy. And this it was. Despite the obviously genuine enthusiasm of some rock guitarists – Shawn Phillips, Big Jim Sullivan, George Harrison, and Brian Jones – by 1968 a sitar sound had become a simple off-the-shelf route to exoticism and mystery. The pop machine turned out production-line 'pretend Indian' hits just as the building industry had thrown up mock-Tudor houses a few decades earlier. It was a cheap sonic fashion accessory, and pop

An advert for Danelectro's electric sitar, "the outstanding new instrument of 1968."

fashions don't last long. The Danelectro brand died as the 1960s drew to a close, and with it its two electric sitars. This mirrored the decline in interest in Eastern influences in pop. By the early 1970s, the sitar and its imitators had become just a trigger for nostalgic recollections of the psychedelic era, along with paisley, kaftans, flowers, long hair, the Maharishi, and LSD. Every now and then in the ensuing decades someone would dust down their Coral electric sitar – Yes, Rory Gallagher, Paul Young – but such events were anomalies.

Yet for all that, the sitar craze did mark a decisive step in the continuing cross-pollination between the musical cultures of the world. Now, if a major pop act uses world music instrumentation, as Blur did on *Think Tank*, for example, the response is mild interest, warranting maybe a few sentences in a review. The fact that it is not big news, and that audiences are accustomed to such experiments, can be attributed in part to the sitar craze.

If nothing else, the work of the pop sitarists told British and northern European audiences a little about Indian music, even though the message was cheapened, corrupted, and confused by fashion. And separated from its cultural connotations and considered simply as a sound, the sitar and its electric impersonators made for some fascinating music.

In the genre blending 1990s, as boundaries between the styles of preceding generations progressively eroded, and as the sounds of world music have advanced ever further into Western pop, and vice versa, the sitar and electric sitar had started to appear more regularly again, not for any cheap mystical Eastern associations, but for the sake of the sound. Or they appear, in a conscious act of redressing the balance, in the hands of bands like the Anglo-Asian Cornershop, who use sitars and other Indian instruments in their own East/West crossover music that undermines the flimsy pseudo-Indian products of earlier times.

Several copies of the Coral electric sitar are now on the market, with modified bridges that eliminate the tuning problems of the original. Of the Indian musicians who played important parts in the pop sitar era, Nazir Jairazbhoy lives in retirement in Los Angeles. Harihar Rao runs the Music Circle, also in

A further 1968 take on the electric-sitar idea, this one from the Rajah Zeetar Corp.

Los Angeles, promoting Asian music, and continues to teach. Ravi Shankar still performs internationally. Of the first generation of pop guitarists still living who experimented with the instrument in the 1960s, only Shawn Phillips retains any active interest in playing Indian musical instruments, currently using a surbahar, a similar instrument to a sitar, although with a broader neck. Big Jim Sullivan still has a sitar in his house. He hasn't played it for many years and it has no strings.

APPENDICES

ENDNOTES

Introduction
1 *Melody Maker*, May 28th 1966

● ●

Chapter 1 > Waves in the ether
and good vibrations
1 http://www.thereminworld.com
2 Andrew Smith, *Moondust* (Bloomsbury 2005).
3 Liner notes from *Waves In The Ether* (Revola CD
   Rev 58), written by Joe Foster, and liner notes to
   Basta Records' *Theremin* 3-CD box-set, written by
   Albert Glinsky.
4 BBC Radio 4, October 21st 2004.
5 Albert Glinsky, speaking on BBC Radio 4, October
   21st 2004.
6 Author's interview, October 9th 2004.
7 Author's interview, October 9th 2004.
8 Author's interview, February 9th 2004.
9 Keith Badman, *The Beach Boys* (Backbeat 2004).
10 Author's interview, February 9th 2004.
11 Author's interview, February 9th 2004.
12 Author's interview, October 9th 2004.

● ●

Chapter 2 > French Connection
1 Author's interview, July 2004.
2 *New York Times*, December 14th 1930.
3 *The Guardian*, March 22nd 2005.
4 *The Guardian*, March 22nd 2005.
5 *The Guardian*, March 3rd 2004.
6 *The Guardian*, March 3rd 2004.
7 Author's interview May 9th 2005.
8 http://www.jeanjacquesperrey.com
9 Author's interview, February 9th 2004.
10 Author's interview, April 27th 2005.

● ●

Chapter 3 > A full orchestra at your fingertips
1 Alan Young & Mark Vail, *The Hammond Organ:*
   Beauty In The B (Backbeat 1997).
2 Author's interview, April 29th 2004.
3 *New York Times*, August 10th 1952
4 *Music Trades*, November 1952.

5 John Repsch, *The Legendary Joe Meek* (Cherry Red
   Books 2000), and Barry Cleveland, *Creative Music*
   Production – Joe Meek's Bold Techniques (Mix
   Books 2001).
6 Andy Babiuk, *Beatles Gear* (Backbeat Books 2001).
7 Author's interview, January 30th 2004.
8 Author's interview, January 30th 2004.
9 Author's interviews, March 29th 2003 and January
   30th 2004
10 Author's interview, January 30th 2004.
11 Author's interview, January 30th 2004.
12 Author's interview, January 30th 2004.
13 Author's interview, April 8th, 2003.
14 *Sounds*, October 5th, 1974.

● ●

Chapter 4 > Magnetic tape
1 *New York Times*, March 15th 1959, discussing
   tape music.
2 *Los Angeles Times*, February 26th 1956.
3 Mark Lewishon, *The Complete Beatles Chronicle*
   (Pyramid Books 1992), and *The Complete Beatles*
   Recording Sessions (Hamlyn 1988).
4 http://www.mellotron.com
5 Mark Vail *Vintage Synthesizers* (Backbeat 2000).
6 Andy Babiuk, *Beatles Gear*, revised edition
   (Backbeat 2002).
7 *New Musical Express*, June 3rd 1972

● ●

Chapter 5 > Aces and Kings
1 Some of the following chronology is derived from
   two articles published by Gordon Reid in *Sound*
   On Sound about the history of Korg and Roland,
   in October 2002 (Korg) and November 2004
   (Roland).
2 Liner notes for *Hotcakes And Outtakes* (Rhino,
   2000) by Little Feat.
3 *Melody Maker*, 28th June 1969
4 Gibb Songs website
   http://www.columbia.edu/~brennan/beegees/
5 *Mojo*, February 2003
6 *Melody Maker*, 11th December 1971
7 *Sounds*, 17th June 1972

Chapter 6 > Doctors and Captains

1 Author's interview, July 28th 2004.

2 Desmond Briscoe and Roy Curtis-Bramwell, *The BBC Radiophonic Workshop – The First 25 Years* (BBC 1983).

3 Desmond Briscoe and Roy Curtis-Bramwell, *The BBC Radiophonic Workshop – The First 25 Years* (BBC 1983).

4 'Radiophonic Ladies,' by Jo Hutton: www.sonicartsnetwork.org

5 Author's interview, July 28th 2004.

6 For a detailed account of the genesis and realisation of the *Dr Who* theme, see http://ourworld.compuserve.com/homepages/ Mark_Ayres/DWTheme.htm

7 Author's interview, April 17th 2002.

8 http://ourworld.compuserve.com/homepages/ Mark_Ayres/DWTheme.htm

9 Author's interview July 28th 2004.

10 Author's interview July 28th 2004.

11 'Radiophonic Ladies,' by Jo Hutton www.sonicartsnetwork.org

12 Author's interview, April 17th 2004.

13 Author's interview, July 28th 2004.

14 *Boazine* 7 – Scottish music and culture fanzine

15 Author's interview, July 28th 2004.

16 Author's interview, July 28th 2004.

17 *The Guardian* – obituary for Delia Derbyshire by Brian Hodgson, July 7th 2001.

18 *Surface*, American art and culture magazine, May 2000.

19 Author's interview, June 30th 2004.

20 *The Wire*, February 1992.

21 Author's interview, June 30th 2004.

22 Barry Miles, *Paul McCartney: Many Years From Now* (Henry Holt 1997).

23 Author's interview, June 30th 2004

24 *Boazine* 7.

25 Author's interview, June 30th 2004.

26 http://abbeyrd.best.vwh.net/carnival.htm

27 Author's interview, June 30th 2004.

28 Author's interview, June 30th, 2004.

29 Many of the biographical details here were provided by Ralph Titterton.

30 *SoundTrack*, September 1993. Interview conducted by Randall D. Larson in 1982.

31 *SoundTrack*, September 1993. Interview conducted by Randall D. Larson in 1982.

32 *SoundTrack*, September 1993. Interview conducted by Randall D. Larson in 1982.

33 Session and broadcast information supplied by Ralph Titterton, January 25th 2005.

34 Account of retrieval of archive from author's interview with Cathy Ford, April 25th 2004.

■ ■

Chapter 7 > Oscillations, Oscillations, Electronic Evocations

1 Thom Holmes *Electronic And Experimental Music* (Routledge 1985).

2 Author's interview, January 21st 2004.

3 Author's interview, January 21st 2004.

4 Author's interview, January 21st 2004.

5 Author's interview, January 24th 2004.

6 Author's interview, January 23rd 2004.

7 *Ptolemaic Terrascope* fanzine, 1996/97.

8 Author's interview, January 23rd 2004

9 Author's interview, July 6th 2004

10 From notes supplied by Joseph Byrd to Sundazed Records, 2002

11 From notes supplied by Joseph Byrd to Sundazed Records, 2002

12 Author's interview, July 6th 2004.

13 Author's interview, July 6th 2004.

14 Author's interview, July 6th 2004.

15 Author's interview, July 6th 2004.

16 *Jimpress* fanzine, winter 2003/04.

17 *Zigzag* magazine 30.

18 Andrew Sandoval, *The Monkees* (Backbeat 2005).

19 Author's interview, January 21st 2004.

■ ■

Chapter 8 > May The Circuit Be Unbroken

1 *Billboard*, November 6th 1971.

2 Optigan owner's manual.

3 www.kraftwerkfaq.com

Chapter 9 > Whatever makes a noise

1 Author's interview, May 26th 2004.
2 www.austinchronicle.com
3 www.austinchronicle.com
4 www.kazooco.com
5 Author's interview, March 15th 2005.
6 *Melody Maker*, December 14th 1957.
7 *Melody Maker*, May 17th 1958.
8 Author's interview, August 2004.
9 www.austinchronicle.com
10 Author's interview, May 14th 2005.
11 *Magnet*, issue 38 (Jan/Feb 1999).
12 *Magnet*, issue 38 (Jan/Feb 1999).
13 Liner notes to *The Eternal Dance*, by Earth Wind & Fire (Columbia Legacy CD boxed set).

Chapter 10 > Toy Stories

1 For a detailed history of Hohner and the harmonica, see http://www.matth-hohner-ag.de/en/default.asp.
2 Letter from Martin Häffner, Director of Deutsches Harmonika Museum, February 18th 2005.
3 Doug Hinman, *The Kinks* (Backbeat 2004).
4 Author's interview, April 8th 2004.
5 Sean Egan, *The Guys Who Wrote 'Em* (Askill Publishing 2004).
6 Author's interview, April 8th 2004.

Chapter 11 > String-Driven Things

1 Jean Ritchie, *The Dulcimer Book* (Oak Publications 1974)
2 Jean Ritchie, *Dulcimer People* (Music Sales 1975)
3 *Dulcimer Players News* Vol. 25 No. 4, November 1999-January 2000.
4 *Dulcimer Players News* Vol. 25 No. 4, November 1999-January 2000.
5 *Beat Instrumental*, June 1966.
6 Philip Norman, *The Stones* (Corgi 1985).
7 Alan Lysacht *The Rolling Stones: An Oral History* (McArthur 2004)
8 *Beat Instrumental*, Oct/Nov 1966.
9 Author's interview, January 26th 2005.
10 Author's interview, January 26th 2005.
11 Author's interview, January 26th 2005.
12 Eddi Fiegel *John Barry: A Sixties Theme* (Boxtree 2001).
13 Author's interview, April 2nd 2005

Chapter 12 > Full of Eastern Promise

1 *Beat Instrumental*, June 1966.
2 *Uncut*, September 2004.
3 Mark Lewisohn, *The Complete Beatles Chronicle* (Pyramid Books 1992); Andy Babiuk, *Beatles Gear*, revised edition, (Backbeat 2002); George Harrison, *I Me Mine* (WH Allen 1982).
4 *Music Maker*, September 1966.
5 *Melody Maker*, June 28th 1966.
6 *Melody Maker*, June 11th 1966.
7 *Music Maker*, September 1966.
8 Author's interview, May 20th 2005.
9 Author's interview, May 4th 2005.
10 Session chronology supplied by Richie Unterberger.
11 Author's interview, March 8th 2004.
12 Kieron Tyler, liner notes to *Sitar Beat* (RPM).
13 Author's interview, May 5th 2005.
14 Author's interview, May 6th 2005.
15 Author's interview, February 19th 2005.
16 Author's interview, February 19th 2005.
17 Annette Carson, *Jeff Beck: Crazy Fingers* (Backbeat 2001).
18 Annette Carson, *Jeff Beck: Crazy Fingers* (Backbeat 2001).
19 *Melody Maker*, May 7th 1966.
20 *Beat Instrumental*, July 1967.
21 *Beat Instrumental*, June 1966.
22 *Beat Instrumental*, June 1966.
23 *Melody Maker*, June 28th 1966.
24 Author's interview, May 20th 2005.
25 *Record Collector*, April 2005.
26 Author's interview, May 17th 2002.
27 Author's interviews, October 2001.
28 Author's interviews, October 2001.

TIPS FOR BUYING AND PLAYING THE STRANGE SOUNDS INSTRUMENTS

Chapter 1 > Theremin and electro-theremin

Of all the early electronic instruments in this book, you will have least trouble buying a Theremin. There are many on the market, from simple hand-held models with a pitch antenna only, starting at under $175/£100, to expensive professional models. If you simply want to make wiggly noises, a cheap hand-held model will do fine. But if you want to try to *play* a Theremin the best model to go for is the Moog Etherwave. It is well made, reasonably priced, and coming as it does from Bob Moog, a man who has been making Theremins for 50 years, you have the pleasure of knowing that you are buying into the Theremin's heritage.

Making evocative spooky noises on a Theremin is easy. Pitching notes and playing tunes isn't. Unless you are willing to put a lot of work into practicing, you might want to consider following in the footsteps of Paul Tanner, and getting hold of an instrument that sounds like a Theremin but can be accurately pitched more easily.

The Tannerin is a copy of Tanner's original electro-theremin, built by Tom Polk with David Miller, and was first commissioned in 1999 by Darian Sahanaja of The Wondermints, for use with Brian Wilson. The Tannerin and Polk can be found at www.tompolk.com/Tannerin/Tannerin.html.

Chapter 2 > The Ondes Martenot and Ondioline

The Ondes Martenot was never mass-produced and the last models were made in the 1980s. Consequently, finding one for sale will be very hard, and even if you succeed you will be looking at spending thousands to buy it. It is technically complicated, too, and the early tube models in particular will need care and maintenance.

There are several alternatives to actually buying an Ondes Martenot. An Akai-format sample CD-ROM called *Vintage* includes some Ondes samples. Then there's the Persephone, a new French-built instrument that uses a touch-sensitive ribbon controller (www.eowave.com).

Alternatively, you could consider the Analogue Systems French Connection, as used by Jonny Greenwood of Radiohead. This gives the best approximation of the main control features of the Ondes Martenot, although it is a controller only, and does not actually generate its own sounds (www.analoguesystems.co.uk).

As for playing the Martenot, there are two methods of selecting notes: with the monophonic keyboard or the ribbon controller. Getting interesting and accurately pitched sounds is easy using either method. But playing the instrument in the *proper* sense, as conceived by Maurice Martenot himself, involves tuition and much practice. Much of the skill lies in coordinating the right hand – operating the keyboard – with the various sensitive hand- and foot-operated expression controls.

Ondiolines are not as rare as the Ondes Martenot, but the total number ever made was probably only a few thousand, and the newest of these is more than 30 years old. During the course of researching this book I saw one for sale, at a price of $3,000/£1,700. It was described as 'needing attention'. This ominous seller's euphemism will apply to most Ondiolines now, as they were never the best-made instruments, and need regular maintenance to keep them working to their full potential.

The lucky few who own working Ondiolines are evangelical about the instrument's sounds. It certainly has a broader sonic palette than the Clavioline, to which the Ondioline is sometimes compared. Like the Clavioline, it is a monophonic keyboard with small keys, which lend themselves to playing rapid scales.

Chapter 3 > Clavioline, Musitron, Univox, and Maestrovox

The Clavioline was the best selling piano attachment, and consequently is the most widely available now. During the two years or so I spent writing this book I checked eBay regularly, and more often than not there was at least one for sale – either an American Gibson, a British Selmer, or sometimes one of the rarer versions from Germany, Italy, or France.

The problem is not so much finding a Clavioline, but finding one that works. The newest Clavioline is now 40 years old, the oldest over 50 years. Many that come up for sale now have been languishing somewhere damp and dusty for decades, which doesn't help the tube electronics. I recently viewed two Claviolines for sale at around $350 /£200, both advertised as in 'working order'. They did both make noises, but many of the switches didn't work at all, keys crackled, notes sounded intermittently, and tuning drifted. At best, instruments like these require a thorough clean up of all contacts; at worst they need substantial refurbishment and the replacement of many components. Most instruments offered at this sort of price will need substantial work. You'd have to double your money to get one that functions properly, and pay more again for one in immaculate cosmetic condition.

A Clavioline sample CD is available from www.clavioline.com. It is an audio CD with just one sample note per sound, but at just $15 /£8.50 it is worth a try.

Of the other piano attachments, the Solovox is relatively common in America and the Univox in the UK, although neither are as numerous as the Clavioline. The Maestrovox is very rare. The Musitron was a one-off adapted Clavioline that was made by Max Crook.

All the piano attachment keyboards are monophonic, so playing them is a matter of picking out tunes with one hand. The keys are small, and the action light, so trills and rapid runs are easy. The amplifiers that are an integral part of the piano attachment packages are puny by today's standards, so if you want to use one in a live setting, extra amplification will be needed.

Chapter 4 > Magnetic Tape and Tape Replay Keyboards

If you really want to get into tape editing and manipulation, rather than the easier digital approximations that use a sampler, then any old tape recorder will do. Reel-to-reel recorders are best because the tape can be easily unspooled for splicing, but even an old cassette portastudio is useful. Most had vari-speeds, and all you need to do to get a backwards sound is to record something, flip the cassette over, and play it back.

Finding an original 1960s Mellotron or Chamberlin is hard work, as few were made and those that survive are highly prized. New Mellotrons are now being made in limited numbers, advertised at www.mellotron.com for "the original 1973 American price of $5,200.00 [£3,000] plus shipping." The same site also offers a Mellotron CD-ROM for $199.00 /£113.

Chapter 5 > Early drum machines

More than any of the other instruments in this book, early drum machine can be replaced by samples. Most hardware and software drum machines on the market at the moment have sounds that are either samples of the first generation of drum machines, or close recreations of them. You can even get sampled patterns and one-off hits for free on the Internet.

Going down the sample route means that you lose the tactile pleasure of the clunky buttons found on Rhythm Aces and Rhythm Kings. If that's important to you, then the sampling technology indirectly helps you because it has driven down the prices of the original machines. Rhythm Aces and Rhythm Kings were made in their thousands, and are robust and have lasted well. Maestro's Rhythm King is more common in America; the Rhythm Ace, often badged as a Bentley, more so in the UK. If you shop around, $175/£100 should get you a good example of either.

Chapter 6 and 7 > Test oscillators

These are still made, although most current models are small digital devices. If you want to get something that looks like it has come from a 1950s lab, with a big dial on the front, there are many secondhand options to choose from. About $70/£40 should be enough. As these devices tend to produce just a sine wave and a square wave they all sound the same.

Playing a test oscillator involves manually turning the dial to alter the pitch of the note. While this is feasible for a simple glissando between two notes, playing anything more complicated than that isn't really an option.

Chapter 8 > various electronic instruments

The Omnichord's descendent, the Qchord, is still made by Suzuki. A considerably more sophisticated instrument than its forebear, with the benefit of a MIDI interface, it nonetheless retains all of the features that make the Omnichord such an easy-to-play gadget. If you want authenticity, original models can be found on eBay for less than $175/£100. All Omnichords and Qchords have a line out, so they can easily be played live as well as in the studio. This is the easiest of all *Strange Sounds* instruments to play, and doesn't even need tuning.

Secondhand Optigans turn up for sale in America frequently, although they are rare elsewhere. These instruments are notoriously unreliable, though, so another option to consider is the sample CD-ROM from www.optigan.com, at $199/£110. Although this doesn't give you all of the real instrument's quirky playback features, you do get all of the sounds.

The original Casio VL-Tone, the VL 1, was sold in tens of thousands and finding one now for a few pounds is easy. The later polyphonic VL-5s are much rarer, but as they lack the programmable function of the earlier model they are not as interesting, so the VL 1 is the one to go for. It is this feature that makes the VL-1 worth seeking out, as all sorts of odd little noises can be created. Most of the presets – both rhythm and lead – sound cheap and nasty, but they do have ultra lo-fi appeal. Actually playing tunes on the VL-1 is quite fiddly, as the monophonic keyboard is a set of tiny little buttons.

Stylophones were made in tens of thousands, too, and working basic models can be picked up for a few pounds. You can buy reconditioned examples for a lot more money, but it probably isn't worth it, as broken ones are so easily replaced. Fewer of the luxury 350S models were made, but they still turn up regularly on eBay, normally selling for less than $175/£100.

Playing Stylophones is simple, of course. All you do is touch the stylus to the keypad. On the basic model there are only two sounds, with or without vibrato, but that thin buzzing tone you hear through the Stylophone's integral speaker becomes much more rounded when connected directly to an amplifier. The 350S has quite a broad range of sounds. Although it isn't programmable as such, there is plenty of scope for variation by combining different features. The reiteration facility is particularly enjoyable. This breaks the otherwise continuous tones into a rapid series of staccato stabs.

The Bee Gees Rhythm Machine was an odd piece of pop merchandising but must have sold reasonably well for a while, as secondhand examples turn up frequently. Prices seem to vary enormously, but be warned that this is a very limited instrument and so doesn't warrant a price tag of much more than you'd expect to pay for a Stylophone or a Casio VL-Tone, unless you happen to be a collector of Bee Gees memorabilia. The monophonic keyboard only has one voice. It's a good one, admittedly, and Kraftwerk did use it, but that's all you get. It is hard to envisage anyone making good musical use of the three rhythm presets.

Chapter 9 > Improvised acoustic instruments

Specialist musical saws are still made, and antique ones can be found, but the easiest way to get into sawing is to do what Joel Eckhouse, who played with Mercury Rev, does: "I play on a Stanley 'Thrifty' crosscut saw that I bought … for $4.49. I use a fiberglass cello bow with real horsehair (synthetic hair doesn't cut it). I have several 'musical' saws that I paid good money for, including an antique musical saw with gold plating and rhinestones, but I like the Stanley better. It's a bit more flexible and has a beautiful tone. I can get over two octaves on it; that's enough for me."

Pitching accurately enough to play tunes on a saw takes practice, although just creating eerie noises can be achieved almost immediately.

In theory any vessel with an aperture at one end will serve as a musical 'jug'. It's best to get something quite big, though, as the larger acoustic chamber gives a fuller sound.

Washboards can easily be found secondhand, or you can buy one new from the only American company that is still manufacturing them, at www.columbuswashboard.com. When playing, wearing thimbles is a good idea as they give extra percussive attack and protect the end of your fingers.

Metal and plastic kazoos can be picked up from music and toyshops for small change. Actually playing a tune on one depends on how well you can pitch notes as a singer, as the instrument doesn't produce sounds itself, but rather modifies the sound of the voice.

Now normally sold as jaw's harps, jew's harps cost a few pounds and can be played by anyone. Useful in recording, but hard to amplify live.

Finding a kalimba or something similar is easy enough, as many such instruments are sold all over the world. Although there are several properly constructed versions available, many others are cheap 'ethnic' gifts, which may be impossible to tune properly. Getting a simple twanging effect is easy, but playing tunes and rhythms in the manner of Maurice White from Earth Wind & Fire takes considerable dexterity. As with most simple acoustic instruments, getting them heard in a live setting is hard. White fitted a contact pickup to his, which did the trick.

Chapter 10 > Bass harmonica, Melodica, and ocarina

Hohner still produces a full range of Melodicas, including the original soprano and alto button models, with prices starting at well under $175 /£100. Many other manufacturers also offer similar instruments. Most general music stores, particularly those that cater for children, will stock at least one version. Their secondhand value tends to be very low because most people think of Melodicas as toys rather than proper instruments. Only the very early wood and metal Hohner instruments, and the Hohner and Yamaha electric models, are hard to find.

Melodicas are versatile instruments. Someone with no keyboard skills can easily pick perform a simple tune with a far greater degree of expression than with other beginners' instruments like the recorder or ocarina. This is because pitch isn't altered by how hard you blow, and fingering is simply a matter of pressing keys.

Bass harmonicas are still made, but can be expensive. The luxury Hohner 268/78 Double Bass-Extended Harmonica has a list price of over $1,000 /£570, for example. Playing any harmonica well takes work, despite the instrument's reputation for accessibility.

Ocarinas can be had for under $18 /£10. Like harmonicas they have a reputation for accessibility that isn't wholly deserved; pitching notes depends not just on correct fingering but also on how hard you blow.

Chapter 11 > Mountain dulcimer, autoharp, zither, Marxophone, and other hybrid instruments

There are many types of mountain dulcimer on the market. Most acoustic music shops will have several to choose from, ranging from cheap mass-produced models from Europe that start at about $175 /£100 to much more expensive custom hand-made models. Budget models are fine for beginners and occasional use, but like all cheap fretted instruments they tend to suffer from poor intonation and fret buzz.

Mountain dulcimers are the easiest fretted stringed instruments to play. As the traditional style involves fretting one string only, there are no complicated chord shapes to learn. And because of the intervals between frets, assuming you don't need to change key during a song, it is impossible to play 'wrong' notes.

There are dozens of types of hammered dulcimer and plucked zither, from many different cultures. These range from cheap 'ethnic' instruments for the tourist market to sophisticated hand-crafted professional instruments. Picking out simple tunes is easy enough, but anything more isn't. For a quick-fix zither-type sound, an autoharp is the best bet. There are many new Oscar Schmidt models on the market around $250 /£140-plus, but far cheaper secondhand ones can be found. Playing an autoharp is easy – all you do is hold down a chord button and strum. Electric examples are available; standard instruments respond quite well with an after-market pickup fitted, so there are options for playing them live. As with all zither-like instruments, the big problem is tuning them.

The secondhand price of Marxophones, Ukelins and other hybrids seems to be variable, but they still turn up regularly in America. Most of these instruments were sold on the promise that they were easy to play, which is a long way from the truth. Having said that, the hammer operation on the Marxophone, for the distinctive Doors sound that most people will be interested in, is simple enough.

Chapter 12 > Sitar, electric sitar, and electric tambura

As is the case with all common musical instruments, there are many different sitars available, from very cheap examples for beginners to expensive professional and antique models. How much you spend on a sitar should be determined by how serious you are about playing it.

Any guitarist can pick out a few scales and drones on a sitar, but playing the instrument properly requires years of tuition and hard work. You also have to move the frets to play in different keys. Sitars record well, and you can now get real sitars – as opposed to electric sitars like the Coral – with pickups, so getting the instrument heard in a live setting isn't the problem it once was.

Original Coral and Danelectro baby electric sitars are now rare and expensive collectors' items, and not very usable with it because of the tuning problems caused by their bridges. There are many later copies of the Coral on the market, which attempt to resolve this problem, with varying degrees of success.

If you're not concerned about 1960s authenticity, the best bet for an electric sitar sound comes from Germany. Eyb Guitars has developed a bridge with individual string saddles that solves the tuning problem while keeping a Danelectro-style sound. The guitars to which they fit these bridges look generic euro-axe and won't be to everyone's taste, and prices start at about $1,800 /£1,000. Alternatively, you can get one of the Eyb bridges and fit it yourself to whatever guitar you want.

There are several electric tamburas currently available, starting at about $175 /£100. You don't really play them – you just set the parameters and turn them on.

SOUND AND VISION

Chapter 1 >

theremin

Films
Spellbound (1945)
Directed by Alfred Hitchcock.
Original music by Miklos Rozsa (and Audrey
Granville [uncredited]).
Theremin played by Dr Samuel Hoffman.

The Lost Weekend (1945)
Directed by Billy Wilder.
Original music by Miklos Rozsa.
Theremin played by Dr Samuel Hoffman.

The Day The Earth Stood Still (1951)
Directed by Robert Wise.
Original music by Bernard Herrmann.
Theremin played by Dr Samuel Hoffman.

These are the three best examples of Hoffman's
Theremin film soundtrack work.

The Song Remains the Same (1976)
Directed by Peter Clifton and Joe Massot.

The Led Zeppelin in-concert movie shows Jimmy
Page playing the Theremin during 'Whole Lotta
Love,' making the most of the theatrical possibilities
conducting the air around the Theremin's antennae.

Theremin: An Electronic Odyssey (1994)
Directed by Steven M Martin.

A documentary telling the story of Leon Theremin
and the instrument that bears his name.

Simon & Garfunkel: Old Friends Live On Stage (2004)
Keyboard player Rob Schwimmer plays a Moog
Theremin solo on 'The Boxer'.

Albums
*Music Out of the Moon / Perfume Set To Music / Music
For Peace Of Mind*
Dr. Samuel J Hoffman
Released 1947-8; reissued 1999.
Basta CD 2427; re-issued again 2004 Rev-Ola CD
Rev 58

Safe As Milk
Captain Beefheart And His Magic Band
Released 1967.
Kama Sutra BDS 5001 (US) / Pye International
NPL 28110 (UK)

electro theremin

Singles
'Good Vibrations'
The Beach Boys
Released 1966
Capitol 5676 (US) / Capitol CL15475 (UK)
US #1 / UK #1

Albums
Music For Heavenly Bodies
Andre Montero and his Orchestra, featuring Paul
Tanner.
Released 1958.
OSL-4 omega DISK (US)

"Heavenly Bodies, whether it be the type that whirl
about us in space, or those that have the glitter of
Monroe, Mansfield or Bardot, have always had a
magnetic attraction for man ..." (from the sleeve
notes).

Music From Outer Space
Andre Montero and his Orchestra, featuring Paul
Tanner.
Released 1962.
Warner Bros W1463 (US)

"The Music of whirling satellites, brilliant galaxies,
streaming comets, mysterious planets, and the eerie
reaches of space in-between – all these take on

startling musical and dramatic life in this remarkable suite …" (from the sleeve notes)

Pet Sounds
The Beach Boys
Released 1966
Capitol T2458 (US & UK)
US #10 / UK #2
(Electro-theremin used on 'I Just Wasn't Made For These Times.')

Wild Honey
The Beach Boys
Released 1967
Capitol T2859 (US & UK)
US #24 / UK #7
(Electro-theremin used on 'Wild Honey.')

Smile
Brian Wilson
Released 2004
Nonesuch 79846 (US & UK)
US #13 / UK #7
(Tannerin)

This album makes use of the Tannerin, the replica Electro-theremin created by David Miller and Tom Polk.

Chapter 2 >

ondes martenot

Film

Lawrence of Arabia (1962)
Directed by David Lean.
Original music by Maurice Jarre.

Mad Max (1979)
Directed by George Miller.
Original music by Brian May.

Albums

Et Cetera
Et Cetera
Released 1976.
Apostrophe AP-800

As Time Goes By
Bryan Ferry
Released 1999.
Virgin 812138 (US) / CDVIR167 (UK)
UK #6

Kid A
Radiohead
Released 2000.
Capitol 27753 (US) / Parlophone CDKIDA1 (UK)
US #1 / UK #1
(Ondes Martenot used on 'Kid A,' 'The National Anthem,' 'How To Disappear Completely,' 'Optimistic,' and 'Motion Picture Soundtrack.')

Amnesiac
Radiohead
Released 2001.
Capitol 32764 (US) / Parlophone CDFHEIT45101 (UK)
US #2 / UK #1
(Ondes Martenot used on 'Pyramid Song,' 'You And Whose Army,' and 'Dollars And Cents.')

Hail To The Thief
Radiohead
Released 2003.
Capitol 84543 (US) / Parlophone 5845432 (UK)
US #3 / UK #1
(Ondes Martenot used on 'Where I End And You Begin.')

ondioline

Films

Spartacus (1960)
Directed by Stanley Kubrick.
Original music by Alex North.

Singles
'No Time Like The Right Time'
Blues Project
Released 1967.
Verve Folkways 5040 (US)
US #96

This track is also featured on the *Nuggets*
compilation. The Ondioline is played by Al Kooper.

Albums
Soul Surfin' (later reissued as *More*)
Kai Winding
Released 1963.
Verve V6-8551 (US & UK)
US #67
Mondo Cane, No. 2
Kai Winding
Released 1963.
Verve V6-8573 (US & UK)

I Must Be Seeing Things
Gene Pitney
Released 1965.
Musicor MS3056 (US)

Ondioline played by Al Kooper.

The In Sound From Way Out
Kingsley-Perrey (Gershon Kingsley & Jean Jacques
Perrey)
Released 1966; reissued 1995.
Vanguard CD 79222 (US)

*The Out Sound From Way In! The Complete Vanguard
Recordings* (3-CD set)
Perrey-Kingsley
Released 2001.
Vanguard 184/86 (US)

*The Amazing New Electronic Pop Sound Of
Jean Jacques Perrey*
Jean Jacques Perrey
Released 1968; reissued 1996.
Vanguard CD 79286 (US)

Moog Indigo
Jean Jacques Perrey
Released 1970; reissued 1996.
Vanguard CD 6549 (US)

Adventure
Television
Released 1978.
Elektra 6E133 (US) / K52072 (UK)
UK #7
(The Ondioline is heard on one song, 'The Fire')

Chapter 3 >

clavioline

Singles
'Telstar'
The Tornados
Released 1962.
London 9561 (US) / Decca F11494 (UK)
US #1 / UK #1

Albums
Atlantis
Sun Ra
Released 1969.
Saturn 507 (US)

The prolific Sun Ra used the Clavioline on many
albums in the 1960s.

Stringbeat
John Barry Seven
Released 1961.
Columbia (UK) SCX3401
Re-released 1982
Cherry Red BRED51 (UK)

musitron

Singles

'Runaway'
Del Shannon
Released 1961.
Big Top 3067 (US) / London HLX 9317 (UK)
US #1 / UK #1

Many Del Shannon hits featured the Musitron, so any comprehensive 'Best Of' compilation will include plenty of examples.

maestrovox

Deceit
This Heat
Released 1981.
Rough Trade ROUGH26
Reissued 1991.
These Records heat2cd

This Heat's Charles Hayward says of his Maestrovox: "It blew up some time before This Heat began and it was quite a problem getting replacement valves [tubes]. During the recording of 'Cenotaph' on the *Deceit* album it blew up again. In fact the track starts out with two tracks of Maestrovox and by the end there's only one because it stopped working during the overdub."

Chapter 4 >

magnetic tape

Albums

I Hear A New World
Joe Meek
Released 1991.
RPM 103 (2001 reissued as RPM 502)

RPM was responsible for the first full issue of *I Hear A New World* in the early 1990s. The later informatively-annotated repackaging of that issue

includes a 35-minute audio monologue recorded in 1962, in which Meek talks about his life, his studio, and his "activities making pop records for the commercial market." With the knowledge of Meek's gruesome and tragic end, hearing his West Country burr through 40 years of hiss is eerie and poignant. A brief CD-ROM clip from a *World In Action* documentary recorded two years later follows the monologue, and is an interesting, though less revealing, curiosity.

Revolver
The Beatles
Released 1966.
Capitol ST2576 (US) / Parlophone 7009 (UK)
US #1 / UK #1

(Backwards guitar on 'I'm Only Sleeping;' various tape manipulations on 'Tomorrow Never Knows.')

The Beatles (aka *The White Album*)
The Beatles
Released 1968.
Apple 101 (US) / Parlophone 7067 (UK)
US #1 / UK #1
(Tape collage on 'Revolution No.9')

An Electrical Storm
White Noise
Released 1969.
Island 9303 (US) / ILPS 9099 (UK)
Experimental rock by Radiophonic Workshop staffers Delia Derbyshire and Brian Hodgson, with David Vorhaus.

mellotron

Singles

'Strawberry Fields Forever'
The Beatles
Released 1967.
Capitol 2653 (US) / Parlophone 7027 (UK)
US #1 / UK #1

This is the most famous use of Mellotron on record, but there are dozens of other examples from the late 1960s and early 1970s, including all Moody Blues albums from that period.

Chapter 5 >

early drum machines

Singles
'Saved By The Bell'
Robin Gibb
Released 1969.
Atco 45-6698 (US) / Polydor 56337 (UK)
UK #2

Albums
Robin's Reign
Robin Gibb
Released 1970.
Atco SD 33-323 (US) / Polydor 184 363 (UK)

There's A Riot Goin' On
Sly & The Family Stone
Released 1971.
Epic 30986 (US) / EPC/40 64613 (UK)
US #1 / UK #31

Naturally
JJ Cale
Released 1972.
Shelter 8908 (US) / A&M AMLS68105 (UK)
US #51

Journey
Kingdom Come (Arthur Brown)
Released 1973.
Passport ppsd98003 (US) / Polydor 2310254 (UK)

Chapter 6 >

Films
Dr. Who And The Daleks (1966)
Directed by Gordon Flemyng.

Original music by Barry Gray & Malcolm Lockyer.

Daleks' Invasion Earth 2150 AD (1966)
Directed by Gordon Flemyng
Original music by Barry Gray & Bill McGuffie.

Gray is credited with producing 'electronic music' for these spin-off movies from the popular BBC television series, although his contributions are more accurately described as sound effects. He is responsible for the electronic interjections during the title themes for both films (neither film used the classic *Dr Who* theme); and various bleeps and hums during the films themselves, usually to denote the workings of some futuristic piece of equipment. He was effectively occupying the role taken by the BBC Radiophonic Workshop in the television programmes.

Island Of Terror (1966)
Directed by Terence Fisher.
Original music by Malcolm Lockyer.

Fahrenheit 451 (1966)
Directed by Francois Truffaut.
Original music by Bernard Herrmann.

On both of these films Gray provided additional electronic music.

Doppelganger. (aka *Journey To The Far Side of The Sun*) (1969)
Directed by Robert Parrish.
Original music by Barry Gray.

Singles
'Time Beat' / 'Waltz In Orbit'
Ray Cathode (BBC Radiophonic Orchestra)
Released 1962.
Parlophone 45-R 4901 (UK)

Neither a commercial nor an artistic success, this curiosity is notable nonetheless, because it was produced by George Martin, shortly before he started working with The Beatles.

Albums

Radiophonic Workshop 21
(various BBC Radiophonic Workshop composers)
Released 1979.
BBC Records REC 354 (UK)

A compilation of work by 18 workshop composers
to celebrate the 21st anniversary of its founding.

30 Years at The Radiophonic Workshop
(various BBC Radiophonic Workshop composers)
Released 1993.
BBC Records CD 871 (UK)

A document of the Workshop's aural contributions
to the popular, long-running TV series *Dr Who*. This
album contains the classic original realization of
Ron Grainer's evocative theme by Delia Derbyshire
and Dick Mills, and dozens of sound effects and
atmospheric noises with titles like 'Reactivation' and
'Laboratory Rises.'

BBC Radiophonic Music
(various BBC Radiophonic Workshop composers)
Released 2002.
BBC records REC25MCD (UK)

The Radiophonic Workshop
(various BBC Radiophonic Workshop composers)
Released 2002.
BBC Legends CD 196 (UK)

These are expanded issues of albums originally
released in 1968 and 1974 respectively. The earlier
album showcases the *musique concrète* techniques
employed by many of the first generation of
radiophonic composers, including Delia Derbyshire
and John Baker. The second demonstrates how the
1970s generation of composers absorbed the new
synthesizer technology into their music.
Radiophonic Workshop archivist Mark Ayres
contributes informative liner notes to both albums.

Captain Scarlet (Original TV Soundtrack)
Barry Gray
Reissued 2003.
Silva Screen 607 (UK)

Chapter 7 >

durrett electronic
music synthesizer

Albums

Pleasures Of The Harbor
Phil Ochs
Released 1967.
A&M SP 4133 (US) / AML913 (UK)
(The Durrett is heard on one song, 'Crucifixion.')

The United States Of America
The United States Of America
Released 1968.
CBS 9619 (US) / CBS63340 (UK)

simeon

Albums

Silver Apples
Silver Apples
Released 1968.
Kapp KS-3562 (US)

Contact
Silver Apples
Released 1969.
Kapp KS-3584 (US)

Silver Apples' original two albums were reissued on
CD by MCA in 1997 (MCD 11680).

Chapter 8 >

stylophone

Singles
'Space Oddity'
David Bowie
Released 1969.
Mercury 72949 (US) / Philips BF1801 (UK)
US #15 (1973 reissue) / UK #5 & #1 (1975 reissue)

'Pocket Calculator'
Kraftwerk
Released 1981.
Warners 49723 (US) / EMI EMI 5175 (UK)
UK #39

Albums
Astronaut
Duran Duran
Released 2004.
Epic 92900 (US) / 5179208 (UK)
US #17 / UK #3
(Stylophone 350S featured on 'Nice.')

casio vl-tone

Singles
'Da Da Da'
Trio
Released 1982.
Mercury CORP5 (UK)
UK #7

omnichord

Albums
The Joshua Tree
U2
Released 1987.
Island 90581 (US) / CIDU 26 (UK)
US #1 / UK #1

Oh Mercy
Bob Dylan
Released 1989.
Columbia 45281 (US) / CBS 465800 (UK)
US #30 / UK #6
(Omnichord featured on 'Shooting Star.')

bee gees rhythm machine

Singles
'Pocket Calculator'
Kraftwerk
(*See under Stylophone for details.*)

optigan

Albums
13
Blur
Released 1999.
Virgin 99129 (US) / Food FOOD 29 (UK)
US #80 / UK #1
(Optigan featured on 'Optigan 1.')

Chapter 9 >

jug

Albums
The Psychedelic Sounds Of …
The Thirteenth Floor Elevators
Released 1966.
International Artists IALP1 (US)

Easter Everywhere
The Thirteenth Floor Elevators
Released 1967.
International Artists IALP5 (US)

washboard

Singles
'Rock Island Line'
The Lonnie Donegan Skiffle Group
Released 1955.
London 1650 (US) / Decca F 10647 (UK)
US #8 / UK #8

kazoo

Singles
'So Long Baby'
Del Shannon
Released 1961
Big Top 3083 (US) / London HLX 9462 (UK)
US #28 / UK #10

The 'bass saxophone' line on this single is played on
Max Crook's Musitron.

'Hooligan'
Embrace
Released 1999.
Hut C/CD123 (US)
UK #18

Albums
Anthem Of The Sun
Grateful Dead
Released 1968.
Warner Bros 1749 (US) / K46021 (UK)
US #87

Unplugged
Eric Clapton
Released 1992.
Reprise 45024 (US) / Duck-Warners 480 (UK)
US #1 / UK #2

musical saw

Albums
Deserter's Songs
Mercury Rev
Released 1998.
V2 27027 (US) / VVR100277 (UK)
UK #27

This album also features use of the tape replay
instrument, the Chamberlin.

jew's harp

Albums
Songs From A Room
Leonard Cohen
Released 1969.
Columbia 9767 (US) / CBS CBS63587 (UK)
US #63 / UK #2

Dear Heather
Leonard Cohen
Released 2004.
Columbia 92891 (US) / 5147682 (UK)
US #131 / UK #34

kalimba

Albums
Head To The Sky
Earth Wind & Fire
Released 1973.
Columbia 32194 (US) / CBS CBS/40 65208 (UK)
US #27

improvised percussion

Singles
'Have I The Right'
The Honeycombs
Released 1964.
Interphon 7707 (US) / Pye 7N 15664 (UK)
US #5 / UK #1

Chapter 10 >

bass harmonica

Albums
Pet Sounds
The Beach Boys
(see 'Electro-theremin')
(Bass harmonica on 'I Know There's An Answer.')

Sgt Pepper's Lonely Hearts Club Band
The Beatles
Released 1967.
Capitol 2653 (US) / Parlophone PMC 7027 (mono)
PCS 7027 (stereo) (UK)
US #1 / UK #1
(Bass harmonica on 'Being For The Benefit Of Mr Kite.')

melodica

Singles
'Sunny Afternoon'
The Kinks
Released 1966.
Reprise 0497 (US) / Pye 7N 17125 (UK)
US #14 / UK #1

Albums
Born In Mississippi, Raised Up In Tennessee
John Lee Hooker
Released 1973.
ABC Records ABCX768
(Electric Melodica is featured on the title track.)

Heavy Weather
Weather Report
Released 1977.
Columbia 34418 (UK) / CBS 81775 (UK)
US #30
(Melodica is featured on 'Birdland' and 'Teen Town.')

Movement
New Order
Released 1981.
Factory FACT50 (UK)
UK #30
(Melodica is featured on 'Truth.')

Vanishing Point
Primal Scream
Released 1997.
Reprise 46559 (US) / Creation CRE 178 (UK)
UK #2
(Melodica featured on 'Star,' which reached Number 16 when issued as a single [CRECS245] in the UK.)

ocarina

Singles
'Wild Thing'
The Troggs
Released 1966.
Fontana 1548 (US) / TF689 (UK)
US #1 / UK #2

Chapter 11 >

mountain dulcimer

Albums
Celebrations For A Grey Day
Richard & Mimi Farina
Released 1965.
Vanguard 79174 (US) / Fontana 6060 (UK)

Reflections In A Crystal Wind
Richard & Mimi Farina
Released 1965.
Vanguard 79204 (US) / Fontana 6075 (UK)

Memories
Richard & Mimi Farina
Released 1968.
Vanguard 79263 (US)

Aftermath
The Rolling Stones
Released 1966.
London 451 (US) / Decca LK/SKL4786 (UK
mono) KSKC4786 (US stereo)
US #2 / UK #1
(Dulcimer featured on "Lady Jane" and 'I Am
Waiting')

Hark! The Village Wait
Steeleye Span
Released 1970.
RCA SF8133 (UK)

Please To See The King
Steeleye Span
Released 1971.
B&C CAS1029 (UK)
UK #45

Ten Man Mop (Or Mr Reservoir Strikes Again)
Steeleye Span
Released 1972.
Pegasus PEG9 (UK)

Tim Hart played electric dulcimer on many of the
songs on these three albums and all of the other
Steeleye Span albums until he left in 1982.

hammered dulcimer

Films
The Ipcress File (1965)
Directed by Sidney J Furie.
Original music by John Barry.

This soundtrack makes use of the cimbalom, a large
Hungarian hammered dulcimer. It also includes
uncredited electronic music.

Albums
A Ghost Is Born
Wilco
Released 2004.
Nonesuch 79809 (US & UK)
US #8

zither

Films
The Third Man (1949)
Directed by Carol Reed.
Original music by Anton Karas (who also plays the
zither).

autoharp

Albums
Do You Believe In Magic
Lovin' Spoonful
Released 1965.
Kama Sutra KLP/+S 8050 (US) / Pye International
NPL 28069 (UK)
US #32

Daydream
Lovin' Spoonful
Released 1966.
Kama Sutra KLP/+S 8051 (US) / Pye International
NPL 28078 (UK)
US #10 / UK #8

Hums Of The Lovin' Spoonful
Lovin' Spoonful
Released 1966
Kama Sutra KLP/+S 8054 (US) / KLP 401 (UK)
US #14

The Lovin' Spoonful's John Sebastian was pop's
primary autoharpist, using the instrument on many
tracks on these and other albums.

Fairport Convention
Fairport Convention
Released 1968.
Cotillion SD 9024 (US) / Polydor 583 035 (UK)

Original Fairport Convention singer Julie Dyble
used electric autoharp on this album.

marxophone

Albums
The Doors
The Doors
Released 1967.
Elektra EKL/EKS 74007 (US & UK)
US #1
(Marxophone featured on 'Alabama Song (Whiskey
Bar),' which was also issued as a single in the UK
[EKSN 45012], but failed to chart.)

The Birds, The Bees And The Monkees
The Monkees
Released 1968.
Colgems 109 (US) / RCA Victor RD/SF 7948
(UK)
US #3
(Marxophone featured on 'P.O. Box 9847.')

i
Magnetic Fields
Released 2004.
Nonesuch 79683 (US & UK)
US #152

Chapter 12 >

sitar

Singles
'Paint It Black'
The Rolling Stones
Released 1966.
London 901 (US) / Decca F 12395 (UK)
US #1 / UK #1

Albums
Rubber Soul
The Beatles
Released 1965.
Capitol 2442 (US) / Parlophone PMC 1267 (UK
mono) PCS 3075 (UK stereo)
US #1 / UK #1
(Sitar featured on 'Norwegian Wood.')

Sunshine Superman
Donovan
Released 1966.
Epic LN 24217 (US mono) / BN 26217 (US
stereo)
US #11

Mellow Yellow
Donovan
Released 1967.
Epic LN 24239 (US mono) / BN 26239 (US
stereo)
US #14

Sitar Beat
Big Jim Sullivan
Released 1968.
Mercury 61137 (UK)/ Reissued 2002 RPM 242

Transition
Zoot Money's Big Roll Band
Released 1968.
Direction 8-63231

Raga Rock
The Folkswingers
Released 1966.
World Pacific WPS-1846

Raga Rock is of the first and best 'sitarploitation' albums. The Folkswingers were a studio ensemble created by George Tipton. The sitar is played by Harihar Rao, alongside seasoned Los Angeles studio veterans like drummer Hal Blaine. It features instrumental versions of all the key early sitar-pop songs, including 'Norwegian Wood' and 'Paint It Black.'

Mutations
Beck
Released 1998.
Geffen Ged 25184
(Sitar and tamboura featured on 'Nobody's Fault But My Own.')

electric sitar

Singles
'Cry Like A Baby'
Box Tops
Released 1968.
Mala 593 (US) / Bell BLL1001 (UK)
US #2 / UK #15

'The Games People Play'
Joe South
Released 1969.
Capitol CL 15579
US #12 / UK #6

Albums
Pop Goes the Electric Sitar
Vinnie Bell
Released 1967.
Decca DL-74938

A kitsch cash-in by the inventor of the Coral electric sitar.

New Adventures In Hi-Fi
R.E.M.
Released 1996.
Warners 9362 46320 (US & UK)
US #2 / UK #1
(Electric sitar featured on 'E-bow The Letter.')

electric tambura

Albums
Vanishing Point
Primal Scream
(see 'Melodica' section)

miscellaneous

Films
Forbidden Planet (1956)
Directed by Fred M Wilcox.
Original music by Bebe Barron & Louis Barron.
The first all-electronic music score.

Performance (1970)
Directed by Donald Cammell and Nicolas Roeg.
Original music by Jack Nitzsche.

Mord Und Totschlag (aka *Degree Of Murder*) (1967)
Directed by Volker Schlöndorff.
Original music by Brian Jones.

Two movies with Rolling Stones connections. *Performance* includes early use of Moog on its soundtrack, alongside mountain dulcimer. It also features what is probably a shakuhachi, a Japanese flute, played by Lowell George, later of Little Feat. George is listed in the film credits, and at the time was the only shakuhachi player registered in Los Angeles, where the soundtrack was recorded.

The music for *Mord Und Totschlag* was composed by Brian Jones and recorded with the help of British session veterans including Jimmy Page and Nicky Hopkins. The music is competent without being exceptional, but the film warrants investigation for two reasons: its soundtrack is the closest Jones got to recording a solo album, and in it he used his full range of instruments – sitar, marimba, dulcimer, and so on – alongside conventional rock instrumentation.

Singles
'Goin' Back' / 'Change Is Now'
The Byrds
Released 1967.
Columbia 44362 (US) / CBS 3093 (UK)_US # 89

The first pop hit to feature Moog.

Albums
Silver Apples Of The Moon For Electronic Music Synthesizer
Morton Subotnick
Released 1967.
Nonesuch H-71174 (US & UK)

The Nonesuch Guide To Electronic Music
Paul Beaver & Bernard L Krause
Released 1968.
Nonesuch HC-73018 (US & UK)

Two early electronic music albums that were released just as pop was becoming aware of the possibilities of electronic instruments. The *Nonesuch Guide* consists mainly of test tones demonstrating different wave-forms.

The Zodiac Cosmic Sounds
Composed, arranged, and conducted by Mort Garson, words by Jacques Wilson, spoken by Cyrus Faryar.
Released 1967.
Elektra EKL 4009 (mono) EKS74009 (stereo)

The Zodiac Cosmic Sounds is the sort of record that could only have been made during a few months in 1967. It consists of Garson's weird light orchestral instrumentations, overlain with folk singer Cyrus Faryar's spoken words. It is very rare and has never been issued on CD. The back cover states that the

LP "must be played in the dark." Paul Beaver plays Moog, possibly the first time the instrument featured on a recording.

Notorious Byrd Brothers
The Byrds
Released 1968.
CBS 9575 (US) / CBS63169 (UK)
US #47 / UK #12

Pisces, Aquarius, Capricorn & Jones Ltd.
The Monkees
Released 1967.
Colgems COM-104 (US) / RCA SF 7912 (UK)
US #1 / UK #5

Two albums recorded at almost exactly the same time, both featuring Moog.

Between The Buttons
The Rolling Stones
Released 1967.
London 499 (US) / Decca LK/SKL 4852 (UK mono) KSKC 4852 (UK stereo)
US #2 / UK #3

Their Satanic Majesties Request
The Rolling Stones
Released 1967.
London 2 (US) / Decca TXL/TXS 103 (UK mono) KTXC 103 (UK stereo)
US #2 / UK #3

Along with *Aftermath*, these two Stones albums bear the fruits of Brian Jones's fascination with exotic instrumentation. An audio test oscillator is audible on 'Please Go Home' (*Buttons*) and the instrumental fragment before 'She's A Rainbow' (*Majesties*). There's a kazoo on 'Cool, Calm And Collected' (*Buttons*). On *Majesties* there are many other unusual sounds that are hard to identify, including bell-like chimes, wind instruments, and plucked stringed instruments (maybe the oud).

The Incredible String Band
The Incredible String Band
Released 1966.
Elektra EKS 7322 (US) / EUK 254 (UK)

The 5000 Spirits Or The Layers Of The Onion
The Incredible String Band
Released 1967.
Elektra EKS 74010 (US) / EUK/+S7 257 (UK)
UK #26

The Hangman's Beautiful Daughter
The Incredible String Band
Released 1968.
Elektra EKS 74021 (US) / EUK/+S7 258 (UK)
UK #5

Wee Tam / The Big Huge
The Incredible String Band
Released 1968.
Elektra EKL/EKS7 4036/7 (US & UK)

All Incredible String Band albums (these are the first four) feature a very wide range of world music, jug, and skiffle instruments alongside more conventional rock fare. This eclecticism became an integral part of the band's identity, to the extent that adverts promoting them in the British music press in the early 1970s featured outline drawings of many of the instruments used by the band.

Side Trips
Kaleidoscope
Released 1967.
Epic 26304 (US) / 48513 (UK)

A Beacon From Mars
Kaleidoscope
Released 1968.
Epic 26333 (US)

The Incredible Kaleidoscope
Kaleidoscope
Released 1969.
Epic 26467 (US)

Bernice
Kaleidoscope
Released 1970.
Epic 26508 (US)

In terms of varied instrumentation, Kaleidoscope can be seen as the American counterparts of the Incredible String Band. The band used many unusual acoustic instruments alongside conventional electric ones.

Lost In Space
Aimee Mann
Released 2002
Supergo Records/United Musicians VVR 1020882

A recent album that features many *Strange Sounds* instruments, most played by guitarist Michael Lockwood, including autoharp, zither, Theremin, Omnichord, Marxophone, and Chamberlin.

sources

Interviews

Paul Tanner, François Evans, Bob Williams, Al Kooper, Dave Amels, Mark Vail, Max Crook, Dick Mills, Mark Ayres, Brian Hodgson, Ralph Titterton, Cathy Ford, Joseph Byrd, Simeon Coxe, Richie Unterberger, Joel Eckhouse, Robin Williamson, Martin Häffner, Reg Presley, Tim Hart, Michael Lockwood, Big Jim Sullivan, Giorgio Gomelsky, Harihar Rao, Nazir Jairazbhoy, Larry Tamblyn, Elizabeth George, Shawn Phillips, Gary Talley, Jean-Jacques Perrey, Jim McCarty.

Books

Modern Music – A Concise History (revised edition)
Paul Griffiths
World of Art
0-500-20278-8
1994

The New Music – The Avant-Garde Since 1945 (2nd edition)
Reginald Smith Brindle
Oxford University Press
0-19-315468-4
1995

The Dulcimer Book
Jean Ritchie
Oak Publications
0-7119-0386-7
1974.

Dulcimer People
Jean Ritchie
Music Sales
0-8256-0142-8
1975

The Stones
Philip Norman
Corgi
0-552-12487-7
1985

The Rolling Stones: An Oral History
Alan Lysaght
McArthur & Company Publishing
1-552-78392-8
2004

John Barry: A Sixties Theme
Eddi Fiegel
Boxtree
0-7522-20330-9
2001

Electronic And Experimental Music (2nd edition)
Thom Holmes
Routledge
0-415-93644-6
2002

The Beach Boys
Keith Badman
Backbeat
0-87930-818-4
2004

The Monkees
Andrew Sandoval
Backbeat
1-87154-786-5
2005

The Kinks
Doug Hinman
Backbeat
0-87930-765-X
2004

Elevator Music: A Surreal History Of Muzak, Easy-Listening, And Other Moodsong
Joseph Lanza
Quartet Books
0-7043-0226-8
1995

The Legendary Joe Meek
John Repsch
Cherry Red Books
1-901447-20-0
2000

The BBC Radiophonic Workshop, The First 25 Years
Desmond Briscoe and Roy Curtis Bramwell,
BBC Books
0 563 20150 9
1983

Electronic Music
Andy Mackay
Phaidon
0-7148-2176-4
1981

Creative Music Production: Joe Meek's Bold Techniques
Mix Books
1-931140-08-1
2001

The Hammond Organ: Beauty In The B
Alan Young & Mark Vail
Backbeat
0-87930-705-6
1997

Follow The Music
Jac Holzman and Gavn Daws
First Media
0-9661221-1-9
1998

Skiffle
Chas McDevitt
Robson Books
0-86105-140-9
1997

The Guys Who Wrote 'Em
Sean Egan
Askill Publishing
0-954570-1-6
2004

Vintage Synthesizers
Mark Vail
Backbeat
0-87930-603-3
2000

Beatles Gear (revised edition)
Andy Babiuk
Backbeat
0-87930-731-5
2002

The Complete Beatles Chronicle
Mark Lewisohn
Pyramid Books
1-85152-975-6
1992

The Complete Beatles Recording Sessions
Mark Lewisohn
Hamlyn
0-600-55798-7
1988

Jeff Beck Crazy Fingers
Annette Carson
Backbeat
0-87930-632-7
2001

The Ukulele
Jim Beloff
Backbeat
0-87930-758-7
2003

The Unknown Paul McCartney
Ian Peel
Reynolds and Hearn
1-90311-40-4
2002

An Incredible String Band Compendium
Ed. Adrian Whittaker
Helter Skelter
1-900924-64-1
2003

Unknown Legends of Rock'n'Roll
Richie Unterberger
Backbeat
0-87930-534-7
1998

Urban Spacemen And Wayfaring Strangers
Richie Unterberger
Backbeat
0-87930-616-5
2000

Turn! Turn! Turn!
Richie Unterberger
Backbeat
0-87930-703-X
2002

Eight Miles High
Richie Unterberger
Backbeat
0-87930-743-9
2003

Positively 4th Street
David Hadju
Bloomsbury
0-7475-5826-4
2001

The Yardbirds
Alan Clayson
Backbeat
0-87930-724-2
2002

Reference Books
The New Grove Dictionary Of Musical Instruments
Macmillan
0-333-37878-4
1984

Electric Guitars: The Illustrated Encyclopedia
Tony Bacon
Balafon/Thunder Bay
1-871547-66-0
2000

Rock: Rough Guide (2nd Edition)
Ed. Jonathan Buckley, Orla Duane, Mark Ellingham,
Al Spicer
Rough Guides
1-85828-457-0
1999

All Music Guide (4th Edition)
Ed. Vladimir Bogdanov, Chris Woodstra, Stephen
Thomas Erlewine
AMG/Backbeat
0-87930-627-0
2001

The Penguin Encyclopedia of Popular Music (2nd
Edition)
Ed. Donald Clarke
Penguin
0-14-051370-1
1998

The Oxford Companion to Musical Instruments
Anthony Baines
Oxford University Press
0-19-311334-1
2002

Musical Instruments
Horniman Museum/London/London Education
Authority
0-7168-0292-9
1977

Magazines, Newpapers and Periodicals
The Music Trades
The New York Times
The Los Angeles Times
Electronics & Music Maker
Melody Maker
Record Collector
Sounds
New Musical Express
Billboard
Rolling Stone
Guitar Player
Mojo
Uncut
The Guardian
Sound On Sound
The Wire
Boazine
Surface
Sound Track

Ptolemaic Terrascope
Jimpress
Zig Zag
The Austin Chronicle
Magnet
Dulcimer Players News
Beat Instrumental
Keyboard

Websites

www.kraftwerkfaq.com
Information on Kraftwerk's instrumentation.

www.optigan.com
An excellent single instrument site for the Optigan.

www.spaceagepop.com
A reference source for exotica and related genres.

www.richardandmimi.com
An unofficial but very well informed site for
Richard and Mimi Fariña.

www.kazooco.com
The official site for the Kazoo Company.

www.vintagesynth.com
www.synthmuseum.com
Two good reference sites for old synths.

www.electrotheremin.com/PTE-TPage.html
David Miller's site devoted to Paul Tanner's electro-
theremin.

www.hohner.com
The official Hohner site.

www.delia-derbyshire.org
www.sonicartsnetwork.org
Two sites with information about Delia Derbyshire
and the Radiophonic Workshop.

http://ourworld.compuserve.com/homepages/Mark_Ayres/
DWTheme.htm#
The full story of the Dr Who theme tune.

www.fanderson.org.uk
The Gerry Anderson fanclub site, which includes
information about Barry Gray.

www.jewsharpguild.org
Contains much useful information about the history
of the jew's harp.

www.korg.com
The official Korg site.

www.broadwaymusicco.com/beatbox1.htm
An informative vintage drum machine site, including
samples.

www.clavioline.com
A single instrument site dedicated to the Clavioline.

www.audities.com
The on-line home of Audities, a collection spanning
the history of electronic instruments.

www.jeanjacquesperrey.com
The official site of the Ondioline and Moog
pioneer.

www.thereminworld.com
A thorough Theremin site.

www.columbia.edu/~brennan/beegees/
Contains information about Robin Gibb's solo
recordings.

www2.netdoor.com/~rlang/marxo/marxop.htm
www.usd.edu/smm
Marxophones, Ukelins and other odd hybrids found
here.

www.mellotron.com
A thorough site with histories of the Chamberlin
and Mellotron.

www.washboards.com
A general history, buying and playing site.

www.miniorgan.com
A madcap collection of Stylophones, Bee Gees
Rhythm Machines, and dozens of other toy organs.

PICTURE CREDITS

12 Miki Slingsby. 14 Redferns. 15 Courtesy of David S Miller. 21 Miki Slingsby. 24 Courtesy of Jean-Jacques Perrey. 32/33 Balafon Image Bank. 37 Strange Sounds Archive. 40/42 Courtesy of Max Crook. 51 Redferns. 52 GRM archives. 60/61 Korg Inc. 63 Miki Slingsby. 64 Strange Sounds Archive. 72 BBC Photo Library. 73 Miki Slingsby. 81 Miki Slingsby. 87 Courtesy of Simeon Coxe. 89 Courtesy of Simeon Coxe/Barry Bryant. 92 Courtesy of Dorothy Moskowitz. 98 Miki Slingsby. 99 Strange Sounds Archive. 100 Miki Slingsby. 101 Miki Slingsby. 102/103 Eric Schneider. 107 Record Collector. 109 Miki Slingsby. 115 Redferns. 116 Miki Slingsby. 117 Redferns. 121/122 Strange Sounds Archive. 123 Miki Slingsby. 131 Miki Slingsby. 132 Balafon Image Bank. 136 Miki Slingsby. 137 Balafon Image Bank. 138/139 Ian Nansen. 143/144 Redferns. 146 Courtesy of RPM Records. 148 Redferns. 151/152/153 Balafon Image Bank.

THANKS...

...to all the musicians, producers, instrument makers, researchers and writers who contributed to this book >
Paul Tanner, François Evans, Bob Williams, Al Kooper, Dave Amels, Mark Vail, Max Crook, Dick Mills, Mark Ayres, Brian Hodgson, Ralph Titterton, Cathy Ford, Joseph Byrd, Simeon Coxe, Richie Unterberger, Joel Eckhouse, Robin Williamson, Martin Häffner, Reg Presley, Tim Hart, Michael Lockwood, Big Jim Sullivan, Giorgio Gomelsky, Jim McCarty, Harihar Rao, Nazir Jairazbhoy, Larry Tamblyn, Elizabeth George, Shawn Phillips, Gary Talley, Jean-Jacques Perrey.

...and to everyone else who helped along the way >
Eric Schneider, Michael Simmons, Teflon Fonfara, David Miller, Tom Polk, Joel McIver, Andy Rogers, Nick Halliwell, Josh Hillman, Andy Babiuk, Warren Brandt, Kieron Tyler.

...and of course everyone at Backbeat UK for their enthusiasm and tolerance >
Tony Bacon, Phil Richardson, John Ryall, Tom Jerome, Nigel Osborne.

Special thanks to >
John Morrish, Tim Conway, David Sheppard, Darren Hayman, John McEntire, and Madeleine and Georgia.

TRACK LIST FOR ACCOMPANYING CD

Track 1
Theremin
Spooky effects with reverb.

Track 2
Ondes Martenot
Cone speaker glissando up low.

Track 3
Ondes Martenot
Cone speaker glissando down low.

Track 4
Ondes Martenot
Cone speaker scale up high.

Track 5
Ondes Martenot
Cone speaker scale down high.

Track 6
Ondes Martenot
Cone speaker scale down low.

Track 7
Ondes Martenot
Palme speaker scale up mid.

Track 8
Ondes Martenot
Palme speaker scale down mid.

Track 9
Ondes Martenot
Metallique speaker glissando up high.

Track 10
Ondes Martenot
Metallique speaker glissando down high.

Track 11
Ondes Martenot
Metallique speaker glissando up low.

Track 12
Ondes Martenot
Metallique speaker scale up high.

Track 13
Ondes Martenot
Metallique speaker scale down high.

Track 14
Ondes Martenot
Metallique speaker scale up low.

(Tracks 3 to 15 by François Evans)

Track 15
Clavioline

Track 16
Clavioline
Using volume swell.

(Tracks 15 and 16 by Warren Brandt)

Track 17
Musitron noises
Recorded live with The Sounds Of Tomorrow, 1968
(by Max Crook)

Track 18
Backwards guitar

Track 19
Ace Tone FR2 Rhythm Ace

All of the 16 preset beats on the FR2 Rhythm Ace
drum machine, played consecutively by manually
switching between presets as the machine is playing.
The beats are, in the order they appear: march,
shuffle, cha-cha, mambo, samba, rumba, beguine,
tango, swing, foxtrot, bossa nova, slow rock,
rock'n'roll, western, dixieland, waltz.

Track 20
Ace Tone Rhythm Ace

Another Rhythm Ace track demonstrating the preset combining and cancelling functions. The track starts with the rock'n'roll preset only, to which the rumba preset is added. The cymbals, claves and snare are then cancelled one by one.

Track 21
Farnell Audio Test Oscillator
Sine wave 440Hz and 150Hz.

Track 22
Farnell Audio Test Oscillator
Square wave 440Hz and 150Hz.

Track 23
Farnell Audio Test Oscillator
Sine wave swoop.

Track 24
Farnell Audio Test Oscillator
Square wave swoop.

Track 25
Stylophone
Directly inputted, plain voice first, followed by vibrato voice.

Track 26
Stylophone
Recorded through the instrument's integral speaker, plain voice first, followed by vibrato voice.

Track 27
Stylophone 350S
Woodwind sound, high octave only.

Track 28
Stylophone 350S
Woodwind sound, all octaves.

Track 29
Stylophone 350S
Woodwind sound, all octaves, slow vibrato.

Track 30
Stylophone 350S
Strings sound, high octave only.

Track 31
Stylophone 350S
Strings sound, all octaves.

Track 32
Stylophone 350S
Strings sound, all octaves, fast vibrato.

Track 33
Stylophone 350S
Woodwind sound, all octaves, fast reiteration.

Track 34
Stylophone 350S
Strings sound, all octaves, slow reiteration.

Track 35
Omnichord
Arpeggios using the instrument's strum plate.

Track 36
Bee Gees Rhythm Machine
Rhythmic presets.

Track 37
Bee Gees Rhythm Machine
Solo voice.

(Tracks 36 and 37 by Andy Rogers)

Track 38
Casio VL-Tone VL1
Piano voice.

Track 39
Casio VL-Tone VL1
Fantasy voice.

Track 40
Casio VL-Tone VL1
Violin voice.

Track 41
Casio VL-Tone VL1
Flute voice.

Track 42
Casio VL-Tone VL1
Guitar voice.

Track 43
Casio VL-Tone VL1
Sample programmed sound.

Track 44
Casio VL-Tone VL1
Rhythm presets: march, waltz, four-beat, swing, rock
1, rock 2, bossa nova, samba, rumba, beguine.

Track 45
Jew's harp

Track 46
Kalimba

Track 47
Bowed saw
Mussehl & Westphal musical saw played with a cello
bow.
(By Josh Hillman)

Track 48
Hohner Melodica Piano 26

Track 49
Angel Melodyhorn

Track 50
Mountain dulcimer

Track 51
Banjo-uke

Track 52
Autoharp
(By Nick Halliwell)

Track 53
Marxophone

Track 54
Ukelin
(Tracks 53 and 54 by Michael Simmons)

Track 55
Six-string Eyb electric sitar

Track 56
Ten-string Eyb electric sitar

(Tracks 55 and 56 by Teflon Fonfara: www.electric-
sitar.com)

Track 57
'Improvisation On Ondes Martenot' (Evans)
Written and performed by François Evans:
www.lampmusic.co.uk
(c) copyright La.M.P. Limited
(p) copyright La.M.P. Limited

Track 58
'Omnichord Theme' (Brend/Conway)
The Strange Sounds Orchestra

Track 59
'A Strange Sense Of Liberty' (Brend/Conway)
The Strange Sounds Orchestra.

All instrument demonstrations recorded by Mark
Brend and Tim Conway, except where indicated.

All selections (p) and © Mark Brend and Tim
Conway, all rights reserved, except where other
performers are indicated, in which cases, (p) and ©
rights are reserved by the performer indicated.

The Strange Sounds Orchestra was formed in
September 2004 to write and record a musical
soundtrack for *Strange Sounds*. Apart from occasional
use of bass guitar, The Orchestra's music is composed
and realized on a selection of the instruments
featured in this book.

Further recordings by The Strange Sounds Orchestra
are available from Static Caravan records. For further
information, see *www.staticcaravan.org*